PRAISE FC

destressifying

"This is a very high-powered book. Stressful thinking is wreaking havoc on the lives of so many in our fast-paced world. davidji offers a comprehensive course written in a language that you can grasp and apply immediately, all within the covers of one book. I loved it and am recommitted to in-the-moment destressifying."

— **Dr. Wayne W. Dyer,** #1 *New York Times* best-selling author of *I Can See Clearly Now*

"I love the genuineness and raw simplicity of davidji's powerful message. His style is inclusive and inviting rather than exclusive and elitist. Bottom line: I want to have an outlook on life just like davidji."

— **Laurent Potdevin,** CEO, lululemon

"davidji is a master teacher who illuminates a better way to be human by bringing bleeding-edge research to life and showing practical ways to change your mind-set about stress."

— **Shawn Achor,** happiness researcher and *New York Times* best-selling author of *The Happiness Advantage*

"davidji is a wonderful teacher who brings joy and awareness to the world."

— **Deepak Chopra, M.D.,** *New York Times* best-selling author of *The Future of God*

*"davidji has written a powerful, practical, and inspiring manual to help us understand and radically transform our relationship to stress. Written with a brilliant blend of clarity, compassion, and wisdom, it enlightens the mind and uplifts the heart. I highly recommend **destressifying** as essential reading for anyone who wants to live a more peaceful and joyful life!"*

— **Dr. Barbara De Angelis,** #1 *New York Times* best-selling author of *Soul Shifts*

destressifying

ALSO BY DAVIDJI

Book

*Secrets of Meditation: A Practical Guide to Inner Peace and Personal Transformation**

Audio Books narrated by davidji

*destressifying: The Real-World Guide to Personal Empowerment,
Lasting Fulfillment, and Peace of Mind**

Secrets of Meditation: A Practical Guide to Inner Peace and Personal Transformation

Audio and Digital Downloads

davidji: Come Fly with Me: The Passenger's Guide to Stress-Free Flying

davidji: Mindful Performance at Work & Home

davidji: Emotional Intelligence, Team-building & Leadership

davidji Guided Affirmations: Making Conscious Choices in Life and Love

Discovering Your Dharma: The Key to Finding Deeper Meaning in Life

davidji Life Tools: 40 Days of Transformation

davidji Guided Meditations: The Awakening Series

davidji Guided Meditations: destressifying your life

davidji Guided Meditations: Emotional Healing

*davidji Guided Meditations: Fill What Is Empty; Empty What Is Full,
featuring Snatam Kaur and Damien Rose*

davidji Guided Meditations: Opening to Love; Healing Your Heart

The Five Secrets of the SweetSpot: Rituals for Daily Meditation

The Meditation Room at davidji.com

*davidji Guided Affirmations: Fill Your Chakras,
inspired by the Tulku Jewels Chakra Amulet Collection*

The Goddess Meditations

*Journey to Infinity: Music, Mantras & Meditations:
An Ayurvedic Opera with SacredFire**

The Secrets of Ayurveda

The davidji SweetSpot YouTube Channel

*Available from Hay House

Please visit:

Hay House USA: www.hayhouse.com®
Hay House Australia: www.hayhouse.com.au
Hay House UK: www.hayhouse.co.uk
Hay House South Africa: info@hayhouse.co.za
Hay House India: www.hayhouse.co.in

destressifying

THE REAL-WORLD GUIDE TO PERSONAL EMPOWERMENT, LASTING FULFILLMENT, AND PEACE OF MIND

davidji

HAY HOUSE, INC.
Carlsbad, California • New York City
London • Sydney • Johannesburg
Vancouver • Hong Kong • New Delhi

Published and distributed in the United States by: Hay House, Inc.: www.hayhouse.com® • *Published and distributed in Australia by:* Hay House Australia Pty. Ltd.: www.hayhouse .com.au • *Published and distributed in the United Kingdom by:* Hay House UK, Ltd.: www .hayhouse.co.uk • *Published and distributed in the Republic of South Africa by:* Hay House SA (Pty), Ltd.: info@hayhouse.co.za • *Distributed in Canada by:* Raincoast Books: www .raincoast.com • *Published in India by:* Hay House Publishers India: www.hayhouse.co.in

Cover design: Angela Moody • *Interior design:* Pamela Homan
Interior illustrations (pgs. 10 and 52): Courtesy of the author
Maslow's Hierarchy of Needs chart (pg. 115): Abraham Maslow, "A Theory of Human Motivation," *Psychological Review,* Vol. 50 #4, pp. 370-396, © 1943

The author gratefully acknowledges and credits the following for the right to reprint material in this book:

"On Work" from *The Prophet* by Kahlil Gibran, copyright © 1923 by Kahlil Gibran and renewed 1951 by Administrators C.T.A. of Kahlil Gibran Estate and Mary G. Gibran. Used by permission of Alfred A. Knopf, an imprint of the Knopf Doubleday Publishing Group, a division of Penguin Random House LLC. All rights reserved.

The Invitation by Oriah Mountain Dreamer, copyright © 1999 by Oriah Mountain Dreamer. Used by permission of Oriah Mountain Dreamer, with deep gratitude and appreciation for the magnificent work of this brilliant author and teacher. All rights reserved.

"Your Seed Pouch" from *The Gift: Poems by Hafiz, The Great Sufi Master,* Penguin Compass, August 1, 1999, translated by Daniel Ladinsky, the greatest Sufi poet of our time. With profound awe and indebtedness for the authentic heart of love that Daniel has flowed into my life and the millions of hearts that taste his words. Copyright © Daniel Ladinsky. All rights reserved.

Nonviolent Communication^{SM} & *NVC*^{SM} are copyrighted service marks of *The Center for Nonviolent Communication*^{SM}. Their work adds inestimable value to the conversation of peace and conflict resolution on our planet. They share their material freely, but you can make a donation to *The Center for Nonviolent Communication*^{SM} by visiting www.CNVC.org.

Library of Congress Cataloging-in-Publication Data

Davidji.
  Destressifying : the real-world guide to personal empowerment, lasting fulfillment, and peace of mind / Davidji. -- 1st edition.
    pages cm
  ISBN 978-1-4019-4800-9 (tradepaper : alk. paper) 1. Stress (Psychology) 2. Stress management. 3. Self-actualization (Psychology) I. Title.
  BF575.S75D277 2015
  155.9'042--dc23
                                                                      2015011243

Tradepaper ISBN: 978-1-4019-4800-9

10 9 8 7 6 5 4 3 2
1st edition, August 2015

Printed in the United States of America

This book is dedicated to anyone who has ever experienced the pain in their belly, the tightness in their chest, the weight on their heart, the throb in their temple, the clench in their jaw, the closing of their throat, the holding in of their breath, and the <u>not</u> holding in of a harsh word.

. . . and to all those who breathe in stress every day only to have it fulfill them, to inspire and motivate them to be the best version of themselves.

contents

Preface

It all begins with awareness.

Several years ago, Michael Nila—a retired commander and 29-year veteran of the Aurora, Illinois, police department—approached me to teach his core team of Blue Courage police officers the practice of *destressifying*. He felt cops around the country would really benefit from my teachings, but he had concerns regarding how members of law enforcement would receive the word *meditation*. I emphasized to him that awareness was the goal, and that meditation was simply one of the tools we would use to get us there.

I shared with him one of my earliest experiences as a stress-management trainer. I had been invited to share some destressifying tips after a day at the beach with a few friends in the military. They suggested we leave the sand and head over to join an impromptu meeting already in progress a few miles away at Camp Pendleton—the Marine Corps' largest West Coast expeditionary training facility, spanning more than 125,000 acres of Southern California terrain and home to more than 30,000 residents.

They made a few calls, and we made our way down a series of winding dirt roads and through various security checkpoints to arrive at what seemed like a sweet small town with a coffee shop, restaurants, a medical clinic, even a swimming pool. We then drove deeper into the compound, leaving the innocence behind and nearing the training facilities where soldiers, sailors, Marines, and Special Forces learn to fight, shoot, and master the art of warfare. I felt more and more like a stranger in a strange land, passing training facilities, firing ranges, and mock-ups of buildings used to simulate raids. I was out of my element. In the distance, I could hear gunfire, helicopters, drill sergeants barking, and the nonstop sound of explosions.

We pulled up to a wooden shack, where my friend opened the door with a broad grin and ushered me forth. We stepped inside and he announced, "Here's a guy who thinks he can help us destressify."

The snickers were audible as I slowly walked to the front of the space, and there I was, standing in a room full of 15 arm-crossed Marines with high and tight "jarhead" haircuts. My long, white hair flowing past my shoulders, along with my signature Superman T-shirt with an "Om" in the middle of the emblem instead of an S, were probably not the best starting points.

As I shifted my gaze from one set of steely eyes to the next, I uttered out loud, "What was I thinking?"

In this room were some of the bravest and best-trained beings to ever walk our planet . . . perfect physical specimens with multiple tours of duty under their belts, fresh from a ten-mile run. And mentally, these guys were considered the toughest of the tough. I was in awe and a bit embarrassed about whether I could teach these heroic Marines anything about life. Most of them had witnessed, engaged in, and experienced more moments of uncertainty, pain, pressure, violence, courage, death, and destruction than the rest of us could ever conjure in the darkest corners of our minds. I must have seemed like a really bad joke. And in that moment, I was positive that I had stepped into the wrong classroom. They didn't know whether to laugh, leave, capture me, or shoot me.

And then I began to talk about Kandahar and the soldiers there who meditated every day with me for two months to stay sane between missions in the dusty heat of the day and their frigid nightly patrols . . .

I shared my story of a friend who was blinded by shrapnel from an IED on the side of the road in Tikrit—and how two of my students in an infantry regiment, scheduled for redeployment, instead were incinerated in their older-model Humvee the day before their departure, during an ambush in the northern Iraqi town of Hajiawa . . .

I spoke of the work I had done with an elite team of Dutch Special Forces on the eve of their mission into Syria and the benefits that so many of these warrior guardians had gleaned to remain whole throughout their various operations in the face of the unspeakable.

Slowly, the Marines' arms uncrossed. They relaxed a bit more in their seats. Their stern faces melted into tolerance . . . and then acceptance. They began to reveal that they were also fathers and brothers, husbands and teammates, and these were areas of their lives where they sought wholeness. They politely allowed me to teach them how to meditate to dial back the stress hormone surges, slow their bodies' raging chemical responses, and ease their relentless state of hypervigilance—all so critical for survival and performance in the heat of battle, and so distracting and damaging in their noncombat lives. Even Marines can benefit from replenishing their sense of calm, rebuilding their resilience, and clearing their minds at the end of a grueling or unthinkable day rather than self-medicating or numbing themselves to noncombat life.

They shared with me that throughout their deployment, they had made life-or-death decisions, pondered their morality, fought boredom, leapt into action, gone on autopilot, had their patience tried, snapped at their colleagues, tested their resolve, pushed their bodies and their minds to the brink—and beyond. Many had been involved in firefights, mortar attacks, and ambushes that sometimes raged for hours as they watched their comrades get wounded, lose limbs, and even get picked off by snipers. Others had desensitized their physiology by repetitively firing M16 "thunder makers" that had left them barely able to hear, barely able to feel . . . anything. Some had been shaken so completely by the relentless pounding of incoming mortar fire that the cells in their bodies felt liquefied. And others felt strengthened by the "what doesn't kill you makes you stronger" reality of surviving multiple deployments.

Several Marines admitted to having daily surges of panic and reactivity under nonthreatening circumstances since returning home. Others couldn't shake their nonstop state of hypervigilance. They opened up about the challenge of figuring out how to better communicate with loved ones and how the true battle actually began once they were back stateside, sitting in traffic alone with their memories or walking through life's daily activities off base.

Together we explored the core elements of destressifying, and I shared a few destressifying practices to help them ease the violent visions that visited them most nights in their dreams. We practiced a few core breathing techniques to help them wind themselves back down and connect to the present moment. We even practiced a body-scan meditation to help them awaken emotions that had become deadened over multiple tours.

When the impromptu class was finished, each Marine shook my hand and hugged me. Some of them even became emotional with gratitude. We had just scratched the surface, but they hankered for deeper destressifying tools and invited me to keep working with them for several weeks afterward. The results were profound. *Oorah! Semper fi!*

The depth of the transformation for all of us was palpable. It remains one of the most transformational days of my life; but throughout our game-changing few hours together, I never once used the word *meditation*. Instead, I spoke of the concept of awareness and introduced them to awareness tools and powerful destressifying practices to help them better understand and interact with themselves, their environment, and those around them. It was then that I coined the term *tactical breathing*, which to this day is used by members of law enforcement and the military, including Special Forces, to begin their process of destressifying.

• • •

As Nelson Mandela is reported to have said, "If you talk to a man in a language he understands, that goes to his head. If you talk to him in his own language, that goes to his heart." This was a huge Aha! moment for me, as I realized that the transformational power of these teachings rests in their translation. And so over the decade following that insight, I immersed myself in a body of knowledge that spanned thousands of years. I studied with some of the greatest masters of our time; I explored age-old scholarly texts; I traveled throughout the world gleaning insights from Eastern philosophies and ancient practices. In time, as lead educator of the Chopra Center and the first dean of Chopra Center University, I was privileged to teach large groups at weeklong retreats and smaller gatherings in workshop settings, where *translating timeless wisdom into real-world practical application* became my mission.

Over the years, my students numbered in the tens of thousands, and they came from every walk of life—highly successful executives and their assistants, movie stars and the homeless, soldiers and yogis, judges and convicts, children and their nannies, musicians and engineers, nurses and hospital patients, investment bankers and Wall Street occupiers, professional athletes and soccer moms, entrepreneurs and construction workers, artists and philanthropists, welfare recipients and mayors, taxi drivers and commuters, politicians and neuroscientists.

After ten years as lead educator, COO, and dean of Chopra Center University, I stepped down to travel the world and inspire the thousands of teachers I had certified during my tenure—and to lead by example. My unique background—a 20-year fusion of real-world business, modern science, and timeless wisdom—had equipped me to help individuals and organizations move in directions they craved but had never envisioned. I began my new mission of translating this vast body of knowledge into 21st-century life wisdom. I launched my own teacher trainings and empowerment workshops, where I taught others to apply these powerful teachings to modern-day situations. And in time, I began training high-stress, highly pressured businesspeople, lawyers, doctors, healers, stay-at-home parents, directors, managers, advisors, and entrepreneurs to become masters of destressifying, as well as teaching members of the U.S. military, Dutch Special Forces, Canadian Mounties, and U.S. law enforcement through Michael Nila's Blue Courage initiative with the support of the Department of Justice.

Over the years, these students of destressifying have leveraged the principles into the way they run their processes, their teams, their units, their departments, their businesses, and their own lives in the big and smaller moments.

• • •

You are probably not a Marine, even though you may wake up some mornings feeling like you're going into battle. And maybe after reading this, you feel as though your issues pale in comparison to those of someone who has experienced the horrors of war. But even for us regular folk, life can still be grueling; confusing; painful; disappointing; and filled with struggle, critical decisions, battles of the heart, nagging issues, and relentless waves of stress.

Most likely, you are a regular person like me who wakes up each day in the comfort of your home. Maybe you walk your dog or dress your kids, make yourself a cup of coffee or a bowl of cereal. You shower, you dress, and you head out to work to begin your day. Before all that, you check your messages upon waking. The e-mails flow into your inbox . . . the texts stack up . . . you go through the same conditioned daily rituals you have for the past decade—but at a faster pace than you did last year. You burn through the day—sometimes on autopilot—return home, eat dinner, and then collapse. Your life unfolds at high velocity as you try to live each moment with purpose and meaning, try to make the best decisions, try to show up and be the best version of yourself, try to add value to the world . . . to your life . . . and to the lives of others.

Some days it flows more easily than others. But every few hours throughout the day, you experience moments where your needs are not met, your expectations don't unfold as predicted, or someone or something throws you for a loop. You say or do something you wish you hadn't; what once seemed clear is now filled with a swirl of confusion; you keep running out of time; you start taking shortcuts when you should have thought through a solution more carefully. And your bigger issues, your career, health, money, and relationships—and even your lifelong dreams—seem to take a backseat to the hundreds of less profound but necessary daily chores, responsibilities, and commitments.

As you try to juggle all these lower- and higher-value tasks with everything else swirling around in your life, the result is stress. And the consequences can be devastating as you end up sacrificing the clarity of your thoughts, the impeccability of your words, the brilliance of your decision making, the potential of high performance, and the fulfillment of your dreams and desires.

But these harmful aspects are not the only side of stress. The most recent science is now demonstrating that stress can also strengthen us, build emotional resilience and mental toughness, help us forge deeper relationships, and teach us profound lessons. This was my inspiration to share the practices of destressifying with you, as the newest studies have opened a door to understanding stress as multidimensional—a destroyer of mental and physical health *and* a life-affirming and healing force. It's all a function of our perception in the moment.

destressifying is not simply another book about meditation. I already wrote that book—it's called *Secrets of Meditation*. It's now translated into 12 languages and has even won awards (hopefully you've read it). And while mastering your awareness is an important building block in the foundation of destressifying, meditation is only one component. It's the tool for setting the table for all that is to come. But more important, it's what you unfold in your life *outside* of meditation, when your eyes are wide open and you're back here with the rest of us—what you think, what you say, how you live, and what you do in the face of stress—that determines the fabric of your existence!

The reason I wrote *destressifying* is to share with you a vast, untapped body of knowledge that's been cloaked in mystery and has remained relatively inaccessible to most people, including:

- ancient empowerment teachings found exclusively in the oral tradition

- the newest brain-scan technology on the positive and negative impact of stress in all sorts of situations

- long-hidden insights and techniques to shift consciousness and communicate more effectively

From this wisdom, I have carefully crafted *a time-tested transformation process,* translated into a language you understand and using a fresh mind-set in order to move you from where you are to where you'd like to be—emotionally, physically, mentally, materially, in your relationships, and on your path to deeper fulfillment.

destressifying is my way of sharing these profound and deeper "secrets" with you in order to help you transform the way you live your life. There are more than seven billion people on the planet right now; and at the end of our lives, when we leave this physical earth plane and get to the top of the mountain, we'll look down and realize that there are more than seven billion paths to get there. Each of us has a different access point to timeless wisdom. Hopefully I'm speaking your language right now!

destressifying is not a term we often think about, but it is essential to our wholeness as individuals. It is our capacity to prepare for, recover from, and adapt in the face of uncertainty, overwhelm, disappointment, stress, adversity, trauma, or tragedy. We're not simply talking about bouncing back *after* we've faced a challenge, but rather *mastering our perception of the moment and cultivating our natural ability to seize that moment and express our best version of ourselves* in the face of a demanding, difficult, and taxing situation. In that process, we self-actualize, we grow, and we thrive.

You don't need to be living life on the edge to destressify—you simply need to be human and to have the desire to express yourself at the highest level. We are all conditioned beings with ancient, primal, biological responses deeply embedded in our DNA. Our emotional defensiveness and reactivity have been woven into the fabric of our thinking by our culture, our parents, our siblings, our schooling, our experiences, our bosses, our colleagues, our children, our partners, our exes, and the early authority figures present during our wonder years. The ripples of those relationships flow through us every day.

We all face stress and we will continue to—in our big moments and our quiet contemplations. *destressifying* will allow you to face it; move through it; transcend it with grace and ease; and come out the other side stronger, calmer, braver, clearer, more powerful, and masterful in living life on planet Earth.

· · · · ·

Introduction

It's pernicious . . . it's diabolical . . . it creeps into every moment in our lives. We've been told about its evils since we were children. It influences our relationships, impacts our physical body, works its way into our conversations, sparks non-nourishing behaviors, forces us to do things we'd never want to do. It's infectious; it's contagious; it's relentless . . .

It's *stress!*

We know it. We all have it. We all experience it. It's the human condition—especially when you learn its simple definition:

Stress is how we respond when our needs are not met.

Human beings experience this phenomena 8 to 15 times a day. And assuming our typical eight hours of sleep, that's an unmet need every one to two hours! But it's what we do with it, it's *how we respond to our unmet needs*—what we think, the words we speak, and how we react to each other and our unmet needs—*that determines the fabric of our life.*

Stress is universal because our needs are universal.

Yet the individual way each of us responds to having our needs met, and how we respond when they aren't met, become this unique mosaic we call our reality.

As we sway relentlessly between the realms of our met and unmet needs, the world swirls around us. And in critical moments when we crave clarity, the spontaneous right thought, word, or action . . . when we wish it could just slow down a bit so that we could make the best, most conscious choice for ourselves and everyone around us . . . *boom!* Instead, we may find ourselves swept up in a tsunami of thoughts, fears, confusion, overwhelm, regrettable behaviors, knee-jerk emotions, and conditioned reactions. Hormones and chemicals surge through our body, constricting our blood vessels, shallowing our breathing, thickening our blood, heightening our sugar levels, and suppressing our immune system.

But wait—the most recent scientific research now points to the fact that stress is not necessarily bad for us. It may even add value to our lives. Stress has now been proven to enhance performance by focusing us and pushing us forward in the direction of our goals, and with this stress-driven motivation comes increased productivity and greater satisfaction. Severe stress—such as in the aftermath of a trauma—has even been credited with birthing many of our Aha! moments, reinforcing our relationships, and elevating our journey of personal development. It's even been confirmed that stress has restorative properties that can increase health and rejuvenate cells after the initial ordeal.

But the long-term implications of stress are all based on our perceptions of it. Under the guidance of Dr. Richard J. Davidson, researchers at the University of Wisconsin–Madison performed an eight-year study on perception of stress and its impact on mortality. More than 25,000 participants were asked to rate their stress levels over the past year and rank how much they believed this stress influenced their health. Over the next eight years, public records were used to record the death of any subjects. The test subjects who (1) self-reported high levels of stress *and* (2) believed stress had a large impact on their health had a 43 percent increased risk of death.

However, the test subjects who self-reported *a lot of stress* but *did not interpret its effects as negative* had the fewest deaths over the eight years.

The main reason most people suffer with stress is because they don't have the right tools to address it. It is the reason I twisted for more than 20 years in the corporate world, struggling with restless sleep, living without balance, feeling overwhelmed, and searching for deeper fulfillment that rarely seemed to come . . . and was fleeting when it did. I didn't know what the tools were—nor did I have the manual on how to use them. *I didn't even know there were tools!*

But right now you're way ahead of where I was, and I have spent the past 14 years compiling the research and studying the wisdom needed to live a destressified life. There are five keys to living a destressifying life:

1. Mastering your awareness

2. Mastering your needs

3. Mastering your emotions

4. Mastering your communication

5. Mastering your purpose in life

You've already taken the most important step by joining me on this journey. And in these pages, we will walk together through each of the masteries until they are embedded within. Once these life tools are part of your thoughts, they will become your internal dialogue . . . and as they entrench themselves into every fiber of your being, they will become your outer dialogue, the way you express yourself with your words and actions. Your perspective on your entire existence will shift. You will become destressified effortlessly.

destressifying transcends the conversation about whether stress is good or bad for you by transporting you to a new and empowered state of consciousness that places you back in control of your emotions, your perception of the world around you, and your interpretation of a stressful moment. Stress is always in the eyes of the beholder! And by adopting a destressifying game plan for life, *everything* changes—from the very seeds of thought that trickle into your awareness to the chemical and hormonal pulses that drive your emotions to the steps you take with your words and actions.

A Clarification on destressifying

I realize that you may be wondering why the word *destressifying* is always in lowercase. destressifying has no capital letters because it is a graceful and easy present-moment process. It requires no announcement that it is unfolding; it seamlessly flows into your every word, thought, and action. When we discuss the process, it will look like this: destressifying. When I am referring to the word itself or to the book you are reading right now, it will look like this: *destressifying.*

The Blueprint for Our Journey

I've divided our journey together into three sections so that you can easily access the content and continue to use this book as a real-life owner's manual.

— *Part I* will teach you everything you ever wanted to know about stress—how it presents itself, the science behind it, and the biological and emotional reactions we have to it—while laying the foundation to a life that transcends stress.

— *Part II* is the essence of destressifying, where you will actually experience mastery in the core areas of your life—your awareness, your needs, your emotions, your communication, and your purpose.

1. First, I will teach you to *master your awareness* through the power of accessing the present moment. If you are new to meditation or have never meditated, do not be afraid—I have taught the toughest of the tough and the meekest of the meek to weave this easy tool into their lives. Having the skill to drift into stillness and silence when all else around you is loud and kinetic is a profound ability, and I will show you how to master it so the other benefits of destressifying have a bigger impact in your life. We'll do it in very small doses, and incrementally your practice will evolve. But that's just one piece of the process; the full practice of destressifying takes you deeper into other core aspects of your being . . .

2. So after you've mastered awareness, you will learn to understand your needs at the deepest level and the motivations behind them. You'll learn to *master your needs* by looking at your life through the lens of the *Five Realms*—a powerful tool to help you let go of what doesn't serve you *and* to bring deeper fulfillment into the physical, emotional, material, relationship, and spiritual aspects of your being.

3. Next, you will learn how to *master your emotions* as you cultivate your emotional awareness, heighten your emotional intelligence, and start to shift the way you respond to the world around you. This process alone will transform every interaction, collaboration, transaction, and communication you have from this moment forward.

4. And to enhance these exchanges between you and others, we'll embed the critical practice of conscious communication into your vocabulary, and you'll start to *master your communication*. You'll actually begin to listen more, express yourself more clearly, increase the likelihood of your needs being fulfilled, and interact with others at a higher level.

5. You will also learn to use daily tools to help you *master your purpose* in life as we uncover answers to the age-old questions *Who am I?* and *Why am I here?*

Upon finishing Part II, you will be comfortable using your tools, and you will have crafted your blueprint for living a destressifying life.

— Lastly, *Part III* is designed to help you keep the practice alive in your everyday life—at home, at work, when you travel, and in any given stressful circumstance. Filled with more in-the-moment stress-busters and guidance on how to keep destressifying flowing in your life on a daily basis, you will settle into destressifying as a proactive lifestyle.

Expanding beyond and blossoming from Part III, I've also created an online portal exclusively for readers of *destressifying* that will allow you to continue destressifying with me in a real-time, interactive, on-demand format. This resource is filled with updated videos, more powerful stress-busting meditations, a bonus chapter on using your five senses to destressify, and the newest scientific research on stress. I invite you to journey with me on a regular basis and reinforce the practice in those moments when stress feels threatening rather than challenging.

Embracing the Stress Paradox

Remember, stress can help us focus, take action, identify our needs that are not being met, enhance our performance, improve our memory, and manage a crisis more effectively. Stress can also push us over the deep end, filling us with anxiety, sadness, and overwhelm; testing our relationships; constricting our emotions; distracting us; and confusing us. This is called the "stress paradox."

We now know that the same biological response that prepares us for battle when we sense a threat can have positive consequences, in addition to the obvious negative physiological and health-related effects. According to the 2012 research paper "Rethinking Stress: The Role of Mindsets in Determining the Stress Response," by Alia J. Crum and Peter Salovey of Yale University and Shawn Achor of GoodThink, "the experience of stress elicits anabolic hormones that rebuild cells, synthesize proteins, and enhance immunity, leaving the body stronger and healthier than it was prior to the stressful experience."

This continuing game-changing research is taking us into uncharted territory regarding our perception of stress and sparking an entirely new dialogue regarding the paradoxical—sometimes counterintuitive—impact it has on our lives. In fact, new terminology is taking shape as stress-related *growth* is now being referred to in some scientific circles as post-traumatic growth (PTG). Science is now finding that weathering the storm of extreme stress can cultivate our inner resilience ("what doesn't kill us . . ."), making us mentally stronger after the fact and leading us to forge deeper relationships as we recover and connect with others. In the aftermath, we see the world with new eyes. We're empowered and brought to a place of deeper understanding of gratitude and purpose.

This doesn't mean that stress is all good or that it doesn't damage, debilitate, and wound us, but it suggests instead that there is a fine line of interpretation during *and* after the stressful moment where *we actually get to choose* whether stress is harming us or helping us.

This foundational paradox is why the process of destressifying makes so much sense. It's a mind-set, a lifestyle—not simply arresting stress in the moment, but proactively shifting the way you receive, interpret, and respond to life by cultivating a deeper awareness of it and yourself. Ultimately, destressifying means learning to be your best and express yourself at your highest level in *every* situation. So whether stress is good or bad matters *less* than what you do with the moment when stress appears and what you do with your life from this moment forward.

So are you ready to destressify? Are you ready to allow the best version of you to shine forth? Right now, in *this* moment, I invite you to join me on this death-defying, destressifying journey. Are you in? Then let's get busy!

• • • • •

PART I

Stress and destressifying

What Is destressifying?

destressifying is our ability to easily adapt to stressful situations and to adversity without experiencing the physical and emotional *negative* repercussions of stress. The most recent science has confirmed that those who deal with daily stresses *as challenges rather than threats* grow from them and can also more easily manage major crises with greater courage, clarity, strength, and grace. After becoming destressified, some of us even experience *greater* calm in the face of changes and surprises.

destressifying can easily be cultivated with a few lifestyle shifts, positive perceptions, and utilization of the daily tools through mastery of our awareness, our needs, our emotions, our communication, and our purpose. Even if you are naturally more sensitive to life's difficulties, if you give yourself permission to embrace the teachings, you can and will destressify.

destressifying occurs on many levels:

- *Physical* destressifying is reflected in our physical health and conditioning; our diet; our exercise; our hygiene; our sleep patterns; and our body's flexibility, balance, endurance, and strength.

- *Emotional* destressifying is reflected in our ability to self-regulate our emotions and reactions to the world around us, temper our highs and lows, cultivate our emotional intelligence, elevate our ratio of positive to negative emotions, muster our courage, heal our heart, and deconstruct our conditioned knee-jerk responses.

- *Mental* destressifying is reflected in our resilience, our thoughts, our perseverance, our attention span, our ability to stay focused, our mental flexibility (finding new, creative solutions to problems), and our level of optimism.

- *Relationship* destressifying is reflected in enhancing the quality of our relationships, winding down those that don't serve us, and redirecting our attention to those that are nourishing.

- *Spiritual* destressifying is reflected in our core values, our intuition, our awareness of something bigger than the self, our purpose, our acceptance of differing values and beliefs, and our self-actualization, which includes being of service to others.

Our performance at work, at home, and in the face of daily surprises is directly linked to our capacity to prepare for, recover from, and adapt to stress—to manage our awareness, needs, emotions, communication, and purpose under pressure and be the calm amidst the storm. And guess what? As long as we live, we will have surprises. Transcending them—actually interpreting them as challenges to be overcome rather than debilitating threats—and expressing ourselves with grace and ease is one of the keys to our self-actualization and rests at the core of destressifying.

• • • • •

CHAPTER I

Stressed Out?

*"Do you have the patience to wait until your mud settles
and the water is clear? Can you remain unmoving
till the right action arises by itself?"*

— LAO-TZU

When was the last time you snapped at someone or the last time you spoke words that you regretted? When's the last time you made a knee-jerk decision that you wish you could take back? Have you ever shut down to spite whomever you were talking to? Have you recently reacted to something in a way that made you feel horrible? How about the last time you felt burned out or overwhelmed?

Most likely the cause was *stress*. Your emotions were swirling. Your heart was pounding. Your mind was awash with a thousand thoughts. You were feeling defensive or protective or acting from anger or fear—and then you said or did something that didn't serve anyone, not you or the other person.

Modern science has termed stress as *any type of change that causes physical, emotional, or psychological strain*. But even that places a bit of a negative slant on it. So let's be more evenhanded and use this definition: *Stress is how you respond when your needs are not met.* All animals have a stress response, and it can be lifesaving. But repetitive or consistent stress can cause both physical and mental harm.

There are five basic types of stress:

1. **Good stress** (known as *eustress*, pronounced *"you*-stress"): a form of short-term stress that occurs when we perceive a stressor as a positive challenge instead of as a negative threat, such as striving to meet an attainable but challenging goal. Examples include playing sports, working toward the completion of a project, following through on an intention, or pursuing a lifelong dream. Eustress occurs when we interpret stress as life enhancing rather than life debilitating.

2. **Routine stress:** the pressures we experience every day at home, at work, at meals, and in between—from our restless sleep through our morning rituals and routines, into whatever regularly fills our day till dinnertime through winding down and back into bed. It's related to the pressures of work, family, and other daily responsibilities. Ideally, the stress from these abates moments after the event; if not, it becomes chronic stress (see item 4).

3. **Acute (short-term) stress:** an experience that delivers an unfavorable surprise that requires a quick response, such as getting a flat tire, spilling coffee on our new shirt, or missing our connection at the airport. But it can also be triggered by one of life's major challenges, such as when we lose something dear to us—a job, a loved one, a marriage, our youth, an important relationship, or even our health upon receiving a negative medical diagnosis. How we receive the information and what we do with it in the short term is our acute stress response. Sometimes news can throw us for such a loop that we remain frozen in a state of shock as the surge of thoughts, feelings, chemicals, and hormones simply overwhelms us.

4. **Chronic (long-term) stress:** the type of stress that *seems* relentless, never ending, and unavoidable. This includes the longer-term realities of—and attempts at coping with—the life challenges of loss, death, career, and love that I mentioned above.

The *day-to-day* realities of having been diagnosed with an illness, losing a job, harboring a deep secret for an extended period of time, feeling trapped in a non-nourishing relationship, or working in a relentless, high-demand position are just a few scenarios where you might feel imprisoned in the land of chronic stress.

5. **Traumatic stress:** the result of an accident, assault, attack, or devastating event that embeds itself so deeply within that even after the threat has subsided, all the physiological pain and emotional damage continues to live on within us. Sometimes numbing us deeply and other times resting dormantly *inside*—waiting for a trigger—traumatic stress can impact a person non-stop, expressing itself as chronic stress or being randomly triggered by sensory reminders such as sound, aroma, images, and even touch. The newest scientific findings point to the victim's ability to recover and grow from stress-related trauma as another outcome (post-traumatic growth, or PTG, which I mentioned in the Introduction)—but only if the right support systems are in place after the fact.

We all feel stress in different ways. Some of us get headaches, experience sleeplessness, bark at others in anger, have indigestion, bite our nails, run to the bathroom, cultivate addictions, or torture ourselves by directing our frustration inward. Some of us shut down and become depressed, remote, irritable, impatient, overwhelmed, or frozen. In chronic stress situations, we can feel as if we are just treading water—desperately trying to stay afloat—as life's waves relentlessly pound us until our will gives way to exhaustion. In the process, our health becomes compromised as we succumb to high blood pressure, extreme weight changes, restless sleep, sugar cravings, bouts of sadness, hardening of the arteries, nervous behaviors, and a weakened immune system.

With all these symptoms and non-nourishing biological reactions to unmet needs, stress gets a bad rap. But in fact, not all types of stress are harmful or even negative. Some are actually good for you. Yes, that's right—as you just learned in the description of eustress, there's *good* stress and *bad* stress. We rarely hear people say, "I'm loving this stress!" But some stresses actually help us feel alive, motivated, satisfied, and fulfilled.

There Really Is Something Called Good Stress

As I briefly described, good stress is the thrill that we experience when we feel excited but not really threatened—taking on a challenge that is a bit beyond our reach but attainable *if* we give it our all. In a classic eustress scenario, our goal is in sight; but to achieve it requires a commitment of time, energy, and will. In the process, we dig deep to summon perseverance, courage, determination, or motivation. And in these core moments of deep immersion into the experience, we are fully present in the task or mission.

Often described as being "in the zone," the eustress experience creates a scenario where we have no sense of time. In those moments of what modern science refers to as *flow,* we become the fusion of focus, chemical rushes, and feelings of accomplishment. We've all been there—performing some challenging task with such deep absorption that we feel we are one with whatever we're doing. These are the times we've said the perfect words at the perfect moment, run the perfect race, held the room captive as we've told the most entertaining story, played tennis like Federer, gardened as if we were one with the earth, cooked as if we were master chefs . . .

There are so many archetypal superstars we have admired and drawn inspiration from over the course of our lives who have publicly exhibited that state of flow in the extreme. Some of them may also have had their demons; but in their peak performance moments, they tapped into a brilliant, dynamic, creative flow that impacted the world and set them apart from their peers. In basketball, we look to Michael Jordan; in media influence, we think of Oprah Winfrey; in hockey, Wayne Gretzky; in dance, Mikhail Baryshnikov; in comedy, Robin Williams and Richard Pryor; in technology, Steve Jobs; in the world of inventions, Elon Musk; in social change, Martin Luther King, Jr. The list goes on and on. But those are only a few of the more famous people who have thrived in the moment of their eustress. There are billions who do it every day.

The triggers for eustress can be simple activities such as working on a crossword puzzle, riding a roller coaster, writing a letter, or planting a garden; trying anything new where the outcome is unknown, such as knitting a scarf or assembling a do-it-yourself piece of furniture; more technical activities such as competing in a tournament, participating in a spelling bee, or performing surgery; work-related projects such as developing a proposal, pitching a new idea, or engaging in a project; physical challenges such as athletic training, racing a motorcycle, surfing a wave, or playing sports; and at the most extreme level, piloting a plane or climbing a mountain.

We can even reinterpret what we feared as a threat to be a challenge and shift our mind-set from "Oh no!" to "Bring it on!" Ideally, when the goal has been reached, we feel deep satisfaction, which rewards the effort. But these are the three key aspects of eustress:

- We interpret the stressor as a positive experience (this is critical).
- We consider it a worthy endeavor.
- We believe the activity will increase our skill level.

The Eureka! Moment

During and after the stressful period, we are physically and emotionally rewarded with a surge of one of our feel-good chemicals—the success hormone dopamine—which creates the feeling we have succeeded at something. I refer to it as the *Eureka! Hormone*, from the famous exclamation of "Eureka!" (which means "I've found it!"), attributed to the ancient Greek mathematician and inventor Archimedes.

The legend goes that as Archimedes sat in his bathtub pondering how to determine the density of objects—in this case, the king's gold crown—he watched water splash over the edge of the tub, brimming from the density of his own body. In a flash, the answer came to him. We now know it as *Archimedes' principle*, which states that when a body is immersed in water, it experiences a kind of force we call buoyancy. This force is equal to the weight of the water displaced by the body. The story continues that in that moment, he leapt from his tub and ran through the streets naked, shouting "Eureka!" ("I have found it!") His brain must have been surging with dopamine!

For eustress to retain its positive impact, the activity must be relatively short-lived and perceived primarily as a good experience. If the stress period goes on too long or happens too frequently, it will devolve into chronic stress, which is never good. You've probably experienced eustress in the past week—meeting someone who makes your heart race, rushing to get to a party or a concert and feeling giddy when you get there, making a big presentation and basking in the afterglow, playing some competitive sport and feeling like an Olympic athlete, or finishing a project or a chore you've been delaying and feeling the tingling of relief and reward simultaneously.

Our pulse quickens, our breath becomes short and shallow, and hormones surge through us. We can even get a bit light-headed at times as the chemicals in our body shift around. We may feel a little scared about some aspect of the activity, but the rush of excitement is short-lived, and we are challenged but never feel an actual threat to our lives.

In fact, the newest brain science has revealed that short-term acute stress actually nourishes and readies the brain for improved performance. In their landmark study at the University of California–Berkeley's Helen Wills Neuroscience Institute, Daniela Kaufer, a professor of integrative biology at the University of California, and Elizabeth Kirby, a UC Berkeley postdoctoral fellow at the time, were able to demonstrate that significant—*but brief*—stressful events caused stem cells in rats' brains to multiply and mature into new nerve cells that *improved* their mental performance. It takes about two weeks for a stem cell to grow into a new nerve cell; and through the process of microlabeling each stem cell, the researchers were even able to determine that *the nerve cells involved in learning new tasks were the exact same neurons triggered by the acute stress two weeks earlier.*

Brain Fact

Science now confirms that momentary surges of stress hormones experienced by humans during acute stress situations help grow our hippocampus—the part of the brain responsible for learning, memory, and spacial orientation. Every fact and event you've ever absorbed into your mind had its birth in your hippocampus. That's not where memories are stored (we now know that memories are distributed throughout the brain), but the hippocampus is where they are formed. And for thousands of years, this timeless brain development system and reinforcement process has taught billions of humans how to stay alive—specifically, the places and situations to stay away from and the behaviors and scenarios that lead to solutions, breakthroughs, and deeper fulfillment.

I witnessed this brain chemistry firsthand with my dog, Peaches, soon after she came into my life. We were walking past a field that she had consistently ignored for about six months. But on this day, there were three rabbits nibbling grass right in the middle of the field. She had never seen a rabbit before, and the moment she spied them, she bolted off the leash to check them out. They quickly scattered into the forest, and she sniffed around in search of her "mirage." For weeks, every time we passed that field, her eyes stayed trained on the space where the rabbits had grazed. But after about six weeks, she stopped looking because the memory had faded since there was no reinforcement. Five years later—and we walk past that field every day—she pays it no mind.

Whether you are a dog, a rat, or a human, that surge of eustress must be short-lived or else it turns into chronic stress, which *elevates* glucocorticoid stress hormones, which then *suppress* growth, *impair* memory, and actually *stunt* us!

This may sound like gobbledygook to you, but bear with me for a moment because I want to share something that's truly amazing. When you experience acute stress, a burst of the stress hormone corticosterone stimulates astrocytes (the cells composing most of your brain), which then release fibroblast growth factor 2 (FGF2). This nourishes your stem cells, turning them into new neurons and increasing the gray matter in your hippocampus. This leads to faster learning, better retention, and expanded awareness.

It works like this:

How Stress Builds New Nerve Cells

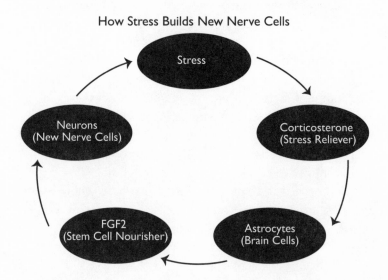

But the power of FGF2 doesn't end there. We now know that this magical growth factor contributes to wound healing by kick-starting the development of new blood vessels; and even more powerfully, it has an impact on lessening depression. So yes, a little stress (and I emphasize the word *little*) can brighten up your gloominess.

In the wild, animals experience acute stress on a constant basis, and this process helps them become more attuned to their environment so that they can more easily determine the nature of a threat. That's how even a domesticated dog quickly learns that a bunny can't hurt it, but a coyote can. Yet any *human* continually in a state of hypervigilance (perhaps that's *you* right now) will experience the negative effects of repetitive acute, intense stress, which over time can lead to chronic stress and, ultimately, to burnout.

The Life-Affirming Benefits of Good Stress

In our daily lives, some of us crave moments of short-term stress and satisfy the urge with activities that have a hint or an aspect of danger, such as racing a motorcycle, going out on a blind date, surfing, bungee jumping, riding a WaveRunner, wearing a scandalous outfit, cliff diving, hang gliding, sending an e-mail to a high school flame, rock climbing, scuba diving, or even jumping out of a plane wearing a parachute. At some deep level, we know all the twists, turns, and rapid descents can be life threatening; but in our heart of hearts, we don't sense that death or injury will be part of the experience. In fact, many thrill seekers have described their euphoria as being so close to death that *they feel totally alive*. We can have flickers of a threat to the body as we sidle right up to the edge of a death-defying activity.

But in most scenarios, during and after the fact, these experiences can be life affirming. Whenever we push the limits of what we think we can do—and this can be simply trying something we've never dared before, starting a new job, speaking in a conference room surrounded by our colleagues, firing an employee, or having that long-put-off difficult discussion at home—the process expands our boundaries and the breadth of our experience. Eustress keeps life fun, vital, exciting, and chock-full of meaning. It coaxes us to stay motivated—to wake up and do it all over again.

Both your body and your mind are impacted by stress; yet *when the experience itself is clearly defined, is relatively short term, and has a beginning and an end*, we recover quickly. Once it has ended, your *bodymind* (a term showing that your body and mind are a single, integrated whole) signals the "all clear" alert, and all the chemicals and hormones triggered by the stressful moment ease back down, leaving you in the afterglow of a feel-good, dopamine orgasm—fist pumping in the air, telling everyone around you about your success, and celebrating your win.

How Good Stress Can Become Bad Stress

We've all heard the expression "Too much of a good thing." And too much good stress can quickly devolve into bad stress. There was a period in my life when I really craved jumping out of planes, strapping on a scuba tank and diving deep, and pushing my motorcycle to the limit. I guess you could call it my adrenaline-junkie phase, where I regularly pursued opportunities to add a little bit of extra "juice" to spice up my life. After a brush with death during an innocent commuter plane flight, I realized that there was enough risk in my regular life to feed all my adrenaline cravings . . . so I traded in my bike and bought a Volvo.

Modern science says these forms of stress are actually beneficial in keeping us motivated and engaged. But for most people, watching an edge-of-your-seat thriller, reading a spy novel, riding a roller coaster, saying yes to a challenge, going out on a date, or making a big presentation can readily take the place of climbing Everest or inserting themselves into harm's way.

And yet . . .

How Much Is Too Much?

If you have too many of these "peak" moments in your daily schedule, your uplifting stress can become overwhelming or addictive, both with disastrous consequences. Yes, even the most exhilarating eustress will begin to accumulate over time and turn into harmful chronic stress, because your bodymind's stress response is not designed to be revving 24/7. So watching a three-hour marathon of violent or scary TV shows or playing video games every day will definitely create a negative ripple in your life and potentially turn into chronic stress.

But even if you've never touched a video game and don't care for violent movies, the state of feeling overwhelmed and its subsequent tsunami of emotions creates a foundation of inertia—procrastination at the lowest levels and burnout at the highest levels. Sometimes we can see this as a motivational force to "get on with it already!" and step through the challenge. But in most instances, the consistent overflow of stress hormones that impacts our physiology and the nonstop swirl of thoughts clouding our mind create a state of consciousness where we simply become stuck, frozen, as if in a voodoo trance.

Some of us have a subtle, unwitting addiction to this extreme stress (which can be as nefarious as being addicted to cigarettes, cocaine, or alcohol) that builds on our brain's craving for adrenaline and dopamine and can lead to extreme imbalances. Like any other addiction, you can begin sacrificing everything dear to you in exchange for a few bursts of adrenaline that come with racing down a slope, having an affair, gambling with your nest egg, shooting at a cartoon threat, or taking unnecessary risks to spike a stress response.

Which is worse? Overwhelm or addiction? In the end, they both will end in imbalance, depression, illness, and possibly death. Remember adrenaline junkie Bodhi, played by Patrick Swayze in the 1991 movie *Point Break*? So possessed was Bodhi, he ultimately chose death over prison by surfing a 100-foot wave.

Whether you are an adrenaline junkie, a new parent, a type-A personality, an overachiever, a perfectionist, starting a business, taking on a new position, juggling too many responsibilities, or somebody who simply likes to live on the edge, celebrate that you have stepped out of the epinephrine brainwashing just for a moment and into this twinkling of clarity: When it comes to stress, short-term *can be good*; long-term *is always bad*. We all need to take a breath once in a while—even from the nonstop roll of life-enhancing stress.

How Routine Is My Routine?

We are all well aware that life on planet Earth is filled with the day-to-day routine pressures of home, work, health, relationships, money, our current desires, and the consequences of our actions. Our mind is filled with ruminations on the past and projections about the future. We are obsessed with contemplating whether we did or said the right thing and how others will respond to our past actions. We are consumed every hour with never-ending predictions about the future.

We relentlessly gaze into the crystal ball and ask and answer strings of questions both important and inane, from *What will I have for dinner?* to *What should I do about this situation?* to *Should I pluck or color that gray hair?* The questions just keep coming: *Was I too harsh? How will they perceive me? Should I eat this brownie? What will happen regarding this decision I made? What time do I need to be there? When can I squeeze in that doctor's appointment? What will they say when they find out? Will I get to the meeting on time? Is he holding a grudge? How will this choice unfold? How do I approach my neighbors about their barking dog? What's my co-pay on this prescription? How should I apologize? Should I send this e-mail now or wait until tomorrow? How will this scenario play out? Can I afford this new house, car, outfit, piece of furniture? When will I fall asleep?* And on and on it goes.

The pressures of our daily responsibilities seem never ending. But we've asked and answered the questions so many times that they become the threads and whispers of routine stress that run in the background of our mind, simply becoming the underlying fabric of our existence. As we destressify, these whispers become fainter and stop relentlessly tugging on our heart and mind. *If we don't,* they devolve into pounding waves of acute stress and turn chronic.

Acute Stress

You don't have to be a daredevil to trigger short-term stress. Outside the realm of euphoria seekers and adrenaline junkies, the rest of us experience short-term stress every day that doesn't necessarily light us up, thrill us to our core, or make us feel great. Seeing the name of someone we don't want to talk to pop up on caller ID, spilling coffee on our clothes, getting lost, bumping into someone we've been avoiding or fighting with, dropping our cell phone, getting caught speeding, getting stuck in an elevator, making a wrong turn, waking up late, finally admitting an error, asking for forgiveness, telling a lie, stubbing our toe, revealing a long-held secret, racing to meet a deadline, rushing to get somewhere on time—these are all examples of what science refers to as short-term or acute stress.

As we've discussed, acute stress can be interpreted positively as *eustress* ("I'm so excited to go to this interview!"); but when it's perceived by us as negative ("I dread having to go to this interview!"), it is called *distress*. But as long as it ends rather quickly, there are no harmful repercussions. In fact, even though distress may bring emotional pain in the moment, if it dissolves within a few minutes, at some basic level it will have helped us develop our brain and expand our realm of experience.

A simple example of the lessons we glean from an acute-stress moment is impatiently sipping a hot cup of coffee and burning our tongue, leading to instant pain, anger, frustration, disappointment, and irritation. The mis-sip has just taught us a valuable lesson (hopefully, it's the first time we've learned that lesson) and will stay with us every time we eat or drink something through the next 24 hours.

But most often, life is filled with more profound examples of acute stress: having an argument, experiencing the consequences of being late, not being prepared, saying the wrong thing, getting into a jam. These all impact us on a deeper emotional level, and we don't let them go so quickly. Each instance becomes a conversation in our head that we hold on to for hours, days, weeks—or even years—and ultimately starts impacting our thoughts, words, and actions.

For wild animals, sporadic acute stress is the bulk of what they experience in the form of physical threats in their direct ecosystem. It takes only a five-second scare to teach an animal "Don't do that again!" Then they move on, having learned the lesson.

This was also the case for humans 20,000 years ago. But the world has become more complex: Our family structure has morphed beyond the simplicity of the village . . . our relationships have become cross-cultural, cross-gender, cross–work/life, cross-geographic, and cross–time zone . . . technology has connected us to people, issues, and situations that are thousands of miles away . . . electricity has plugged us into myriad conversations that go way beyond our basic internal dialogue . . . and our attention is pulled in so many different directions. Now we go far beyond the five seconds of learning from an acute stress moment and hold on to it, often longer than it serves us. We worry, discuss, and ruminate on our experiences (even a burned tongue), which, in turn, can create even more stress.

Any time we interpret a threat to our physical body, our belief system, or our sense of self, the response is acute stress. It doesn't matter if it's real or not—as long as we *perceive* the threat (imagined or actual), all the biological and emotional repercussions of stress will instantly be sparked. We will start to perspire; our breathing will become more rapid, increasing our blood flow, and in turn increasing our blood pressure. A tidal wave of stress hormones will race into our cells, and we will exhibit the biological stress response that psychologists refer to as the *fight-or-flight response*: either physically or emotionally getting aggressive or running away. And in the critical moment when you need to be impeccable with your word, to summon your patience as someone else lashes out at you, or to come up with the nick-of-time solution—when you most need to be reflective instead of reflexive and show up as the best version of yourself—instead you will simply be reactive, responding like a barking dog, a charging rhino, or a skittering lizard that feels threatened. Sound familiar?

When this occurs on a daily basis because you just can't get past all the instances of acute stress that are bombarding you, then you "graduate" to what stress psychologists call *episodic acute stress*. At this point, in every moment, you are at the mercy of what comes at you because you have neither the tools to cope with it nor the mind-set to transcend it. destressifying will arm you with those tools and help you foster a mind-set that places you back in charge of how you perceive the world. If left unattended, however, as the surprises, disappointments, overwhelm, and non-stop threats to your body and mind continue for days, weeks, or months, you will arrive at the harmful lifestyle of chronic stress.

Chronic Stress

Chronic stress occurs over a period of time when we repeatedly face stressors that we believe threaten us in some way. (Imagine that rhino charging at you every hour on the hour, or someone poking you in the chest every 15 minutes.) Whether it's our credit-card debt; our lack of self-esteem (and all the little voices in our head that regret, judge, and hold grievances); a boring or grueling job we dislike or a demanding boss; feeling unsupported in some way; a relationship filled with disagreement, nonstop emotional turbulence, struggles, or toxicity; or daily coping with physical pain, if we are feeling constantly threatened, the impact it has on us is no longer a beneficial jolt of acute stress—it's long-term chronic stress.

When we experience any kind of *distress* with this type of regularity or concentration, our autonomic nervous system can't catch its breath long enough to relax our physiology. The result is that we become captive to a constant state of hormonal overload, fear-based thinking, and lack of clarity.

If you are not there yet, destressifying will help you avoid getting there. If you are already in the throes of chronic stress, *do not despair!* destressifying was specifically designed for you, and by the end of this book, *you will be destressified!*

Traumatic Stress

At the furthest edge of the stress spectrum is traumatic stress. We often think of this in terms of soldiers returning home from multiple tours of duty, but those suffering from the impact of traumatic stress come from all walks of life. In fact, in our vast society, victims of childhood physical, sexual, or emotional abuse are even more numerous than those in the military who've been diagnosed with post-traumatic stress disorder (PTSD); but they don't get the press or same public attention and most likely have been living with their trauma for decades. Traumatic stress was once considered the rarest form of stress, until tens of thousands of men and women stationed in Vietnam, Iraq, and Afghanistan began reintegrating back into a society that didn't understand their trauma or the consequences of the repetitive stress of living under the hourly threat of death.

We have become a country rich in PTSD, with millions of individuals spanning the mildest forms of trauma to the most severe, who display chronic symptoms of insomnia, night terrors, paranoia, reclusiveness, and extreme depression. The most obvious examples are the survivors of physical, sexual, and emotional abuse as children; every survivor from the Twin Towers of the World Trade Center on 9/11; the family members of every nonsurvivor; all the police, fire, and rescue teams who spent that fateful day and the ensuing weeks at ground zero; most of our Vietnam veterans who returned home with no support system; the millions of black Americans who spent their childhoods under the oppression of segregation and the disenfranchisement, horror, and violence that accompanied it; the tens of thousands of kids who have been bullied at school and continue to be tormented online; the tens of thousands of police officers who have been living with the agony of chronic stress for decades; the thousands of victims of identity theft; and the tens of thousands who lost their homes *and* jobs during the financial crisis and subsequent economic downturn of 2007–2010. This list is ever expanding, open-ended, and wide-ranging. Imagine the stress that this broad collective is under.

Chronic stress also impacts those experiencing trauma from natural disasters; assaults; car, train, bus, bicycle, plane, and ferry accidents; robberies; home invasions; and random violence that we see on the news every night. And it all comes from one or multiple events that were so stressful to a person that they then carved themselves deep into the individual's psyche, where the person can't find the "off" switch for the surge of hormones and chemicals that were released into their bloodstream.

Life after Trauma

First reported in the *Bulletin of the Menninger Clinic,* a world leader in psychiatric treatment, research, and education, Drs. C. A. Simpson and G. L. Porter's research of the 1980s revealed almost double the amount of "self-destructive activities" in victims of PTSD compared with those not traumatically stressed. Pioneering research on behavioral reenactment by Bessel A. van der Kolk, M.D., originally published in *Psychiatric Clinics of North America* in 1989, showed that those experiencing a life trauma—especially as children—continue to live in states of profound chronic stress. His research uncovered that these individuals subconsciously replay the traumatizing event over and over, triggering its physiological and emotional stressors. They do so to such an extent that they create similar circumstances to their trauma and reenact it in some way by victimizing someone else in the same way or by playing the victim again and again. This recurrent theme of revictimization and masochism reverberates in almost every victim of PTSD—until they are treated and taught to destressify.

In the following passage from his groundbreaking research mentioned above, Dr. van der Kolk shares an insight from one of his PTSD patients:

> For example, we treated a Vietnam veteran who had lit a cigarette at night and caused the death of a friend by a Viet Cong sniper's bullet in 1968. From 1969 to 1986, on the exact anniversary of the death, to the hour and minute, he yearly committed

"armed robbery" by putting a finger in his pocket and staging a "holdup," in order to provoke gunfire from the police. The compulsive re-enactment ceased when he came to understand its meaning.

This is just one example from the millions who suffer from traumatic stress, which *is* treatable by working with a trained mental-health professional. I have worked with many individuals diagnosed with PTSD, and I know from firsthand experience that it is not a death sentence. Recovery and thriving are indeed likely outcomes for patients willing to seek help; commit to treatment; redefine their lives; and work with a qualified therapist, doctor, nurse, or support organization.

Post-Traumatic Growth

Additionally, the most cutting-edge, current research is revealing new ways to look at stress through the diagnosis of post-traumatic growth (PTG). This means that after the specific trauma or adversity, victims report finding a new gear, comprising inner strength and enhanced abilities, rejuvenation and renewed nourishment in the relationships in their lives, deeper spiritual and purposeful connections, a redefining of their "story," and a reordering of their life priorities. We've all heard someone say, "Being diagnosed with cancer *saved* my life," or "I'm so grateful my husband divorced me," or "Being fired opened new doorways for me that I never imagined."

Groundbreaking research and contributions to the field of PTG have been pioneered by many. But it's most notably the recent work of contributors to the *Handbook of Posttraumatic Growth,* edited by Lawrence G. Calhoun and Richard G. Tedeschi; *Trauma, Recovery, and Growth,* edited by Stephen Joseph and P. Alex Linley; and leading-edge work by brilliant researcher, happiness expert, TED Talk sensation, and author of *The Happiness Advantage,* Shawn Achor, that have advanced the conversation to its current status.

In a 2012 article in *The Psychologist*, Stephen Joseph wrote:

After experiencing a traumatic event, people often report three ways in which their psychological functioning increases:

1. Relationships are enhanced in some way. For example, people describe that they come to value their friends and family more, feel an increased sense of compassion for others and a longing for more intimate relationships.

2. People change their views of themselves. For example, developing in wisdom, personal strength and gratitude, perhaps coupled with a greater acceptance of their vulnerabilities and limitations.

3. People describe changes in their life philosophy. For example, finding a fresh appreciation for each new day and re-evaluating their understanding of what really matters in life, becoming less materialistic and more able to live in the present.

Transforming Bad Stress to Good Stress

Using the proper destressifying tools, we can shift our perception of the moment and transform bad stress into good stress. It's not an exercise in denial or rationalization, and it may appear magical when you first experience the shift, but it's real. It's also scientifically documented by brain scans and MRIs, as well as hormone and chemical analyses of what happens in our bodies and brains when we no longer have the experience of perceiving a threat to our physiology or to our ego.

Taking Your Stress Pulse

A valuable step for anyone fearing they are experiencing acute distress, chronic stress, overwhelm, or stress addiction is to stop the wild ride just long enough to take a self-assessment and see where they stand. So let's find out right now where *you* are, stress-wise. Simply take your stress pulse by answering the following questions. Are you:

- Irritated by little things or small interruptions in your flow?
- Impatient or restless (waiting for something to happen)?
- Feeling run-down?
- Lacking clarity in your decision making?
- Experiencing agitated sleep?
- Running out of time or missing deadlines?
- Snapping at those around you?
- Feeling like you're walking on eggshells or afraid to speak?
- Quick-tempered?
- Using sarcastic language?
- Feeling hopeless?
- Feeling like life is coming at you too quickly?
- Stuck?

If you answered *yes* to any of these questions and the issue has been going on for a while (more than a week), then there's a good likelihood that stress is taking its toll on you. How exciting! But no worries—you've come to the right place.

Just as sadness is a symptom of being out of balance, your answers to these questions are symptoms of your degree of stress perception and imbalance. The short- and long-term consequences of stress are scientifically proven to lead to disease. If you put down this book right now and choose not to destressify, in time, these symptoms will most likely exacerbate and turn into a full-blown diagnosis of something much more serious.

More important, your mind-set in terms of how you receive and perceive stress will stay stuck in that old-school, glass-half-empty, negative, life-debilitating belief system, which will adversely impact every aspect of your existence.

Stress is here, and *hundreds* of millions of people are struggling with it right now. But by simply continuing this journey with me, you *will* destressify. Some of us have destressifying woven into our DNA, and some of us must cultivate it. Don't worry about whether you are organically destressified. Wherever you are in your life, you can locate it, learn it, strengthen it, cultivate it, and then have its nourishing benefits flow through every cell in your body. To start the process, let's get clear about what stress *really* does to us on a physical and emotional level.

• • • • •

CHAPTER 2

What Stress Does to Your Body: The Fight-or-Flight Response

"We take our shape, it is true, within and against that cage of reality bequeathed us at our birth; and yet it is precisely through our dependence on this reality that we are most endlessly betrayed."

— JAMES BALDWIN

As human beings evolved over the past 20,000 years, we were hardwired with a self-preservation reflex known as the fight-or-flight response. It was first described by American physiologist Walter Cannon in 1929 and explains what happens to our body's most primal brain functions when we perceive a threat to our physical body—essentially how we react when something crosses our boundary of physical safety. When we perceive a life-threatening situation, we react in the moment and choose one of two basic paths of survival: *to fight* or *to run*. This self-preservation mechanism is woven into every animal on the planet and has been for tens of thousands of years.

Essentially, it works like this: Imagine that you're hunting and gathering in a jungle during prehistoric times, when you hear a saber-toothed tiger make a loud hiss. Upon perceiving this threat, your body's limbic system (which controls emotion, behavior, memory, and your sense of smell) immediately responds via your autonomic nervous system, a complex network of endocrine glands that automatically regulates your hormonal chemistry and metabolism. Your autonomic nervous system is the part of your reflex makeup that causes you to unconsciously blink your eyes and lick your lips. Among many other functions, it's essentially your body's maintenance, equilibrium, and survival autopilot.

So you hear the hiss of the saber-toothed tiger and instantly your body knows, *Uh-oh—there's a high likelihood I will be killed or maimed in a few moments!* Your autonomic nervous system goes into high gear because it knows it has only a few moments to save your life. This will be a sprint—not a marathon. You've got just a few minutes to defeat the threat or run from it as the fight-or-flight biological stress response kicks in.

Here's what happens in the first few seconds:

- First, you start to perspire. Your autonomic nervous system knows you most likely will overheat from your response, so it does the one thing it can to cool you: It sweats.

- Then you start to breathe more rapidly, pulling oxygen more quickly into your bloodstream.

- This increases blood flow, blood pressure, your pulse, and stress on your heart.

- Blood leaves all the noncritical aspects of your physiology and moves to the muscles in your arms and legs so that you can either run away or battle the saber-toothed tiger.

- Blood flow to your organs decreases, especially to your digestive tract, so all the food you've eaten stops being digested.

- Then your stress hormones (adrenaline, cortisol, glucagon) start to surge to give you an extra burst of energy and focus.

- Your blood sugar spikes as glucagon tells the pancreas to slow insulin production (so the effect is like eating five Snickers bars at once!). Now you're really hyper, in case you need an additional spurt of energy to fight or run away.

- Your autonomic nervous system shuts down all functions not essential for dealing with the threat, such as your growth hormone (hair, nails, skin, cellular development) and your sex hormones (the health of your entire reproductive system).

- Since you might die from this threat at any moment, your immune system shuts down so as not to waste any unnecessary effort (fighting germs is superfluous under the threat of death!).

- Your platelets (the hard parts of your blood that move through your plasma) become plump and sticky, thickening your blood. Your systems believe the threat is real and perhaps you will be cut by the saber-toothed tiger, so they start the clotting in advance.

All this happens in less than five seconds—and now you are ready to fight the life-threatening situation or run from it. Can you imagine how critical this was when we were living in the wild thousands of years ago?

Okay, now fast-forward to the present day. There are no saber-toothed tigers out there; and unless we're in a war zone, we rarely experience threats to our lives. But don't tell that to your autonomic nervous system. It was designed more than ten millennia ago and has not kept up with the newest technology or extinct animals list. It believes *all* threats are life threatening because 10,000 years ago, they were. Someone needs to update your internal software . . . oh yeah, you're doing it right now!

The fight-or-flight response is referred to as a biological stress response. The term *stress* is short for *distress,* a word evolved from the Latin word *distringere,* meaning "to draw or pull apart." In your most stressful moments, it can sometimes feel as if you are being pulled in a million directions emotionally, physically, mentally, spiritually, and in all other aspects of your life.

Each day we experience small disappointments and larger expectations not being met. Whenever your needs aren't met, you have the potential to respond in many ways. When you respond reflexively instead of reflectively—automatically going into "survival mode" instead of choosing a more thoughtful response— you lower yourself to your most primitive state, which includes the fight-or-flight response hardwired into your DNA. And in that moment, you are ruled by your chemicals and hormones, acting out a long-conditioned pattern.

Are You Wired to Fight or Flee?

The level of testosterone that's in your system will often determine whether you will fight or flee. If you have a high level of testosterone, which is the case with more men than women, then you're prewired to *fight* upon experiencing a threat. Lower levels of testosterone, which is the case with more women than men, will make you more likely to *run away.* An additional factor is hunger. We are actually more likely to fight back if our stomach is empty. When we are famished, the blood flows away from our rational brain functions to our reptilian, survival-based functions, and boom—we are milliseconds away from attacking. But nine out of ten times, our first instinct when we're physically threatened will be to run (or at least move or jump back) before we take our next step, whether we are a man or a woman.

Oxytocin Helps Us Tend and Befriend

In addition to the fight-or-flight reaction, new research shows that there is actually a third response known as *tend-and-befriend*, introduced in 2000 by Shelley E. Taylor, Ph.D., and her research team at UCLA and first described in *Psychological Review*. In crisis, women are more likely to ask for help. (You know the stereotypical conversation when a couple is lost. One partner suggests, "Honey, why don't you ask for directions?" And the other responds, "No. I can figure this out!") That's not because members of the "fairer" sex are weaker, but rather because they have a special relationship with the hormone oxytocin.

The word *oxcytocin* comes from two Greek words: *oksys*, meaning "swift," and *tokos*, meaning "birth"—essentially *swift birth*. Oxytocin is released in large amounts after distension of the cervix and uterus during labor, facilitating birth and maternal bonding, and then the stimulation of the nipples and lactation.

Outside of the direct role it plays in childbirth, oxytocin is known as the love hormone, the feel-good chemical, and the bonding or attachment hormone. It gives you that special feeling of "oneness" when you are with someone you trust. Going back millennia, establishing social alliances helped us survive—but only with people we could trust. This hormone helps us determine whom we believe we can trust in the most primal way.

Oxytocin can be released in response to stressors that trigger what are known as *affiliative needs*, which include maternal tending, sexual connections, bonding with others, protecting our offspring, and seeking social support. Because women are wired to propagate the species and nurture their young, the oxytocin pathway in their brains has been more deeply carved. For someone (such as a mother) who is practiced in tending and befriending, oxytocin virtually forces affiliation under stress. These individuals reach back to their earliest, most fundamental needs of protecting themselves and their children and pursuing social contact to meet the innate maternal drive to shield, defend, and safeguard.

It's theorized that oxytocin increases our desire to approach or avoid someone in a social situation. And research shows that it actually heightens our ability to pay closer attention to any social cues they might express, like body language, facial micro-expressions, and other forms of nonverbal communication. Oxytocin helps us intuitively determine another person's relationship potential—their openness, friendliness, attraction, eagerness, and their all-around "energy." In the subtlest way, it helps us identify relevant social cues and detect nuances in trustworthiness.

Reaching out for help is as relevant now as it was way back in caveman days. Our fear and anxiety responses were designed to protect us by garnering a little more support to help us overcome a challenge. And as we instinctively seek strength in numbers, the complex biological aspects of tend-and-befriend lead to an even greater likelihood that we will survive the potential threat.

When operating during times of low stress, oxytocin physiologically rewards those who maintain good social bonds with feelings of well-being. But when it comes on board during times of high social stress or pain, according to Dr. Taylor, it may "lead people to seek out more and better social contacts." She has surmised that "stress-related manifestation of oxytocin may produce physiological changes that then encourage people to seek contact with others."

Fight or Flight . . . or Freeze?

In 12-step groups throughout the world, a fourth response beyond fight-or-flight is often discussed: the *freeze response*. And yes, oxytocin is responsible for this as well. According to C. Sue Carter, Ph.D., former co-director of the Brain Body Center at the University of Illinois at Chicago, and one of the first to study oxytocin in animals, the freeze response is real. She points to the work of Stephen W. Porges (another trailblazer in this field of study, a professor in the Department of Psychiatry at the University of North Carolina at Chapel Hill), who first articulated that oxytocin, acting in part through effects on the autonomic nervous system, might allow what he termed "immobility without fear."

In other words, oxytocin may in fact protect us from an inappropriate fear response in the face of stressful circumstances, especially those that require freezing or holding still (like coming face-to-face with some underwater denizen while you're scuba diving) rather than fighting or fleeing. According to Carter, "oxytocin may play an important role in helping females manage both emotional and physiological responses during life-altering events such as childbirth—converting potentially stressful experiences into opportunities for expressing joy and love." Pure destressification!

The Real Reason Why Women Are More Intuitive

It's often said that women are the more sensitive gender, and perhaps it's because of their special relationship to oxytocin. Estrogen has been shown to stimulate the release of oxytocin. So the more you have, the more you will be guided to draw a circle around the people you trust and bring them closer and to exclude or avoid those you don't trust by distancing yourself from them. The phrases "women's intuition" and "mother knows best" aren't simply old wives' tales—they are rooted in the power of oxytocin and its estrogen foundations. Studies show that women can actually identify facial expressions of disgust and fear more quickly than men. This goes back to prehistoric days when determining who to trust was a life-or-death decision (and of course, that huge responsibility was interwoven into women, while the men were out hunting). Paradoxically, these oxytocin moments seem to *override* our biological stress responses of elevated heart rate; increased blood pressure; and the release of cortisol, adrenaline, and glucagon. Love overcomes stress!

The Damage of the Fight-or-Flight Response

Over time, repeated triggering of fight-or-flight reactions because of distress can lead to emotional, physical, or sexual dysfunction and increase your chances of getting sick. It may manifest as chronic illness, such as irritable bowel syndrome, fibromyalgia, lupus, Crohn's disease, migraine headaches, skin disorders like psoriasis, or PTSD.

Realistically, how many times do you think you can harden your blood, suppress your immune system, inject yourself with sugar, and strain your heart before you are diagnosed with something much more catastrophic than whatever you were stressed out about?

Add to that the stark reality that our bodies are designed to slowly decelerate the protective response once the perceived threat is gone, *but often don't when we are in the grip of chronic stress.*

Adrenaline Facts

Adrenaline, also known as *epinephrine*, is a naturally occurring hormone. When we perceive a threat, the adrenal glands release epinephrine into the bloodstream, which has these effects:

- Revs us up

- Makes our heart pump harder

- Narrows our blood vessels

- Increases our blood pressure

- Expands the airways in our lungs

- Constricts blood flow in our intestines

- Sends blood to our arms and legs so that we can fight or run

While adrenaline can motivate us to save ourselves in life-threatening situations, throughout the day—when our lives are *not* being threatened—surges of adrenaline are activated in response to perceived threats (that are not really a danger), which leads to feelings of anxiousness, rushes of fear, overwhelm, exhaustion, and ultimately, burnout.

Stress and Health: Implications of Chronic Stress

If we continue to sense threats, very quickly we will start to experience physical symptoms of being in chronic stress. We'll catch colds a little more frequently than we ever did before. This is not a sign of getting older; this is a sign that we are suppressing our immune system with regularity. We can start to experience consistent or regular headaches when we used to have them only in extreme situations. In time, we may notice sexual dysfunction, premature aging, accelerated hair loss, depression, cold sore eruptions, and slow wound healing.

My dear friend and mentor David Simon, M.D., a brilliant neurologist, was known to have said, "90 percent of our physical toxicity is emotionally derived." Our fight-or-flight reactions to stress are creating physical issues, and *our interpretation of stress as a threat rather than a challenge is the culprit.*

Chest pains are also a common sign of chronic stress, since you're continually straining the heart, as are headaches, migraines, twitches, and nervous tics, because you're increasing your blood pressure and moving blood away from your core. A constant lump in your throat or a consistently dry mouth are also symptoms of chronic stress, because your salivary glands are shut down by the autonomic nervous system as they won't help you fight or run.

Since all this blood is being forced into your larger muscle groups, experiencing muscle pain in your legs and tension in your arms—especially at night when you are lying in bed and are most aware of your body—is a common sign of chronic stress. Other signs include impotence, amenorrhea, early onset of menopause (male and female), and many other issues related to sexual function, because your flow of blood and its nourishing nutrients are redirected away from your genitals and reproductive tissues to your arms and legs. A more visible sign of stress is premature aging, skin dryness, and rashes as your growth hormone wanes.

If you find yourself chewing on Tums or Rolaids for indigestion, or Prilosec, Prevacid, AcipHex, Protonix, Zegerid, Nexium, or some other proton pump inhibitor "cure" for heartburn or gastroesophageal reflux disease (GERD), you should be aware that all these issues are related to stress. It comes as no surprise that President Obama was diagnosed with GERD in 2014—his sixth consecutive year of chronic stress. The fight-or-flight response shuts down your digestion, increases acid secretion, and creates ulcers over a period of time, bouncing you between diarrhea and constipation, which then cause you to take Pepto-Bismol and Kaopectate. destressifying can end your dependence on *all* these temporary remedies. Do you realize the size of the industry that has been built on keeping you in the clutches of stress?

The Six Stages of Stress

Stress follows a very clear path to disease, and it moves in six stages.

Stage One: Accumulation

Stress causes toxins produced by improper digestion to collect in the gastrointestinal (GI) tract. The presence of these toxins causes mild and ill-defined symptoms to show. This is the first and most subtle stage, where we have an opportunity to recognize, address, and eliminate the cause instead of ignoring or suppressing it. Most often we are oblivious since we're complacent in our stress, seeing it as normal or temporary.

Stage Two: Aggravation

The accumulated stress toxins amass to such a degree that they begin to get "excited" by our behaviors, the foods we ingest, and our environment. We may have a twinge here or there, but we are still relatively unaware of the cause. And by now we may even be inured to the symptoms.

Stage Three: Spread

The aggravated, accumulated toxins start overflowing. Generally, up to this stage the damage is entirely reversible and restorable through a daily destressifying practice. We may notice that we're experiencing symptoms of malaise or tiredness as our antibodies work overtime to hold back the flood of toxins.

Stage Four: Augmentation

The overflowing toxins begin to migrate, leading to tissue malfunction and structural damage as specific degeneration and sensitivities to more serious infections begin. If we haven't felt physical symptoms before, we will start to feel them at this stage, although they may still be one stage short of a Western medical diagnosis.

If you feel symptoms that can't be detected by modern Western medicine, this does not mean you are crazy. The augmentation stage can be very stealthy. Take an additional step to help get to the root of the matter and seek out an alternative, holistic, or complementary health professional.

Stage Five: Symptom Manifestation

Specific symptoms begin to appear and can now be identified and diagnosed by conventional medical science or a physician. A classic tip-off is that we find ourselves Googling our symptoms or going on websites looking for a diagnosis. Remember that identifying or eliminating symptoms is *not* the same as treating the source of the issue. A committed program of destressifying is necessary at this stage to return our bodies to their healthiest state.

Stage Six: Complications/Differentiation

After years or even decades, stress reaches its final stage of physical manifestation, becoming chronic and ultimately revealing the clear nature of the disease. And then we get officially diagnosed with a physical ailment. Dis-ease has become disease.

Every disease follows this six-stage path. When we chronically succumb to our less-evolved, conditioned, knee-jerk reactions, we may not feel the damage in the moment, but the longer-term health consequences can be devastating. Chronic stress nefariously plants seeds of illness.

The concept of "seeds of illness" was first discussed by the 19th-century French physiologist Claude Bernard when he wrote, "Illnesses hover constantly above us, their seeds blown by the wind, but they do not set in the terrain unless the terrain is ready to receive them." A person in the throes of stress is indeed that fertile terrain waiting for these "seeds of illness" to plant themselves. And as Dr. David Simon often said, there is a cause-and-effect nature of these stress "seeds" as they relate to our modern diagnosis of disease.

Because each of our early warning signals is different, it's important to get in touch with your own response to stress overload. Simply by paying attention, you'll begin to notice the toll that stress is taking on your body and the seeds of illness that are surreptitiously being planted.

Seeds . . . then Disease	
Change in Physiology:	**Leads to:**
Increased blood pressure, heart stress	Coronary heart disease
Increased stress hormones	Anxiety, insomnia, addictions
Increased blood sugar	Diabetes, obesity
Decreased blood circulation in the digestive tract	Digestive disturbances
Suppressed growth and sex hormones	Premature aging
Lowered immunity function	Infections, cancer
Increased stickiness of platelets	Heart attacks, strokes

Now you know what stress does to your body. As if that wasn't bad enough, the direct influence that stress has on your mind, your emotions, your decisions, and your sense of fulfillment is even more profound because that will influence your thoughts, your words, and your actions, which in turn touch everyone and everything around you.

Let's look at the impact that stress has on your mind (and the impact your mind has on stress) so that you can see how it's affecting you and the 60,000 to 80,000 thoughts you have each day.

• • • • •

~~~~~~

CHAPTER 3

What Stress Does to Your Mind: The Reactive or Ego Response

"90 percent of our physical toxicity is emotionally derived."

— DAVID SIMON, M.D.

Since you're not facing a physical threat at this very moment (I hope!), your bodymind isn't triggering the fight-or-flight biological stress response. But you could very easily invoke it in reaction to one of your emotional needs not being fulfilled. When we feel mentally or emotionally threatened, we respond with what is known as the *reactive* or *ego response*. Under these circumstances, we respond with an emotional charge rather than punching someone or physically running away—that is, we get aggressive with our words, our tone, or our body language; or we simply shut down.

It's still a very primitive response, and we use it when we sense a threat to our ego, rather than our life. For example, in this case, there's no saber-toothed tiger triggering our autonomic nervous system; instead, it's the threat of not getting to work on time, being misunderstood, misplacing our phone, being challenged, getting caught in a lie, getting stuck in traffic, losing our keys, losing out on an opportunity, missing a deadline, and so on. When our actual flesh is threatened, the fight-or-flight response kicks in; when our sense of self (our ego) is challenged, the ego response is the most common biological stress response—and carries with it the same physiological reaction as fight-or-flight.

All That I Own

The ego is the realm of *I, me, mine*—it's our sense of self, our sense of ownership of people, things, and experiences. When that ownership is questioned or one of our boundaries is contested or attacked, we lash out to defend it or shut down in resignation. An illuminating example is how we feel when we drive a car. First of all, we feel a strong sense of ownership regarding the vehicle we're driving—even if it's a rental. We think of it as *my* car. Then, of course, there's the lane we are driving in (*my* lane). Then there are the 20 feet in front of us and the 50 feet behind us (*my* personal space!). And how about when another vehicle crosses the line and gets a little too close to our car, or, heaven forbid, cuts us off? (*Jerk!*)

Think of all the things you feel as though you own: your house; your car; your school; your city, state, town, and maybe your country; your partner; your kids (get over that one now); your company; your religion; your office, your neighborhood; your clothes; your TV channel; your musical group; your favorite song; your phone; your shoes; your sport, your athlete, and your team; your show; your actor, writer, or teacher . . . get the point?

You'd need more than 100 hands to hold on to all the things you think you own. But in reality, you own only this sacred, precious moment . . . and now it's gone, but here's another . . . and another. You may have attachments to—and deep fondness for—all these other things in your life, but you don't really own them. Ask yourself right now, *What do I really own?*, and let the answers flow for a few moments.

There was a time when I was actively looking at buying a house in New Jersey that had a magnificent view of the New York City skyline. I looked at so many homes, but when I saw that view, it took my breath away. I remember saying, "How amazing would it be if every morning as the sun comes up, I'm looking across the river at those two amazing Twin Towers?" And since I was working in one of them at the time, I considered Tower 2 to be *my* tower. I built up a whole story in my head that I could watch the sun rise right behind *my* tower. I looked at several homes, and during the process, I always referred to that one as the one with *my* special view.

I didn't buy the house, though. And a few short months later, *my* tower no longer existed. I would have wagered everything that *my* view would have been unchanging forever. In my head, I owned that view. But what do we really own?

Our Spectrum of Emotions

The ego response has the whole spectrum of fight-or-flight reactions woven into its emotional expressions. The *fight* version of the ego response may manifest as reactive, angry, argumentative, caustic, aggressive, or abrasive behavior. The *flight* version of the ego response can be expressed by emotionally closing down, biting your tongue, throwing your hands up, shutting someone out, or withdrawing, such as refusing to converse with another person or giving them only terse replies.

You know those moments where you have to hold your tongue and work so hard to not respond. We've all been there: You have an argument. Your ego was hurt, and you clutch your emotional flight mode with every fiber of your being.

The other person apologizes and then asks, "So are we okay?"

As you're sitting and stewing, holding on to your flight with even greater determination, you reply, "Yup. Perfect." And you are so withdrawn in the moment that you are light-years from anything close to perfect.

The ripple may even follow you into bed, where you lie with arms crossed, jaw clenched.

And the other person inquires again, "So we're good, right?"

And you lie, "Yup. We're good."

It's a bit passive-aggressive considering that in the moment, you are far from "good," but it's textbook flight in the emotional sense. You have shut down to escape the threat—except you haven't escaped it. *You're marinating in it!* More extreme forms of emotional flight are expressed through non-nourishing escapist behaviors such as substance abuse, drinking too much alcohol, excessive television viewing, gambling, and Internet addiction.

Think of a time you were having a heated discussion and found yourself reacting with anger, raising your voice, or even barking a response at another person. And at some point, most of us have reacted with the emotional version of the flight response as we walked away, shut down dialogue, or hung up on someone. It's the classic "talk to the hand" directive when, in resignation, you shut down and mutter, "Whatever!"

When someone challenges you or your ideas; questions your belief systems; dares you; defies you; confronts you; makes a demand; second-guesses you; mocks you; teases you; scolds you; shames you; disappoints you; confronts you; tests you; mimics you; or makes fun of your clothes, your statements, your school, your team, your religion, your values, your associations, your food choices, or anything that matters to you, how you respond makes all the difference. If it hits a hot button or threatens you in any way, your autonomic nervous system revs its engine, the ego stress response kicks in, and you hiss like a snake or quickly slither away. Think of the last time you heard someone say something and you responded by being outraged—that was a classic example of your ego being challenged and you feeling threatened.

Consequences of the Emotional Fight-or-Flight Response

The emotional responses to stress are well documented. Here are just a few of the ways we respond when our needs aren't met or when we detect a threat to our sense of self:

- Harsh or defensive attitude

- Sarcasm or shutdown

- Impatience and reactivity

- Unclear and knee-jerk thinking

- Overwhelm and procrastination

- Surges of anxiety or depression

This emotional version of the fight-or-flight response is triggered by your autonomic nervous system as you detect a threat to the boundaries of your ego, creating the exact same physiological self-preservation reactions we discussed in the previous chapter—as if the saber-toothed tiger had magically reappeared.

When the ego or reactive stress response kicks in, this is what your body does:

- You start to perspire.

- You start to breathe more rapidly.

- Your blood pressure and your pulse begin to stress your heart.

- Blood rushes into the muscles in your arms and legs.

- Your stress hormones (adrenaline, cortisol, glucagon) surge.

- Your blood sugar spikes.

- Blood leaves your digestive tract, so you stop digesting.

- Your growth hormone and sex hormones suppress.

- Your immune system shuts down.

- Your platelets become plump and sticky, thickening your blood.

Sound familiar?

Reaching for SODA

There's a powerful tool I have taught to thousands of highly pressured businesspeople on their way to living a destressified life. I'd love for you to join the club. The tool is called *Reaching for SODA*. I know. It sounds kooky, but it's highly effective in preventing you from blurting out that harsh, unkind, and regrettable word. It will guarantee that you won't send that toxic, nuclear e-mail to someone, copying everyone you both know. And if you're someone who declares, "I say what I think," *Reaching for SODA* will ensure that you say it in an emotionally intelligent way.

We are never our best when we're behaving like a junkyard dog, shutting down, or acting passive-aggressive. This technique might just be the one that saves you in the moment. Let's walk through it together.

The Secret of the Emotional Tell

Each of us has an *emotional tell* that tips us off that we are about to get emotionally constricted—either getting ready to bark at someone or to shut down and withdraw. A *tell* is an unconscious sign that you're feeling a certain way. In poker, it's when you reveal that you have a great hand by unwittingly tugging on your ear, scratching your nose, biting your lip, or talking too much or too little. Someone with evolved emotional awareness instantly picks this up even though you're oblivious to it. Essentially, you reveal the nature of your poker hand simply by displaying with your body what your mind is thinking.

Well, we do this all the time whether we're playing cards or not. We especially do it at the first sign that one of our needs is not being met. Now that we understand the biological stress responses, we can apply them to our own emotional responses in a given situation. Just by getting this far with me in the journey of destressifying, you are more aware of your own feelings, emotions, and physical expressions, so you'll be able to detect your emotional tell very quickly.

Let's identify it. What is the first thing you feel when someone or something irritates you? And where do you feel it? This could be any internal emotional tip-off: your stomach flipping, your body tightening, your palms sweating, your temples throbbing, your jaw clenching, your heartbeat quickening, your throat closing, your chest burning, your pulse increasing, your face heating. Place your hand on that spot now.

For me, I feel a spark of heat in my upper chest right above where the two sides of my rib cage meet. The spark quickly (in less than a second) turns to an ember, and within another second, the fire catches; it starts as a gentle flame, turns into a bonfire, then a blaze, and ultimately a raging wildfire. As the moments progress, the heat begins to take hold and moves up into my throat, traveling to my jaw. I know that I have about three to five seconds before it reaches my jawline, and if it does . . . *I will scorch the village!* I will incinerate everyone in my path. So as soon as I feel my emotional tell—the spark of heat in my chest from an unmet need—I *Reach for SODA,* and everyone (including myself) is saved.

No Need to Scorch the Village: *Reach for SODA*

When you find yourself emotionally constricting in any way and notice your emotional tell, think SODA:

- Stop
- Observe
- Detach
- Awaken

Maybe you are in a heated discussion that's getting hotter. Or perhaps something just occurred that's frustrating or angering you, and you're feeling the need to vent. Or maybe you're typing that nuclear e-mail to someone, and it's laced with zingers. As soon as you detect your *emotional tell*—you feel the anxiety surge into your belly or the tightening come into your chest or the heat rise into your throat—*Reach for SODA*:

Stop whatever you are doing or thinking. Just stop. Silently whisper to yourself, *Stop!* Remember, this whole exercise takes less than 5 seconds.

Observe yourself—where you are, whom you're with, what's going on from a witnessing perspective. Feel yourself rise up to the top of the room, observing yourself with no opinion. Keep rising up until you can objectively see yourself and the other person or irritant and simply view them as two children of God. Sometimes I've had to rise to the top of the building or even the moon before I was able to observe objectively!

Detach—for just a moment—from the drama, charge, and emotion of the situation and take a long, slow deep breath in. At the same time, ever so subtly, step, lean, or (if you are sitting) roll back a few inches. Then take a long, slow exhale, which will bring some release from the turbulence. In this process you've created some energetic distance (through breathing) and physical distance (through leaning or stepping back) between you and the irritant.

Awaken to a better version of yourself, the part of you that makes you feel proud of how you respond to life. Awaken a hidden aspect of yourself—perhaps the part of you that trusts or is brave, grounded, or forgiving—the part of you that's "better than this." Stay in this space for a few seconds and simply breathe. Observe your higher traits such as strength, confidence, and compassion, and let them be introduced into the moment. We've all heard, *"What would Buddha do?"* or *"What would Jesus do?"* At this point in the process, ask yourself, *What would the best version of me do or say right now?* At this moment, the reactive aspect of yourself will transform in seconds to your most relaxed version.

Even at the height of a battle of words, taking some of the emotional charge out of the moment will allow you to think more clearly and make a better choice. *Reaching for SODA* can stop you from having regrets later in the day as your emotional intelligence blossoms and blooms while your stress level eases. Essentially, when you *Reach for SODA,* you introduce a brief interruption in your conditioned stress-response mechanism and stop the trajectory of whatever emotional hostage taking was about to occur. *Reaching for SODA* actually allows you to quickly wind down the emotional charge that was starting to build up.

Once you're on the other side of your deactivated reactive response, infinite possibilities await you, and—with a clearer head—you can make a more conscious choice. destressifying techniques like *Reaching for SODA* are critical in helping all of us transcend the physical and emotional impact of our more primitive responses.

The Truth about Cortisol

The stress hormone cortisol is secreted by the adrenal glands to maintain the body's equilibrium, peaking each morning and ebbing in the evening. Its primary functions are to increase blood sugar; regulate blood pressure; suppress the immune system; decrease bone formation; and aid the metabolism of fat, protein, and carbohydrates.

Cortisol is called "the stress hormone" because it's secreted in its highest levels during the body's fight-or-flight biological response to stress. In that case, it performs these functions:

- Lessens sensitivity to pain
- Delivers in-the-moment surges of energy
- Amplifies memory functions
- Supports homeostasis in the body

These were the magnificent core benefits of cortisol 20,000 years ago when we were hunting and gathering in the wilderness and suddenly encountered a threat to our bodies. But these tremendous benefits also have a hitch. First of all, there's no cortisol "off" switch, so we may hold on to those surges for hours after a fight-or-flight moment. And second, we're not concerned about your life being threatened thousands of years ago—we're talking about your ego or your sense of ownership being threatened in the here-and-now. Prolonged levels of cortisol in the bloodstream *caused by emotional stressors* have been shown to have negative effects:

- Decreased bone density
- Higher blood pressure
- Lack of clarity
- Suppressed thyroid function
- Blood sugar imbalances such as hyperglycemia and diabetes
- Suppressed immunity and inflammatory responses
- Increased abdominal fat

Studies have also shown that people who secrete higher levels of cortisol in response to stress tend to eat more carbohydrates than people who secrete less cortisol. Increased levels of cortisol shrink the hippocampus, impacting memory formation, new brain cell development, and our ability to learn. Simultaneously, cortisol increases the size of our amygdala, keeping us in fear-based learning mode.

Honey, I Shrunk My Medial Prefrontal Cortex!

The newest brain science goes even further, as evidenced in the groundbreaking 2012 Yale stress study published in the journal *Biological Psychiatry*. Researchers found that stressful life events such as divorce or job loss impacted the brains of even healthy individuals, making them less capable of enduring subsequent stressful events by hindering their emotions and self-control.

Prior to this study, the effects of stress on the brains of healthy individuals had been unclear. But after brain scanning 103 healthy subjects who had been interviewed about traumatic stress and adverse life events, such as the death of a loved one, job loss, divorce, or loss of a home to natural disaster, scientists observed across-the-board marked shrinkage in the *medial prefrontal cortex*, the anterior cingulate, and the insula—the parts of the brain responsible for personality expression, emotions, decision making, self-control, and goal achievement. And these parts of the brain shrank with every additional stressful life event a test subject had experienced.

The lead author of the study, Emily Ansell, concluded that "the accumulation of stressful life events may make it more challenging for these individuals to deal with future stress, particularly if the next demanding event requires effortful control, emotion regulation, or integrated social processing to overcome it." And as we now know, the next "demanding" event *will* indeed require those skills.

Neurosurgeons experienced in operating on brain tumors had previously known that eliminating up to two-thirds of the medial prefrontal cortex resulted in concentration issues, judgment and problem-solving difficulties, and inability to think in the abstract. And these are the very same symptoms that we experience in the wake of an intense stressor. We might conclude that stressful life events have a similar impact on the brain as surgery does on the medial prefrontal cortex!

But don't despair—this is not a *One Flew Over the Cuckoo's Nest* moment. One of the most potent benefits of destressifying is the suppression of cortisol so that the body's functions can *quickly* return to normal following a stressful event.

"The brain is dynamic and plastic and things can improve— but only if stress is dealt with in a healthy manner," said Rajita Sinha, the Yale Foundations Fund Professor of Psychiatry and a professor in the Department of Neurobiology. "If not, the effects of stress can have a negative impact on both our physical and mental health."

When it comes to stress and the brain, size really does matter. And right in your hands, you hold the key to dealing with stress in a healthy manner.

Stress and Performance

Understanding the potent impact that stress can have on our brain, our body, and our mind is critical to us showing up and being our best. The other key is truly understanding and mastering our needs: the desires, motivations, and requirements on which we have built our individual lives. In Chapter 6, we will dive deep into identifying and meeting our needs. When we're able to do so on a daily basis, fewer buttons get pushed and we trigger emotional fight-or-flight less frequently, keeping our cortisol and adrenaline levels in check.

As we've previously discussed, a little bit of stress sparks us out of the doldrums, moving us from boredom and malaise into a heightened state of interest and attention. From there, if the stressor is maintained for a short duration (which is different for everyone), we move into our optimal performance space, known as being in the zone or in flow. *Our performance peaks under the heightened activation that comes with a moderate level of stress.* However, if the stressor sticks around too long, our peak performance wanes as it succumbs to anxiety; and if it goes on even longer, we collapse in exhaustion.

That's why it's rare for athletes to be spectacular for every minute of a game, which usually lasts between two and three hours. They will have spurts of peak performance and periods of lethargy as they move through the cycle of hormones, chemicals, brain activation, being in the zone, overload, exhaustion, boredom, and rest . . . and then await the next burst of stress to reinvigorate them. And this is why certain professional and Olympic athletes, such as sprinters, skiers, snowboarders, freestylers, half-pipe competitors, wrestlers, pitchers, batters, surfers, quarterbacks, wide-receivers, pole vaulters, golfers, point guards, gymnasts, biathletes, swimmers, ski jumpers, downhill racers, aerial artists, and even extreme fighters—those who excel by harnessing their brilliance and intensity for short 5- to 30-second bursts of time—continue to push the limits of what's even thinkable as all their training, attention, focus, and hormones peak in a compressed and magnificent crescendo *at the critical moment*. They've mastered the cycle of stress!

The destressified Zone

Remember, as long as the stress isn't prolonged *and* as long as it's perceived as positive (motivating, exciting, growth enhancing), it's harmless—perhaps even a good thing—as those otherwise-debilitating chemical surges instead help us focus, push the limits, and rebuild damaged cells. It's not just the best athletes who have learned to master their cycle of stress. Our most successful actors, businesspeople, cops, performers, entertainers, soldiers, and surgeons—most of the high achievers in our world who know how to activate the best version of themselves—have also mastered their bodymind's responses to stress using the same teachings included here.

Mastering the Cycle of Stress

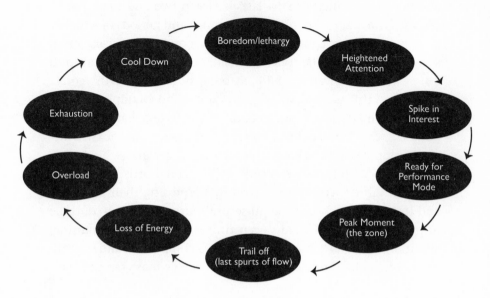

All these individuals know when to prepare, how to experience stress, what it means to their bodymind, how to manage their emotions, how to identify and prioritize their needs of the moment, and how to flow. They also recognize the importance of resting after the fact. Think of any high-performance professional who has to show up every day and be brilliant for months on end. Most successful destressifiers fill their downtime with physical rest and mental rejuvenation, to prevent them from getting burned out.

Downtime and pacing ourselves are critical for us to thrive in our peak moments. Regardless of profession, the model applies to all of us in everything we do. The process of stress sparking us out of a restful state, slowly building, peaking while we are in the zone, then declining, and ultimately leaving us exhausted is a natural process. If we can own it and use it to our advantage, we will thrive and live lives of higher performance and deeper fulfillment.

• • • • •

CHAPTER 4

Beyond Stress: The destressified Response

"The experience of stress can enhance the development of mental toughness, heightened awareness, new perspectives, a sense of mastery, strengthened priorities, deeper relationships, greater appreciation for life, and an increased sense of meaningfulness."

— Drs. C. L. Park and V. S. Helgeson

After practicing destressifying for only a few days, you will transform forever! And now that you fully understand the basics of stress, your increasing knowledge of the realm *beyond* stress will effortlessly unfold. *Those who practice destressifying* (these people are known as *destressifiers,* and you will quickly become one) *have been scientifically proven to respond to the world differently.* destressifiers are calmer, less reactive, less angry, more reflective, more fully present, more creative, more articulate, more intuitive, more efficient, more patient, more productive, happier, more fulfilled, and ultimately more self-actualized.

destressifiers have highly sharpened coping practices that they use in stressful scenarios. Regardless of what's happening in their environment, they moderate their stress levels, keeping them low, which guarantees that the response is short-lived and its impact is negligible. Our society's most visible "performers" have regular destressifying rituals they employ in the face of millions of fans, global TV audiences, screaming detractors, big money, and high-pressure stakes. The next time a big game is on, or you're at a concert or a play, or you're watching a live show, spend a few minutes observing the stars taking deep breaths, closing their eyes for a moment, settling in, anchoring their feet, tightening their muscles . . . then relaxing them. This is all designed to allow them to release stress, calm the mind, relax the body, and be their best in the moment, or what we call *self-actualized*.

squeeze&release

Let's try one of the most powerful destressifying techniques, known as *squeeze&release*.

Think of something stressful that has been troubling you for the past month. Play it over in your mind. Connect to the emotion it makes you feel. Say it out loud. Now locate the feeling of discomfort it creates someplace in your body. Maybe it's your throat, your heart, your chest, your solar plexus, or your belly. Place your fingers or your whole hand on that space. Rate the level of stress it makes you feel on a scale of 1 to 10.

Now take a deep breath in and make a really tight fist with your right hand (it's okay to move your hand away from the "stress spot" where you just had it). Keep holding your breath. Holding that fist tight, tense your right arm from your wrist to your forearm, elbow, bicep . . . right up to your shoulder. Hold this tension and your breath for about ten seconds, and then release both. Next do the same with your left side, starting with taking a deep breath in, clenching your left fist, and then extending the squeeze up through your left arm. Hold that tension and your breath for about ten seconds, and then release both. Shake it out.

Now do the same with your right foot, ankle, calf, and thigh for about ten seconds, taking a deep breath in and holding it as you squeeze all those muscles really tightly. Release your breath and muscles at the same time. Next do the same on your left side, squeezing the muscles in your foot, ankle, calf, and thigh for about ten seconds, taking a deep breath in and holding it as you squeeze all those muscles really tightly. Release your breath and your muscles simultaneously. Shake it out.

Now take a long, slow, deep breath in. Tense your arms and legs on both sides, hold your breath, and then tighten your belly as well . . . just for ten seconds. Hold it. Hold it. Keep holding it. Just a little bit longer. And now release it all—your breath, your fists, arms, feet, legs, and belly. Just rest for a few seconds and let the blood return to the rest of your body. You may actually feel it move back into your head, pelvis, neck, and back. Now take a long, slow, deep breath in through your nostrils, and sigh as you exhale through your mouth. Breathe in and out three more times, and sigh as you exhale. And, when you're done with the last sigh, breathe normally and just observe your body and mind.

That was just under a minute. And in that minute, the tension we placed on our physiology pooled all the blood in our body in those selected areas, chemically simulating a fight-or-flight moment without an external threat. We stressed our body—but only for a minute.

Because we moved that "stressor" around from side to side, from upper to lower extremities, and then tensed our core— surging blood into our belly—we triggered a familiar fight-or-flight physical sensation, connecting with our autonomic nervous system. The amazing thing is that the formal act of *releasing* then sent a signal to our bodymind that the threat was over, *powering down* the fight-or-flight response and all its repercussions.

Didn't you feel a sense of relief as you released the tightness and let go of your breath? The impact isn't just muscular—it's molecular! It impacts the chemicals and hormones in your body as well. Right now, your pulse is slowing, your stress hormones are suppressing, your growth and sex hormones are waking up, and your immune system is igniting as white blood cells surge back into any weakened areas of your body.

In that minute, you "tricked" your conditioned biological response mechanism into thinking there was a momentary threat to the body. Then you interpreted it as a nourishing challenge, which gave your bodymind permission to wind down. You essentially announced to your physiology that the threat was over. After only one minute of *squeeze&release,* you returned your physiology to a post-stress state and manually overrode all the effects and consequences of a longer-term stressful moment.

So, on a scale of 1 to 10, what's your stress level now? Chances are that it's lower than it was only a minute ago. You actually destressified in under a minute. Are your thoughts more relaxed? How does your body feel? Do you notice that you're much more aware of your physiology right now? More aware of your thoughts? Stress has been replaced by relief and clarity. Pretty amazing, right?

You can practice *squeeze&release* throughout the day. The key is to pay really close attention to how your body and mind feel before and after. It's the perfect exercise to do while you're stuck in traffic; waiting in line; about to take a "stressful" call, enter a meeting, or begin a difficult conversation; or whenever you feel the first wave of stress washing over you.

Finding Another Gear: The destressified Response

destressifiers understand their core needs and more consistently meet them; and in those instances when their needs are not met, their bodies and minds respond in a unique way known as the *destressified response.* destressifiers consistently transcend overwhelm, remind themselves of their innate strengths, clearly see the resources available, and leverage the silver lining in the moment, moving beyond any dark clouds they detect on the horizon.

Essentially the counterpart to the fight-or-flight response, the destressified response occurs when the body senses it is no longer in perceived danger and all the functions of the autonomic nervous system return to normal. As we destressify, the body moves from a state of physiological arousal to one of physiological relaxation:

- Breathing slows and becomes quieter.

- Pulse decelerates, easing blood pressure.

- Digestive functions normalize as blood returns to the intestines.

- Stress hormones (adrenaline, glucagon, and cortisol) slow their surges.

- Immune system strengthens.

- Platelets become less sticky, and blood flows more easily.

Accompanying this destressified physiological state of relaxation are powerful emotional benefits that impact our thoughts, how we interpret information, and how we respond to the world. As we begin to destressify, we will notice more and more that we are:

- Less emotionally turbulent

- Less reactive

- Less nervous and fidgety

- More patient

- A better listener

- Less overwhelmed

- More focused and clear

- More creative and solution oriented

- More relaxed

- Truly the calm amidst the chaos

And with each destressifying technique you practice, there is a transformational <u>halo effect</u> that lingers on in your thoughts and words for minutes, hours, even days, as long as you continue to use the tools. Rather than buy into your most constricted and conditioned behaviors, you will suddenly find that you are more fluid in how you respond to life, coming from a less conditioned, less constricted place.

The potent shift into this expanded new gear will change your basic nature. You will respond to life rather than react to it; and because of this internal shift, you intuitively will make better decisions. *By cultivating a daily destressifying practice, you will create this state of restful awareness as your <u>primary</u> biological response to stress!*

16 Seconds That Will Change Your Life

Of all the techniques that I've shared throughout the world, the one with the most powerful effect is perhaps the simplest one. It's a game changer, and I call it "16 seconds to clarity." (Throughout the rest of this book, I'll refer to it as *16seconds*.) Not only does it have a profound destressifying impact in the moment, but it can also be the foundation for a long-lasting daily practice. Let's try it right now. It's okay to keep reading as you go through this exercise with me.

16 seconds to clarity

Think of something that has irritated or bothered you in the past few days . . . a difficult conversation, a disappointment, an unmet expectation. Perhaps someone said they would do something and they didn't, or they said they would meet you at a certain time and they were late, or they unexpectedly shared something about you with another person and it got back to you. (Don't go too deep. This isn't therapy.) But right now, feel free to envision that other person's face . . . maybe replay the moment in your mind's eye, even notice someplace in your body that feels connected to the irritation. Take a few moments to settle into that space.

Now take a long, slow, deep breath in through your nostrils, and as you do . . . slowly count to four, and observe the air as it moves into your nostrils and to the back of your throat. Watch your breath as it moves down your chest and deep into your lungs. Feel your belly expand.

Observe your belly being filled, and hold that breath in to the count of four. And just witness the breath in your belly as you silently count. One, two, three, four.

Now slowly, to the count of four, release your breath and watch it as it moves up into your chest, into your throat, into your sinuses, and out through your nostrils.

And when the last wisp of air is out of you, hold that breath out to the count of four. And observe it, watch it, witness it . . . as it dissipates into the air.

Now breathe normally, and let's try it with your eyes closed. Remember: in four—hold four—out four—hold four. And make sure you follow your breath. Observing it along the way is key to the process. (I'll wait right here . . . it's only 16 seconds.)

I'm guessing you're back right now, eyes open and breathing normally. Well, our whole experience was 32 seconds: 16 seconds with your eyes open and 16 seconds with your eyes closed. And in that half a minute while you were observing your breath (assuming you were playing along), you were totally present. You were not thinking about the past or any of its grievances or regrets, nor moving into the future with all its predictions and projections. You were not thinking about your irritation. You were totally in the present moment. Your mind is a little calmer; your heartbeat has slowed a bit. You've filled your body with heavily oxygenated blood and nourishing hormones, and in the process, you've released a little bit of stress.

In under a minute, you have taken another powerful step into destressifying. The formal terminology for what's happening in the exercises *squeeze&release* and *16seconds* is *introducing a pattern interrupt*. You actually just jammed the brakes on a potential surge of stress hormones and all the negative bodymind reactions you were starting to feel. You broke the flow of conditioned physical and emotional responses. Just the thought of this irritating situation or person triggered a memory of the stressful circumstances, and in 16 seconds you returned to the present moment. Then in the 17th second, you're clearer—beyond the moment of emotion.

The feeling you have right now is the halo effect I was previously referring to. You are a bit calmer . . . a bit lighter . . . a bit easier. Now imagine if you could string together a few minutes of that. Well, you actually do every time you use a destressifying technique such as *16seconds* or any of the other in-the-moment tools we will explore throughout these pages.

Instant destressifying

When we introduce a pattern interrupt into our flow of thoughts, we can gently step aside from the uneasy memories of the past or the anxious thoughts of the future and truly ground ourselves back into the present moment. Our bodymind moves beyond all that irritation, anger, discomfort, anxiety, and less-than or "it's not fair" thinking. The constriction vanishes instantly; and our next thought, word, or action will come from a less conditioned, more expansive place. Now we are primed for greater possibilities, novel solutions, and infinite potential. Whatever limiting belief was holding us back is momentarily suspended.

A classic, very public pattern interrupt happened during a long TV time-out in Super Bowl XXIII. There were three minutes left in the game as the 49ers—trailing the Bengals by three points—stood 93 yards away from the goal line. Every player on the field was awash in constricting stress hormones . . . emotions of fear and overwhelm swirled in their heads . . . and the limiting belief that no one can advance the ball 93 yards and score in three minutes consumed each one of them—except for quarterback Joe Montana, who famously pointed to the sidelines during the huddle and asked teammate Harris Barton, "Isn't that John Candy?" So unexpected and powerful was this pattern interrupt that it slowed the intensity of the moment and took every player out of his head and back into the game. When the TV time-out ended, Montana marched the fully destressified 'Niners down the field and into Super Bowl history.

Once destressifying becomes part of your daily routine, this state of restful awareness occurs naturally. Calm and balance become the norm; and anxieties, anger, emotional turbulence, and knee-jerk reactions drift away as your physical body relaxes and your innate emotional intelligence gently returns to guide your choices. In times of extreme stress, however, when the body experiences constant physiological arousal over numerous perceived dangers that are *not* life-threatening, the destressified response can be created through techniques like the one you just experienced.

When I'm training law enforcement personnel or members of the military, I refer to *16seconds* as "tactical breathing." Whatever you choose to call it, feel free to use it as a daily tool when you feel a bit of anxiety bubbling up or panic sweeping through you. You can even post on Facebook or Instagram or tweet #16seconds to share your destressifying moment! There are tens of thousands of us who use this tool every day, and I'll share many more of these techniques throughout our journey together.

The Big Five

Some of us are actually wired to be a bit more reactive than others. Most likely it's a combination of DNA, childhood influences, and years of reinforcement. If you've been stressed out lately or for a while, you might be thinking, *Oh, that's definitely me!*

Well, don't be so reactive! Okay, okay—I'm only joking. More than likely you're not wired to be so reactive; you've just succumbed to a certain mind-set. But if in fact you are, no worries—you'll just require a bit more dedication to the deconstruction of those patterns and the reconstruction of your new destressified behaviors. Let's explore this concept a bit so that we can understand more about our innate tendencies and those of the people in our lives.

In psychology, the *Big Five personality traits* are five broad domains or dimensions of character and makeup that are used to describe human personality. In psychology circles, they go by the acronym OCEAN to help you better remember them:

- Openness

- Conscientiousness

- Extraversion

- Agreeableness

- Neuroticism

Within each of the five categories, a series of more specific primary factors is found. For example, in the trait of extraversion we find such related qualities as gregariousness, assertiveness, excitement seeking, warmth, activity, and positive emotions; and each of us expresses varying degrees of these characteristics.

The Big Five model was originally defined by several independent sets of researchers studying known personality traits and then analyzing hundreds of measures of these traits to find the underlying factors. The Big Five are pretty accurate and consistent regardless of age, gender, or culture. We could easily spend a lifetime analyzing all the facets of each category, but when it comes to stress, our concern is with the fifth trait, neuroticism, which we'll address in greater depth. But first, here's a thumbnail sketch of each personality trait:

- **Openness to experience:** This trait reflects the degree of intellectual curiosity, creativity, variety of experience, desire for adventure, appreciation of art, and preference for novelty and variety versus a personal preference for strict routine.

- **Conscientiousness:** This trait reflects the degree of preferring to be organized and dependable, show self-discipline, act dutifully, aim for achievement, and have planned experiences versus a preference for random or spontaneous behavior.

- **Extraversion:** This trait reflects the tendency toward outgoing behavior, high energy, positive emotions, assertiveness, sociability, and seeking stimulation in the company of others versus a preference for reserved and solitary behavior.

- **Agreeableness:** This trait reflects the degree to which one's basic nature is trusting, helpful, compassionate, cooperative, and even tempered versus the tendency to be suspicious and antagonistic toward others.

- **Neuroticism:** This trait reflects the likelihood one has of interpreting ordinary situations as threatening or disappointing versus perceiving the world in an easygoing, relaxed manner and as something that can be coped with.

These five overarching domains are assumed to represent the basic structure behind *all* our personality traits, and each category contains the two extremes of the range and all the subtraits in between. But it's neuroticism that is most fascinating when it comes to stress because *people high on this trait's scale are actually more susceptible to interpreting stress as negative*—and we now know the impact of that!

Neuroticism is basically one's susceptibility to negative emotions such as irritation, anger, anxiety, moodiness, and depression. It's sometimes referred to as the domain of emotional stability . . . or instability. We all have emotional triggers, conditioned responses to life, and hot buttons that irk us, irritate us, and downright drive us crazy—and our tendency to succumb to this emotional mind-set determines where we fall along the scale of neuroticism.

In 2007, a groundbreaking study was published in the peer-reviewed scientific journal *Psychophysiology* that proved British psychologist Hans Jürgen Eysenck's 1967 theory of personality, which positively *linked neuroticism with a low tolerance for stress*.

The Neuroticism Scale

The scope of traits within neuroticism range between *volatility* and *calmness*. Examples of *high* neuroticism are reactivity; inability to relax; easily stressed out; seeing yourself as a victim; high frequency of mood changes; easily disturbed or upset; and prone to worry, anxiety, and sadness.

Those who score low in neuroticism are more emotionally stable, less tense, less reactive to stress, and more satisfied with their lives. Those who score high in neuroticism are naturally hardwired to be more emotionally reactive and more susceptible to feeling anxious, fearful, moody, lonely, and worried. They are actually more vulnerable to stress and are more likely to interpret commonplace situations as threatening and minor frustrations as hopelessly problematic—thus spiking their cortisol, adrenaline, and glucagon levels on a consistent basis. They are the outliers when it comes to destressifying.

This group's negative emotional reactions tend to persist for unusually long periods of time, which means they are often in an unpleasant mood, see the glass as half empty, or find a dark lining around every silver cloud. In the workplace, those whose personalities exhibit high neuroticism often express a pessimistic approach, a conviction that their work conflicts with their personal relationships, and a view that the work environment is one of high anxiety. Remember, it's all about our *perceptions* of stress. Those high in neuroticism are interpreting stress as high most of the time because they are usually feeling threatened or victimized!

Those who score high on neuroticism often display increased levels of skin conductivity (just like in a lie detector test), a clear sign of stress, anxiety, and reactivity. Their frequent challenges in emotional regulation and lack of contentment can limit their ability to think clearly, make decisions, and cope effectively with stress.

At the other end of the scale, individuals who score low in neuroticism have much higher thresholds for upset and emotional reactivity. They tend to be calm and emotionally stable. And although they're not necessarily happy and enthusiastic, they are free from persistent negative feelings.

destressifying Eases Neuroticism

Neuroticism has similar aspects but is not the same as being neurotic in the Freudian sense. Some psychologists prefer to use the term *emotional stability* to differentiate this member of the Big Five from the psychological term *neurotic*. But neuroticism is simply another personality trait. As noted earlier, some of us are more prone to high scores of neuroticism, which will directly translate to our level of fulfillment in life.

Science is now demonstrating that a 60-day immersion into yoga and meditation can demonstrably lower scores in the neuroticism personality trait. So whether you or someone you live with, work with, or are friends with is prone to high levels of neuroticism, we now know that a *two-month commitment* to destressifying will positively impact the perception of stressful situations and lessen the irritation, anxiety, and disappointment through which you or they interpret the world. Remember, we can all be rewired through the tools of destressifying.

Are You a destressifier?

As we've previously discussed, those who use the tools on a daily basis and embrace destressifying as a life process are referred to as *destressifiers*. There are approximately eight billion people on the planet and only a few million destressifiers. But our numbers are growing, and those who live a destressified existence seem to share these 15 traits and behaviors:

- They have mastered their breath and use it as a tool.

- They have mastered their emotions and can quickly shift from emotional turbulence to a state of calm; they are emotionally intelligent.

- Their inner dialogue rules their outer world, not the other way around.

- They understand their needs, what's driving them, where there are blockages, and how to transcend them.

- They communicate without emotional charge.

- They live life from a place of gratitude and see the miracles in the mundane.

- They spend more time in the present moment and less time on the regrets of the past or the what-ifs of the future.

- They have a positive outlook on life and see challenges as opportunities and failures as growth experiences.

- They master their time and are not "on call" for the universe or tethered to their electronic devices.

- They embrace social support and know they are stronger and more successful if they leverage the help of others.

- They regularly take quiet time for themselves through prayer, meditation, massage, nourishing behaviors, spending time in nature, or just *being*.

- They don't waste valuable energy resisting other viewpoints or trying to impose their will where it doesn't matter.

- They live purpose-driven lives.

- They sleep soundly and awaken well rested.

- They are self-actualized, meeting most of—if not all—their basic needs (which we'll explore in upcoming chapters, as we go deep into needs).

You may presently display several of these traits and behaviors; and if so, you are already on the path to living a destressified life. It's also quite possible that you remain stuck with only one or two of these behaviors. Fear not! This book *is* an owner's manual for getting you from where you are to where you'd like to be—and by simply being open to the process of destressifying, you will immediately see subtle shifts beginning to unfold in your life. If you just keep breathing, reading, and believing in yourself, then one by one, these powerful, life-affirming traits will become yours.

A Course of Action

Acute stress in itself doesn't take a heavy toll if we find ways to relax quickly after the stressed moment. Once the short-term stressor has been dealt with, we need to return our body to homeostasis, or its pre-stress state, in order to feel balanced again. But the sad reality is that even though the stress itself might last for only a moment, *after that moment*, we often retain a stressful, anxiety-filled dialogue in our head for hours, days, weeks, and even years!

The ripples seem to go on forever as we replay the moment—the words we spoke, the thing we did, the scenario that unfolded, the things we could have said and done differently. And then we project into the minds of others—we calculate their interpretations, what they are thinking and telling other people. We twist and squirm as we try to prognosticate how it will all play out. And although the event has come and gone, these ever-widening ripples begin to extend themselves for longer periods of time, morphing into chronic stress. That's why we need to go beyond the in-the-moment magic bullet to reduce the symptoms of acute stress when it flares up. We need a proactive destressifying mind-set.

destressifying shifts the way you view, interpret, and think about stressors before and after the fact. It's a way of seeing the world with new eyes, expanding your perspective and shifting every fiber of your being until you are evolved to a state of self-actualization where your needs are more consistently met, where your environment supports you, where your potential is actualized, and where you are the calm amidst everyone else's chaos.

destressifying Is a Place of Lasting Transformation

destressifying guides you to walk two paths simultaneously. One path arms you with tools like *16seconds, Reaching for SODA,* and *squeeze&release* to shift your stress response in the moment—what you say and do milliseconds *after* the stressor has reared its ugly head. That is a more allopathic (symptom-based) approach, essentially dealing with the signals of your natural stress-response mechanism during a stressful moment and cooling yourself back down as the surges of adrenaline, cortisol, and glucagon are bathing your bloodstream.

But there is also a deeper path of destressifying that will shift you and every cell in your body forever. This path is holistic and transformational. It guides you to rise above stress and move beyond it by shifting the way you see, interpret, and respond to the world around you, so there are fewer crises and stressful moments. In the process, you'll master your awareness, your needs, your emotions, your communication skills, and your purpose in life. *This* path is destressifying in its purest sense. It is through this real-world transformation that you increase the odds in every moment that you *will not* perceive events as stressful; your core needs *will* be met; and you *will* indeed experience personal empowerment, lasting fulfillment, and peace of mind. By the end of this book, you will have mastered both paths, and you will be destressified!

An ancient sage said, "All that we are arises with our thoughts; with our thoughts we create the world." And whether we believe it or not, we also create our own stress as we interpret, reinterpret, and refine each thought, sensory impression, and physical sensation and then attempt to integrate it with one of our needs in the moment. This applies directly to our interpretation of life and our perception of stress. So let's begin the practice of *destressifying*!

• • • • •

PART II

Mastering the Five Cores of destressifying— the Practice

Well, you have all the basics. You understand stress and all its nuances better than 99 percent of the people on the planet. Now it's up to you and what you do with that knowledge—how you convert it to your own innate wisdom—that is the key to living a destressifying existence.

A brilliant example of a destressified mind-set is exemplified by the words of the late, great ESPN anchor Stuart Scott. Reflecting on his seven-year-long battle with cancer, he said, "When you die, that does not mean that you lose to cancer. You beat cancer by how you live, why you live, and in the manner in which you live." Indeed, *how, why,* and *the manner in which we live* determine the fullness, grace, and beauty of every moment in our lives.

You've learned a few fast tools (*Reaching for SODA, squeeze-&release,* and *16seconds*) for quickly decelerating your bodymind's reaction to stress, and you'll learn many more in the pages that follow. But a more profound, longer-lasting solution is to *shift the way you perceive the outside world*, how you interpret it, and how you are oriented to it.

We are conditioned beings. Since we were babies, we have carved deep grooves into our brains to develop patterned responses. By simply reorienting ourselves to a few of our most fundamental behaviors, we can permanently rewire how and what we think, and transform how we respond to stress.

There are five core components to proactively destressifying, and each can be mastered simply by reading these pages and following along. They're all concepts you know on the surface; but by diving deeper into their makeup and truly understanding them, owning them, and living them, you will subtly start rewiring the circuits in your brain. Very quickly, you will forge new pathways in how you think, how you perceive the world around you, and most important, how you respond to it.

These are the five core components of destressifying:

1. destressifying by mastering your awareness

2. destressifying by mastering your needs

3. destressifying by mastering your emotions

4. destressifying by mastering your communication

5. destressifying by mastering your purpose in life

The concept of mastery may seem intimidating, but ideally that's how you show up for everything you do. You grasp the goal, and then you take action to get as close to it as possible. When you have attained a new level of competence, that once-dreamed-of achievement becomes the new base for your next step. Then you take that proficiency and move forward. It's pure personal evolution!

Some aspects of destressifying will be unfamiliar, so you will take baby steps; others will challenge you and encourage you to take strides; and others, because of your familiarity with them, will allow you to take leaps. As long as you keep reading, stay open, and continue moving in the direction of your personal evolution, you will receive all the gifts of living a destressified life—a life filled with greater passion and purpose, empowerment and fulfillment, emotional freedom and happiness, and clarity and peace of mind.

In the process, you will develop some personal best practices that will serve you as you move along the path; you will also identify those thoughts, words, behaviors, conversations, and situations that don't serve you. And through this process and by using a powerful, time-tested life tool—looking at your life through the lens of the *Five Realms*—you will begin to attract what serves you and release what no longer does. Shedding non-nourishing aspects of your being and acquiring new nourishing skills, capabilities, and perspectives will actually *transform* you. Bean by bean, the bag gets filled.

The following Five Masteries will become the new foundation for who you are; why you are here; how you live; and what you think, say, and do from this moment forward. So let's begin mastering!

• • • • •

CHAPTER 5

destressifying by Mastering Your Awareness

"The ultimate value of life depends upon awareness and the power of contemplation rather than upon mere survival."

— A RISTOTLE

The first mastery of destressifying is *mastering your awareness*. Just as you experienced an increased awareness of your body and mind after you practiced *Reaching for SODA, squeeze&release,* and *16seconds,* once you've mastered your awareness, you will consistently come from a place of stillness and silence—from the present moment—rather than from the past, the future, or some conditioned reaction. Through this first mastery, you will actually open the door to an unconditioned life. And from that moment forward, every step you take will be new, fresh, and purposeful. Heightened self-awareness will be the most obvious shift you feel, then an increase in your awareness of others. But the most amazing shift you will experience is that the world outside of you will begin to slow down. There will be fewer crises and greater clarity as you replace confusion and overwhelm with spontaneous right thoughts, words, and actions.

Our Internal World

When it comes to awareness, there are two major aspects of life that contribute to our daily stress: our internal world and the external world. Our internal world is all about us and includes all our past and present choices—the things we've said and done over the course of our lives; what we're thinking and doing right now; and the continuous rippling from each decision, conversation, and action we've taken. We must never forget the power of this ripple, from our health, diet, and sleep patterns to an innocent conversation in a coffee shop to an interaction with a friend, acquaintance, relative, co-worker, spouse, or ex, to a direction in life we've taken.

Once you activate something from your internal world, you set a ball in motion, and it keeps rolling even if you've forgotten about it. The thoughts you think, the expectations you have (and have had), the words you speak (and have spoken), and the actions you take (and have taken) create your physical and emotional agenda, which fuels how your life unfolds each day. For example, have you ever regretted a commitment you made to someone? Have you ever wished you didn't say or do something? Have you ever been late because it took you longer than anticipated to get out the door? Have you ever ruminated for hours over an upcoming or past interaction? These are a few of the stress makers from your internal world.

Our External World

The second contributor to stress comes from the external world: everything that exists *outside* of our physical body, our emotions, and our intellect. These external stressors are essentially how the world shows up for us and responds to us, and how it proactively unfolds its daily surprises, consistencies, changes, intensities, and shockers into our lives. It includes everything external that we don't have any direct control or influence over, the stuff that is coming *at* us on a daily basis: the weather, other people's health, company or school policies, politics, local traffic, flight delays, technology, the ups and downs of the housing and stock markets, and what goes on immediately around us—what we read, watch, hear, and experience. Most important, it includes the needs, requests, choices, thoughts, words, deadlines, and actions of our friends, family members, colleagues, acquaintances, and even those we randomly encounter.

There is a constant and dynamic interplay between our inner and outer worlds—a cause-and-effect relationship that ripples through every fiber of our being and back out into the environment with our conversations, interactions, and relationships. destressifying is about mastering both worlds. We take charge of *our inner world* through elevating our awareness, understanding our needs and prioritizing them, heightening our emotional intelligence, consciously communicating, and living with purpose.

Mastering our outer world is a bit more challenging, because we don't actually control anything outside of us. Our outer world is all about *our interpretation* of the trillions of moving parts exterior to us and the speed and order they flow at us. *This is where mastering our awareness comes into play.* By heightening our ability to receive the world at a speed and frequency that nourishes us, we can slow the flow; shift our interpretation; and just as in tai chi, we can sidestep experiences that don't add value to our lives.

We know that when we quiet down, we become more sensitive to sounds around us. We also know that when we slow down, we become more attuned to activity around us. When we are in a frenetic state, it's virtually impossible to sense subtleties of movement, emotion, or activity. But when we come from a place of stillness and quietude, all the nuances of life are apparent.

I want to help you get to this space. It's actually possible to live from a much more aware state, where *you* get to choose how fast the world comes at you.

Benefits at Work and at Home

The life-changing tool to awaken that expanded awareness is spending time in stillness and silence—specifically meditation. The Harvard Business School, along with INSEAD, Europe's leading business school, have concluded that the two most effective business tools for 21st-century executives are meditation and intuition. The benefits of meditation in the workplace are cumulative. They build on one another, starting with the way you see the world with a calmer, clearer, more focused attitude; and from there they positively impact your performance and ultimately your business as a whole.

The benefits of meditation in your home life will ripple out in the same fashion, touching everyone you live with and having a positive effect on their lives. You will create a destressifying aura around you, and anyone who comes into your space will feel the calm . . . feel your stillness. And in between work and home, your life will have a new trajectory of peace in which your needs are more frequently met.

So many people have stopped meditating after a few attempts because of their expectations of what was supposed to happen. They didn't see the white light . . . Buddha didn't come to visit them . . . Jesus didn't whisper in their ear . . . or they just didn't see the value quickly enough, and in their impatience, they tossed it away. But after spending so much time in the corporate world, I developed ways to demystify the practice and make it "real world" so that you can quickly feel the results without waiting for the guru to arrive.

Introducing Stillness

Meditation is a time-tested and scientifically verified process for quieting your mind, healing your emotional wounds, and bringing your body back into balance. We live in a realm of constant thoughts, nonstop mental chatter, daydreaming, replaying options, making lists, living in the past, fantasizing, and creating scenarios that we expect to unfold. It starts the moment we open our eyes each morning and does not cease until we surrender into deep sleep at the end of the day. And this goes on from the moment we exit the womb to the moment we take our last breath. According to UCLA's Laboratory of Neuro Imaging, we have 60,000 to 80,000 thoughts every day. That's one thought every 1.2 seconds, and the relentless process continues in every moment, day after day.

By gently introducing some stillness and silence into the onslaught of mental overwhelm, we can interrupt the nonstop activity, causing it to slow down. When we do this with some regularity, the consistent *new* pattern of brief interruptions in the constant flow of thoughts creates a shift in how our brain works and how we interact with the world. With regular practice, rather than experiencing hours of thoughts-activity-thoughts-activity-thoughts-activity, the new pattern of existence evolves into thoughts – stillness – activity – stillness – thoughts – stillness – activity – stillness . . .

What happens next is remarkable. A new foundation begins to form, from which all our thoughts, words, and actions flow. This new arc of our life takes on an entirely different trajectory. It's everything that existed before, except some of the noise, the mental chatter, has quieted; and the velocity of confusing thoughts has slowed down. And then in tiny increments, we start to change . . . to morph into a merged version of our previous self and our current self. It's a slow evolution, and we can feel it. And every time we open our eyes after meditating, we bring back into our world a tweezer pinch of stillness . . . a thimbleful of silence . . . and an eyedropper full of our unconditioned self. Imagine how that compounds and builds up over time.

The Power of the Pattern Interrupt

The process of repeated mini-immersions into stillness and silence is such a profound departure from our conditioned patterns and behaviors that we very quickly start to see the world differently. Each moment carries a little extra stillness—almost as if life is flowing at us in slow motion. We begin to reawaken our natural equilibrium—our organic, unconditioned set point—which connects us effortlessly to the core of our creativity and intuition.

It is from the fertile garden of stillness and silence that true vision, emotional intelligence, crystalline clarity, and infinite possibilities take root. From this field of pure potentiality we get our bursts of inspiration, our most intuitive thoughts, our greatest insights, and our deepest sense of connection to ourselves and to the world around us. Practicing meditation on a daily basis allows you to weave silence and stillness into your mind and body to create a life of greater compassion and fulfillment.

The Science of Meditation

If the definition of stress is how we respond when our needs are not met, then meditation can be viewed as one of the antidotes to stress. After many years of speculation and skepticism, meditation has now been scientifically proven to lower our heart rate; slow and deepen our breathing; increase our growth and sex hormones; suppress cortisol, glucagon, and adrenaline; boost our immune system; help us manage pain; expand our sense of well-being; and slow the fluctuations of our mind, easing the nonstop swirl of thoughts.

A recent meditation study at the University of Massachusetts, in concert with Massachusetts General Hospital (MGH) and Harvard Medical School, tracked changes to the physical structure of the brain using MRI scans over an eight-week period—a mere 56 days. All 16 test subjects meditated on their breath for 30 minutes a day and experienced the following structural shifts:

- An increase in the size of the hippocampus, the part of the brain responsible for learning, memory, and spatial orientation

- A decrease in the size of the amygdala, the part of the brain responsible for fear, anger, and stress

As brain-imaging software develops and improves, we are finally able to look deep into the brain and see what happens when someone meditates. Many other peer-reviewed scientific studies are validating the findings of the Massachusetts research and revealing the healing power of meditation at the cellular level and the influence it has on our chromosomes. Sara Lazar, Ph.D., of the MGH Psychiatric Neuroimaging Research Program and the Massachusetts study's senior author, explained the breakthrough:

> Although the practice of meditation is associated with a sense of peacefulness and physical relaxation, practitioners have long claimed that meditation also provides cognitive and psychological benefits that persist throughout the day. This study demonstrates that changes in brain structure may underlie some of these reported improvements and that people are not just feeling better because they are spending time relaxing.

Amishi Jha, Ph.D., a University of Miami neuroscientist who investigates mindfulness training's effects on individuals in high-stress situations, reinforced this groundbreaking science:

> These results shed light on the mechanisms of action of mindfulness-based training. They demonstrate that the first-person experience of stress can not only be reduced with an eight-week mindfulness training program but that this experiential change corresponds with structural changes in the amygdala, a finding that opens doors to many possibilities for further research on MBSR's potential to protect against stress-related disorders, such as post-traumatic stress disorder.

MBSR stands for Mind Body Stress Reduction, and mindfulness meditation is simply following your breath in and out, as we do when we practice *16seconds*.

Meditation: Why and How?

The practice of meditation is a destressifying journey to the center of your very being, a journey to emotional freedom, and a journey to the reawakening of your unconditioned self. If you show up and meditate every day, you will begin to experience a transformational shift in how you interpret stressful situations; you will experience a consistent calm that helps keep you from "losing it"; your relationships will begin to heal and flourish; you will sleep more restfully; your connection to life will become centered; you will be more productive; and you will find deeper fulfillment in your work, at home, and in your life in general. You will become the stillness inside the storm . . . the calm amidst the chaos . . . the coolness under the collar.

There are many methods of meditation, and the style you choose for yourself has to resonate. I explore many different techniques in my book *Secrets of Meditation,* and if you really want to become a master meditator, I suggest you attend one of my teacher trainings. But for our purposes right now, let's build on what we already know: *16seconds.* The current practice of mindfulness, the ancient Buddhist technique of *Vipassana,* and basic breath awareness are all styles in which the breath is used as the object of your attention.

Before I found my meditation mojo, I practiced meditation on and off for many years. But, over the past decade, I have developed tools and techniques so that I never miss my morning meditation, and I have shared these real-world secrets with hundreds of thousands of people from every walk of life. I originally wrote *Secrets of Meditation* to demystify the ancient teachings and to help remove the stigma that has held so many people back from having a beautiful daily practice. I have written more than 200 articles on the subject, all available on davidji.com, along with an audiobook narrated by me. I also have a page on davidji.com dedicated to meditation resources with downloads, guided meditations, destressifying music, and meditation timers. I encourage you to sign up to be a member of the davidji SweetSpot Meditation Community so that you can have access to the newest technologies; the most cutting-edge research; and my most recent meditations, visualizations, and videos.

You Are Already a Meditator!

We've practiced meditating together using *16seconds,* so you already get the concept—and that was less than half a minute! Just to remind you, our mind processes 60,000 to 80,000 thoughts throughout the 1,440 minutes in every 24-hour day. That's a thought every 1.2 seconds. Ouch! My head hurts just taking that in. And in the midst of the waterfall of thoughts, it's easy to feel overwhelmed, anxious, stressed out, and depressed. The thoughts are coming no matter what we do.

If only there were a technique that disconnected us from all those thoughts—or at least slowed them down—then we would no longer be at their mercy. In fact, we might be more creative because we wouldn't be constricted by conditioning. We might be more intuitive because we wouldn't be so distracted. We might be more satisfied because we would have greater clarity regarding our needs; and we would be healthier because we wouldn't be subject to random surges of fight-or-flight chemicals or reactive biological stress responses.

Well, as you now realize . . . *there is a technique, and it's called meditation.* And you've already done it. Remember: If you don't sense a threat, it doesn't exist at the chemical, hormonal, or biological level. And if it doesn't exist, there is no physical or emotional response to it. That is one of the powerful benefits of destressifying.

The destressified Response: The Meditator's Main Gear

When we meditate, our body's chemistry changes. In fact, we experience the opposite of the physiological effects produced by the fight-or-flight and ego biological responses. We are less inclined to perspire, our breathing and heart rate slow, our body's production of stress hormones decreases, our sex hormone production increases, our growth hormone levels are elevated, our immune system strengthens, and our platelets become less sticky so that blood flows more easily throughout our entire body. As these physiological shifts occur, our mind calms, anxiety lessens, and there is an emotional shift in how we respond to unmet needs.

This state of restful awareness can last for a moment or through the entire meditation. But the beauty of this process is that the state of restful awareness continues to benefit our body and mind even after our meditation session. The *halo effect* continues to ripple outward. And as we meditate on a regular basis, we slowly and gently shift our automatic response mechanism to a more destressified one.

In the state of restful awareness, we move through situations with greater grace and ease. We are more reflective and less reflexive. We're less likely to lash out or have knee-jerk reactions, because we are not coming from a conditioned space. We're less impulsive and more purposeful. We're making more conscious choices, because we intuitively know what the highest choice *is* in a particular moment.

The Benefits of Meditation

Meditation can help us respond to stress constructively instead of acting out conditioned or instinctive patterns of response such as reactive, angry, argumentative behavior; emotionally shutting down; withdrawing; or escaping into isolation or certain addictions.

Meditation has been scientifically proven to counteract the effects of stress in these ways:

- Slowing our pulse and lowering our blood pressure

- Relaxing our breathing and creating a sense of calm

- Reducing our stress hormones, leading to less reactivity

- Decreasing our anxiety, overwhelm, and second-guessing of our choices

- Moderating our sweating and lessening hot flashes

- Diminishing the frequency of headaches

- Strengthening our immune system

- Enhancing our clarity, intuition, creativity, and balance

- Creating more restful sleep

- Developing more conscious choice making

- Generating greater grace and ease and deeper fulfillment

- Allowing us to stay present and focused

Meditation Awakens an Unconditioned Mind-set

Meditation creates a state of restful awareness that trickles into subsequent waking moments, creating room in our awareness for multiple interpretations of a scenario and decreasing attachment to previous interpretations, making our need to defend them become less urgent. We become more aware of the bigger picture—our point of view begins accommodating a more expanded landscape.

Over the first few weeks of daily meditation, this grace, ease, and expanded awareness weave themselves intermittently throughout our interactions. As we continue our daily meditation ritual and spend more time in stillness and silence, each day becomes more comfortable; restful awareness becomes more and more our natural state; and greater clarity begins to unfold. It becomes less important to defend our point of view, because we see greater possibilities and creative solutions emerge from once-daunting challenges.

We become more alert, more creative, more intuitive, and more relaxed. We start having anxiety-free days, and stress becomes more manageable. And our first response to unmet needs is no longer the ego response . . . that's so *last week!*

Our more common response starts to be one of truly resting while we are aware—of silently witnessing before we act out old, conditioned response patterns yet again. We become effortless observers who can then move in any direction we please, untriggered by what might have pushed our buttons in the past. Therefore, we don't respond to everything emotionally. We are more clearheaded. Our senses are heightened, and we begin to experience a new lightness of being. Little things don't irritate us or knock us off course as easily. We become more fluid in our thoughts and actions . . . more intuitive . . . more emotionally intelligent . . . more creative . . . more visionary . . . and then we start seizing new opportunities throughout every day.

Finally . . . Peace of Mind

Experiencing greater peace of mind throughout the day becomes common when you have a daily meditation ritual, as do the additional benefits of more restful sleep, better digestion, and an entirely new level of vitality. You are slowly returned to equilibrium—to wholeness!

It's often been said that 30 minutes of meditation is more restorative than 30 minutes of sleep. If you have an irregular or abnormal sleep pattern, it can normalize in just a few days after you have gotten comfortable with your new meditation routine. Of course, if the thing that keeps you awake is a deeper emotional constriction or pain, meditation will help with the acuteness of the discomfort. However, only a commitment to deeper self-discovery, emotional release, and heightened emotional intelligence will relieve the emotional pain at the core of your insomnia.

Most people embarking on a new meditation practice do so because they are seeking more from life or more from themselves. As they begin to explore their thoughts, dreams, and daily choices, an awareness settles in that they are not just their thoughts or their body—they are more than that. They are pure, unbounded consciousness sealed in a flesh casing for the span of a lifetime.

An Expanded Perspective

That new perspective changes everything because it means that in any moment, anything is possible. Your previous patterns, ruts, roadblocks, conditioned responses, thoughts, and behaviors start becoming less automatic as they are bathed in droplets of your unconditioned self.

The purest and most defenseless and unconditioned aspects of you begin to take hold in your daily routine, and then they weave themselves into your physiology. With each meditation, you move ever deeper into the most universal, infinite facets of your being, those at your very core. You're accessing the best version of yourself . . . your unbounded, unconditioned, most genuine self.

As you continue to meditate, your very foundation expands. And once your starting point for all things is at a higher level, everything that flows from that point vibrates at a higher frequency. You see the world differently; you experience your life with fuller grace and greater ease. As your brain spends more time in this state, you begin to recognize the universal connection we all share. It's as if each of us is a wave in a vast ocean that contains billions of waves—a vast oneness from which we occasionally pop up to individuate ourselves and then, after a few moments, collapse back into the oneness of the unified surf.

The Simplicity of Meditation

I believe that one of the biggest reasons why meditation is not more prevalent is because it's impossible to convey the transformational nature of the practice. People try it, and if they don't have an Aha! moment or achieve enlightenment in a week, they abandon the practice. Osho, the great Indian philosopher and guru, said, "Enlightenment is finding that there is nothing to find. Enlightenment is to come to know that there is nowhere to go."

You don't need to be a guru, yogi, or believer in any one philosophy or religion to incorporate this capability into your life. You just need the willingness to try it. So what's the best path to ultimate awareness? Let's dive in and see. In fact, let's do it right now. We'll take our *16seconds* practice to a deeper level by doing the process 20 times. As a refresher, here's the basic practice:

Sit down, get comfortable, and close your mouth. Now take a long, slow, deep breath in through your nostrils and slowly count to four. Observe the air as it moves into your nostrils, to the back of your throat, down your chest, and deep into your belly. Once your belly is filled, hold that breath in to the count of four as you continue to witness it. Now slowly . . . to the count of four . . . release the breath and watch it as it moves up through your chest and out through your nostrils. When the last bit of air is out of you, hold that to the count of four and observe it as it dissipates into the ether. And then begin the process again. If you drift away to thoughts (and you will), ever so gently drift back to your breath. Keep coming back to your breath.

Ready?

Now gently close your eyes, and let's do it 20 times, or for about five minutes. I'll wait. And if that feels too long for you, start with four times 16seconds so you can at least experience a full minute.

Instant destressifying

Did you notice that while you were observing your breath, you were totally present? Not thinking about the past or moving into the future, but totally in the moment—that is meditation! Your mind is a little calmer; your heartbeat has slowed a bit; you've filled your body with heavily oxygenated blood and nourishing hormones, boosted your immune system, and quieted your breath. And in the process, you've released a little bit of stress.

That's it. Meditation isn't any more complex than what you just experienced in those five minutes. People can make it more complicated, but basic breath-awareness meditation has not changed in more than 2,500 years! The process is simple, gentle, and easy, with no equipment necessary. It only requires that you show up, close your eyes . . . and breathe. It has had many names, but our current society refers to the technique of closing your eyes and following your breath as *mindfulness meditation,* or simply *mindfulness. Essentially, you are taking a break to simply witness and be aware.*

To increase the quietude and extend these destressifying ripples throughout your day, you can repeat your meditation ritual at midday and in the late afternoon. The key is ritualization. And each time you stop and follow your breath, the cumulative impact of destressifying will build. Very quickly you'll find that you're less reactive, more grounded, calmer, breathing easier, and having greater clarity as you move throughout your day. Full-on destressification!

Now take a minute and witness your thoughts in the same way. Just observe . . . no interpretation. Watch yourself as one thought tumbles into another and the list making and priorities begin to develop. Pay attention as the stillness at your core receives the flow of thoughts. There they are again! The beauty of mindfulness meditation is that as long as you keep your attention on whatever is happening in a given moment—and drift back to your breath when you notice you are in the past or future—it will have the destressifying effect.

What Really Happens When You Meditate?

Here's what the experience is like:

You breathe in and follow your breath down into your belly . . . then you hold the breath, watching it the whole time . . . then you release the breath and watch it travel up your chest into your throat and out through your nostrils . . . and then you hold that breath out . . . and suddenly you hear the ticking of a clock, and then your stomach gurgles, your nose itches, you get an image of what you ate for lunch, you remember a conversation you had at lunch, you start replaying the conversation—and then you become aware that you are no longer following your breath as you replay a scenario in your mind. Then you think a bit more about the conversation—and you realize again that you are no longer following your breath but have drifted into the past . . . so you drift back to your breath, which is in the present . . . and you follow your breath for a little bit . . . and then you have a song in your head. It reminds you of a moment, and you feel your body relax . . . and then you start to make a list of things to do—and then you become aware that you are no longer following your breath . . . so you drift back to your breath . . . drifting back and forth . . .

That's all. That's mindfulness: *gently drifting back and forth between your breath in the present moment and your thoughts about the past and future.*

The Object of Your Attention

As long as you stay in the present moment—and you can always return by drifting your attention to your breath—you will experience all the benefits of mindfulness. If you drift into the past or future, that's actually daydreaming, and it doesn't have the same benefits as meditation because you are engaging in activity with nothing to bring you back to center.

So the secret is to have an *object of your attention*—a consistent place to drift back to that doesn't spark thought or pull you into your emotions. Following your breath in and out is an easy object of your attention. Let's practice the most common form of mindfulness meditation right now:

Just gently breathe in and out through your nostrils, and direct your attention to your breath. You'll witness your breath as you inhale, and you'll witness your breath as you exhale. Don't hold it in or out . . . and don't feel the need to count . . . simply keep breathing naturally . . . in a relaxed way. Feel your body relax. Inhale, and then gently exhale and keep observing. Feel yourself start to slow. Just keep breathing. You will notice that you drift away to thoughts, sounds, or physical sensations. When you do drift away, simply drift your attention back to your breathing in and breathing out. You use the breath as the object of your attention . . . so no matter where you drift . . . you come back to the breath. Keep coming back to the breath . . . back to the breath.

Now try it with your eyes closed, and just breathe and witness, watch, observe. There's nothing else to do other than watch the in and out of your breathing. This is mindfulness.

Practice it for a few minutes right now. Take your time. I'll wait . . .

Welcome back. Congratulations! The next time you hear the words *mindful* or *mindfulness,* you will know exactly what they mean. You are a meditator!

We can follow our breath to meditate, or we can use another technique called *mantra meditation.* When we meditate on a mantra, we place our attention not on our breath but on a word or phrase. In the ancient Indian language of Sanskrit, that word or phrase is called a *mantra,* which comes from two Sanskrit words: *man,* meaning mind, and *tra,* meaning vehicle. So a mantra is essentially a mind vehicle. No matter where our mind drifts, as long as we have an object of our attention (such as our breath or a mantra), we will stay present.

Feel free to use any of the techniques mentioned throughout this book. Find one that resonates with you, and use it consistently for 21 days. If you determine that you'd like to use a mantra as the object of your attention instead of your breath, there are some classic universal sounds I recommend in *Secrets of Meditation* and on davidji.com. These include the traditional mantra *Om* and the *So Hum* mantra, which has been used in meditation for more than 3,000 years and was popularized by my teacher, the prolific author, physician, and spiritual icon Dr. Deepak Chopra. As you breathe in, silently repeat *So*; and as you breathe out, silently repeat *Hum*. *So - Hum. So - Hum. So - Hum.*

Try it for a few moments now with your eyes closed. How does that feel? There's no perfect speed; it's whatever feels right in the moment. As you repeat the mantra, it will change. Even though you are repeating it silently, it may get louder or fainter. It may speed up or slow down. It may become jumbled or distorted. It may even vanish. However it changes, continue to repeat it innocently. Just as following your breath works to connect you to the present moment by disconnecting you from thoughts, silently repeating a mantra over and over and over and over accomplishes the same thing.

If you prefer to use an English mantra, you can use the one popularized by the brilliant teacher and author Dr. Wayne Dyer: *I Am.* If you take a few minutes and just repeat *I* as you inhale and *Am* as you exhale over and over and over and over, you will experience the same destressifying benefits as any other meditation technique. Yes, you will have thoughts (no thoughts means you're dead . . . thoughts are okay). You will hear sounds, you will have physical sensations, you might experience deep stillness . . . and you might even fall asleep. But as soon as you realize you have drifted away from *I Am*, simply drift back to it and begin silently repeating it again as your breath moves in and out.

Let's try it now for a few minutes . . .

How do you feel? Does one technique resonate more than another? Do you prefer following your breath as we do in *16seconds,* or practicing basic mindfulness, or repeating a mantra? Feel free to use the mantras offered here or any you find online; and if you'd like to personalize your practice, consider attending one of my workshops, retreats, or teacher trainings.

If you'd prefer to simply follow your breath, make sure you don't force the breath; just let it flow in and out and witness it. You can do this for as long as you like—1 minute, or 5, 10, 15, or 30 minutes—but start small so that you don't quickly get overwhelmed.

I've recorded several free meditation timers that you can download from davidji.com onto your iPhone, iPad, iPod, BlackBerry, Droid, or tablet or right onto your computer. They are perfect meditation timers and give you the option of 5-, 10-, 15-, 20-, 25-, or 30-minute meditations. As you continue in this journey, the method you use can shift and evolve. So keep an open mind and stay with the practice.

Experiences During Meditation

Regardless of the method you are using as the object of your attention, there are only three things that can actually happen when you meditate. And they are all valid experiences.

- You can *have thoughts.*
- You can *fall asleep.*
- You can *experience stillness.*

All three are signs of a verified meditation. As long as you are showing up, you are doing it right.

All our sensory experiences start outside of us and then turn into thoughts. Here are just a couple of examples:

— *Sounds* are a part of the fabric of meditation, and when you hear a sound, it generates a thought. You cannot flip a switch and shut off your ability to hear. When you notice an internal conversation sparked by hearing a sound, gently drift back to following your breath or whatever the object of your attention is during the meditation.

— Various physical *sensations* can arise while meditating. If your legs have gone numb from sitting, uncross them. If your back hurts, stop and rub it for a bit, or stand up and stretch. Then gently reimmerse yourself in the meditation by taking a few breaths and floating back into following your breath. Try to begin in a position of comfort. After all, if the pins and needles start, then your attention is redirected to your physical state, interrupting the flow of the meditation. If you just participated in strenuous physical activity, wait and cool down for a bit to avoid hyperventilating during meditation. Avoid bringing the effects of alternative "medicines" into the experience as well—caffeine, cannabis, or alcohol—for they will detract from the benefit of the experience. They will numb you to the positive aspects of increasing your awareness.

Releasing Stress in Many Ways

Beginners often experience a release of stress that can be expressed in many ways: Some sigh, some smile more, some fall asleep, some cry, some feel the release in their body, some feel more grounded, some have flashes of clarity, some have Aha! moments, some become more sensitive or more emotional, some have feelings of compassion or empathy where they did not previously, and some have visual experiences.

The release of stress can also express itself through the physical body in the form of lightness or heaviness in the upper body, tingling sensations, cold or hot feelings in your hands or feet, pins and needles, and soft waves of energy flowing through certain parts of your body.

To help you connect more deeply to your body, let's practice a powerful technique called *eight destressifications of the spine*. This exercise will proactively release you from bodily stress you may encounter throughout the course of the day and increase your physical awareness.

eight destressifications of the spine

Sitting in a chair with your feet firmly on the ground, gently bend your head forward, curving your spine like a turtle shell— hold it for five seconds. Now do it the opposite way, arching yourself backward—and hold that for five seconds.

Come back to center. Sit straight up. Now take your right hand, reach across your belly, and grip the bottom of the left side of your chair. Hold that pose for five seconds. You'll feel your spine loosen a bit. Now do it the opposite way with your left hand. Remember: Reach only as far as feels comfortable. If you can't reach the chair, reach as far as feels like a comfortable stretch. Hold it for five seconds.

Come back to center. Now reach both arms up to the sky, and hold that for five seconds. Next reach down to the floor, resting your chest on your knees, and hold that for five seconds.

Come back to center. Reach your right hand up to the sky, and gently, with your elbow straight, tilt your right arm as far to the left over your head as possible—reach out as if you are picking an apple from over the left side of your body. Hold that for five seconds. Now do the same reach with your left arm over to the right side, stretching as far as it is comfortable. And come back to center.

You've now just experienced the 40-second exercise *eight destressifications of the spine.* You can start your day with it; do it in the car, on a train or bus, or at your desk. You can even do it standing if you prefer. It's like you are a human stress ball, and by squeezing yourself in different ways, you create a state of restful awareness.

Now that we've taken this short pattern interrupt, let's get back to the other experiences we can have during meditation . . .

Some of us are more visual than others and see images, pictures, geometric shapes, saturations of color, words, symbols, drawings, photographs, or even videos. Some see the faces of people they have never met, as well as faces of loved ones or those who have passed on from this earthly realm.

And yes, you may see nothing and even fall asleep as a result of meditation—an indication that you have relaxed enough to surrender to your bodymind's restoration process. This is a powerful sign of a verified meditation. However, falling asleep *all the time* may indicate that you're not getting enough rest.

Don't try to have some special experience like transcendence or merging into oneness. These are rookie mistakes. And even if you do visit some ethereal other dimension during your meditation, it's probably just another thought. *We don't meditate for the experiences in meditation. We meditate for the destressifying and the peace of mind it brings to our lives when we are not meditating.*

So why isn't everyone meditating?

Excuse #1: I Don't Have Enough Time

The number one excuse people give for not meditating is that they don't have enough time. They have time for watching TV, surfing the Internet, texting, talking, watching movies, writing, hobbies, playing Wii, working late, partying, reading, relaxing, checking e-mail, cooking meals, scrolling through Facebook, bathing, napping, commuting, waiting, flying, tweeting, waiting, brushing their hair, playing with the dog, taking care of the baby, seeing the doctor, waiting, hurrying up, and waiting . . . but no time for meditating!

We determine what activities we fit into each moment of the 24 hours of our day. Of course we have the time to meditate for 30 minutes every day, even if we end up just shaving one minute from each of our morning activities. Time is not some independent being that imposes itself on our schedule. We develop our schedule based on our values and beliefs. We decide what we think is the best use of our life energy and how much time we are willing to allot to various activities.

What I have found is that when you incorporate a meditation practice into your life, you quickly destressify, and suddenly there is time for everything. You approach each moment from a point of greater clarity and ease. Deadlines evaporate as you finish projects ahead of schedule. You experience more restful sleep, which gives you greater vitality and the ability to focus. You become more efficient in all your work, so there is finally some free time and some breathing room. You identify the non-nourishing behaviors you were expending energy on and the unmet needs you were struggling over, and you are able to replace them with more nourishing and more efficient behaviors—ways of living that offer you greater support.

But you have to take the first step, so I suggest that you commit to a week or two or three of a daily meditation practice, and you will see how the time in your life expands to fit everything you want . . . and more. Simply start with *16seconds* and add one solid minute each week for the next four months. This is how I was able to teach police officers and members of the military. Remember: Bean by bean, the bag gets filled.

So start easy with *16seconds,* and the world of meditation will unfold for you. After three weeks, you'll be up to three minutes and 16seconds; after six weeks, you'll have comfortably rolled over the five-minute mark; and at the end of 16 weeks, you will have mastered the practice with very little interruption in your life because of the incremental steps you've taken.

Excuse #2: I Don't Feel the Results

The second most common reason people cite for not meditating is that they think the results are too subtle, so they can't see any value in continuing. Again, this goes back to our misconceptions about what meditation is supposed to be. If your expectations are to levitate and see colors, but you are only aware of drifting back and forth between your breath and thoughts, you will assume it's not working and give up. You may even think you're doing it wrong, because you don't have any Aha! moments during your practice.

Remember, the benefits happen in the other 23 hours in the day, when you're *not* meditating. So be patient and stop looking for the higher state of consciousness to arrive. Day by day, you will find you are struggling a bit less, you are sleeping more restfully, answers come to you more quickly, you are more relaxed, and there are fewer crises. Don't worry about whether you are doing it right. Just keep meditating, and after a few weeks, you will recognize distinct changes in the way you interact with life, stress, disappointments, unmet needs, your emotions, and your own thoughts. The only bad meditation is the one you don't show up for!

Personalizing Your Meditation

Having a meditation practice is no different from doing some form of physical exercise every day. Exercise subtly tightens your body; meditating every day gently eases your mind into a sense of well-being—pure destressifying.

In order to bring this peace and stillness into your life on a daily basis, you must have a practice that supports the process. So many of us have meditated either through a guided meditation audio or CD, lying on our backs at the end of a yoga class, or simply sitting in silence for a few minutes. Each of these experiences brings a sense of calm to our lives but doesn't necessarily shift our consciousness over the long term. Changing the way we view the world, our life, our needs, our emotions, others' words and actions, and our own behavior happens naturally through the destressifying process we're exploring.

To achieve the transformational shift that daily meditation offers requires that you connect to stillness and silence on a regular basis. The optimal duration is 30 minutes, but starting with a few minutes is perfect; the ideal frequency is twice each day—once in the morning and once in the afternoon or evening—but beginning with just once a day is fantastic. In fact, if you can start right now with *16seconds*, you can effortlessly build it up into a full nourishing daily practice. The following sections will help you establish your own destressifying routine.

The Exception to the Rule

New meditators who are high achievers often give meditation the same level of effort, focus, and concentration that they have applied to every other aspect of their lives. We know that such determination often delivers results in business, finance, and so many other aspects of our world. In fact, most of us were taught the following equation at a very young age:

$$focus + effort = success$$

We were also taught that if we increase the effort, our level of success will expand as well. The lesson we absorbed was this: Work hard enough, and we can have whatever we want. For many of us, that's how we achieved everything we cherish, which only reinforces the belief that *focus* and *effort* are the key ingredients to any success.

But as you may have noticed, this doesn't always get results. In fact, in time it becomes more of a personal style—a conditioned way we end up living our life—rather than a success formula we consciously follow. This "natural" law of our society doesn't always translate life's challenges into expansive solutions. In fact, it deludes us into thinking that everything can be solved with focus and effort—when in reality, this conditioned mind-set often leads to constriction, frustration, and stress.

Meditation allows us to step back to—or forward from—a different perspective. When we destressifiers re-immerse ourselves into daily life, we sometimes see familiar aspects of our world with "new eyes," infinitely increasing the possibilities for expansion and growth. This creates the space for old patterns to fall away . . . for old conditioned behaviors to be recognized as having outlived their usefulness.

When Should I Meditate?

In the era when these teachings were first made popular, almost 5,000 years ago, most people were farmers. They rose before sunrise, they washed, they prayed and meditated, and then they went into the fields at the first hint of sunrise. They worked in the fields with their animals, and then they retired for the day before sunset. They meditated before dinner, and they slept as the sun slept. The platform for these techniques was developed long before Las Vegas, Facebook, and the 10 P.M. restaurant reservation—long before night shifts, insomnia, red-eye flights, nightclubs, pulling all-nighters, swing shifts, and round-the-clock emergency rooms. It was refined millennia before planes, trains, and buses moved through the night . . . before our "modern" nocturnal behaviors began to buck our natural circadian rhythms. The great teachers of that time suggested meditating between 5 A.M. and 7 A.M. and from 5 P.M. to 7 P.M.—at the start and end of the solar day. But the developers of this ancient guidance had no idea we would be living in an age when people go out to dinner after it's already dark, and many of us rise long after the sun has come up.

Introducing pattern interrupts into your life throughout the day is a powerful awareness tool, but starting your day from a platform of stillness and silence is *transformational*. Every other moment you experience, every word you speak, and every action you take then comes from a place that's reflective rather than reflexive, that's purposeful rather than knee-jerk reactive, and that's unconditioned—not pulling from your tight, constricted realm of conditioned responses. The awareness that unfolds from simply a few moments of quiet reflection *before* you act will powerfully shift you into destressifying mode.

The Power of Ritual

So when is the right time to meditate? I used to say to myself, *I'll meditate at ten o'clock every morning.* But ten never comes. You know what it's like: The phone rings. The dog needs attention. You're suddenly greeted with information that requires a response. You spend more time than you thought sending an e-mail, going to the store, or dealing with a challenge. And then it's noon, and you have a lunch meeting. You plan for three o'clock, but then you get pulled away, so you promise yourself that you will meditate as soon as you get home. But a friend calls and asks you out to dinner. And then you go to a movie, and then to a club for dancing, and before you know it, it's midnight . . . and you haven't meditated.

The secret is to ritualize your practice so that it will just flow without thought. You rarely skip brushing your teeth because the phone rings, right? We create and maintain our behaviors by ritualizing them. The easiest way to lock in your daily meditation practice—and, most important, your morning meditation—is to make it part of a series of activities that you do based on each one flowing into the next, rather than what time it is while you're performing them.

For example, when you wake up each morning, you look at the clock—then you pee. You don't say to yourself, *It's 6:30—time to pee!* That activity happens as a natural flow of your morning ritual. Then you do the next thing on your invisible list of morning activities, and then the next. Most of us pretty much do the same things in the same order every day. We have between 8 and 15 morning rituals that we deploy in a certain sequence upon waking. Sometimes we have a different ritual for the weekends than for the workweek. These evolve over time, but each of us has this autopilot string of rituals we perform each day like clockwork.

It starts when you wake up—perhaps by alarm or the sun, or maybe you just awaken. The next thing you do is look at the clock to orient yourself. Then you do the rest of these activities in the same ritualistic order you always do, and you do them all like a prearranged dance: You *wake;* you *pee;* you *wash your face;* you *move your bowels;* you *shower;* you *groom yourself* by shaving or putting on makeup; you *do your hair;* you *dress;* you *tend to any children or babies* in the house; you *tend to your pet;* you *interact with your significant other or housemate;* you *watch morning TV;* you *read a newspaper;* you *go online or check your e-mail;* you *make coffee or tea;* and you *eat or serve some form of breakfast.* You perform these activities in the same ritualistic order, on autopilot, and you have done them like that every day for months, years, even decades.

The Effortless Ritual: RPM

To solve the difficulty most meditators have ensuring they get in that first meditation of the day, I developed a ritual that has helped thousands effortlessly lock down their practice. It's known as *RPM*, which stands for Rise, Pee, Meditate. It's based on the fact that you wake up each day. So what time do you wake up?

It's not too big a leap to think that within a few minutes of waking, you're going to pee. Well, you're two-thirds of the way there! If the very next thing you do is sit down to meditate, then within 35 minutes of opening your eyes in the morning, you'll have a half hour of stillness and silence inside you to greet every moment as you move throughout the rest of your day. You'll have created a trajectory of destressifying that is expressed by your being less reactive, more reflective, more creative, more intuitive, more compassionate, more understanding, and more purposeful in your thoughts, words, and actions.

In the first few minutes after you wake up, you have the least amount of active thoughts. But the flow of making meaning out of each moment as you get further into the day quickly accelerates your mind's activity as your needs, emotions, and thoughts of the past and future start to rush into you. If instead the first thing you do when you wake up is meditate, then logically there will be fewer distractions to interfere with your practice.

Couldn't you take one minute from each of your morning ablution rituals and wake up 15 minutes earlier? Then you'd have that sweet, unhurried space of meditation to start your day. If the answer is no, then revisit what time you go to bed, and try going to sleep 15 minutes earlier for a few weeks in a row. It will suddenly be a part of who you are.

You can make this work even if you start with just a few minutes of meditation. Then you will slide effortlessly into this morning ritual as easily as you did into the rituals of watching TV, brushing your teeth, making your morning brew, or taking your morning walk. Pushing RPM to the very front of your morning ritual train will allow you to integrate meditation into your daily routine until it is as much a part of your morning flow as any of your other ablution rituals.

So yes, there is ancient wisdom that says to meditate between the hours of 5 A.M. and 7 A.M., but you have to do what works best for you—whatever that may be! The key is to create a ritual.

RAW: Your Second Meditation of the Day

The meditation at the end of your day is for a different purpose than your morning ritual. This session is to help you release all the stress you've absorbed and to process all the intensity you've experienced over the course of the day. So to further the daily-routine analogy, if the first meditation of the day is to set the table, then the second one is to wash the dishes!

This late-afternoon or evening meditation can be more difficult to squeeze in, because now you have time issues on both sides of your meditation practice, and your mind is very active. For the afternoon or evening meditation, I suggest the acronym *RAW,* standing for Right After Work. Make it the very, very, very last thing you do before you leave work or the very, very, very first thing you do when you get home. This way it's ritualized and there are fewer time pressures. If you spend most of your days at home, then you get to set your own rules for the timing.

If you meditate using the RAW ritual, you will ever so gently coast into your evening before it explodes with activity: dinner, kids, stories of the day, TV, Internet, pets, workouts, and anything else you cram into those last remaining hours you are awake. You will be bringing a bit of stillness and silence into whatever unfolds at home. And you will be in alignment with the timeless rhythms of nature. If you can have your evening destressifying practice under your belt, you will handle home and evening challenges with grace and aplomb. And you won't be bringing the swirl of the day into your evening or sleep regimen. If it feels better for you to meditate closer to your bedtime, do that. Maintain this philosophy: When it comes to your afternoon or evening meditation, do whatever works!

The Myths That Keep Us from Meditating

There are more people who have tried to meditate and stopped than currently *do* meditate. Here are the five myths that keep most people from meditating:

Myth #1: The first thing you need to do is clear the thoughts from your mind or at least still them.

As you now know, we all have between 60,000 and 80,000 thoughts per day, approximately one thought every 1.2 seconds. That's what our brain does! If it's functioning properly, you will have thoughts as all those neurotransmitters fire throughout each moment. The thoughts will continue coming. Remember: no thoughts = flatlining; thoughts = alive!

Do not attempt to erase them, for this merely focuses energy and attention upon them. Treat them as you would clouds—pieces of the scenery that drift passively on by. Do not engage them. When you realize that you are thinking and no longer meditating, simply drift back to the object of your attention.

Myth #2: Something special or transcendent is supposed to happen during meditation.

Nothing special is supposed to happen during meditation. Sure, it is possible for something cool to happen, although it's not the goal. And most likely, any experience you have is simply stress being released or a thought coming into your awareness. The emotional, physical, and spiritual destressifying benefits creep into your day gradually, as subtle shifts that affect your moment-to-moment waking state. Simply let yourself be—bask in the stillness and lack of activity—as opposed to waiting for something exciting or surreal to unfold. Attempting to find significance in the experience means making a shift from stillness to activity, from innocence to intellectualizing. Meditation serves to benefit every other waking moment in which we interact with others and the world. It is not the same as going to the movies!

Myth #3: I don't think I'm doing it right.

People have the common tendency to question, "Am I doing it right?" This is irrelevant when it comes to meditation. Do not aspire toward any perception of what the right way is. Do not be critical of yourself. Don't judge. Simply release, let go, and surrender to the unknown. Allow your sole purpose in meditation to be innocently following your breath or repeating a mantra, depending on the meditation practice you choose in the moment. And yes, as long as you are showing up to meditate, you are doing it right. The only "bad" meditation is the one you don't show up for!

> *Myth #4: If I meditate long enough, I will achieve enlightenment.*
>
> Meditation initiates the restoration of your unconditioned self, very gradually destressifying you as layers of conditioning are peeled away. The rigid patterns of thought, stresses, traumas, and emotional scars that may have built up over a lifetime actually start to deconstruct themselves as you morph into your best version of yourself—the destressified you. Meditation opens your eyes to new possibilities and gradually dissipates the fogginess of your vision so that you see more clearly and act more purposefully. Meditation is not about becoming enlightened, although it will help on your journey of self-discovery and ultimately self-actualization. The practice is simply about destressifying so that you can be happier, more empowered, and more deeply fulfilled.
>
> *Myth #5: If I meditate, I am a superior human being, because I am spiritual.*
>
> There is no spiritual hierarchy of humans based on whether they meditate or for how long. This is the same claim that fundamentalists of all religions and belief systems have used for millennia to elevate themselves and distance nonbelievers. Meditation facilitates the recognition of our universality—our common connection to all people—and this state of oneness awareness is not conducive to making comparisons. And realistically, if you think you are superior . . . you've got some more work to do.

Where Should I Meditate?

I meditate each morning on a fat, round zafu pillow, with my L.A. rescue dog, Peaches, the Buddha Princess, curled up on a pillow right next to me. I refer to her as "the Mindful Morkie." (She has her own Facebook page—please Like her!) I sit in front of a coffee table that I place a digital clock on. I don't use a timer or alarm. I meditate using my breath or one of the mantras I've discussed, and I open my eyes when I am aware I'm thinking about time. When I wonder how long it's been, I open my eyes a crack, glance at the clock, take in the time, and go back into meditation.

What should *you* do? First, leave your bed or sit up with your back against your headboard. Find a spot that you don't connect with other ritualized behaviors. Try not to start off lying down; it will create a Pavlovian connection between sleep and meditation. Pick any relatively quiet place where you can be relaxed and comfortable. In extreme circumstances, meditators have meditated in their bathrooms, their cars, even their closets. I suggest you find a quiet spot that feels somewhat sacred or special, a place you can imagine sitting in every day, and find a cushion, pillow, or chair you can hang out in for at least 15 minutes. Move toward the most comfortable seat and the most comfortable position. Feather your nest. Always keep moving toward comfort, wherever that is.

Feel free to meditate while commuting (as long as you are not driving), at the doctor's office, in the airport, at a sporting event, at a rock concert, or during any long trip you're taking. The next time you have five free minutes, see what it feels like to use those precious moments tapping into the stillness and silence that rests within.

It doesn't matter what direction you face: God is everywhere. I like to face east to feel the first light of morning come into my awareness, which always makes me smile. Usually this is followed by hearing birds wake up, but every day is different, all so special. If you need to peek, peek. If you need to move, move. If you need to stretch, stretch. Do whatever you need to do: sneeze, cough, yawn, scratch, yelp. Always move toward comfort. If you are pulled out of meditation by some disturbance, tend to your urgent situation and then return and meditate for the remaining minutes.

If for any reason you have skipped a day or a meditation, rather than beat yourself up . . . give yourself a hug for noticing. Cut yourself some slack and then dive right back in. The practice is cumulative, so don't worry if you slip away from it—as long as you are willing to slip back in.

The Keys to a Successful Daily Practice

Whether you meditate using your breath or using a mantra as the object of your attention, there are nine basic keys to an effortless and comfortable daily practice:

1. **Put comfort first.** Make sure you are comfortable in every moment. If you're comfortable, you'll continue to meditate; if you're not comfortable, most likely you'll stop. So no matter what the disturbance, don't resist. Stop and deal with it (stretch your legs, look at your watch, rub your neck, turn off your phone, scratch your cheek), and drift back to the object of your attention.

2. **Start slowly.** I've trained thousands of people with regular meditation practices to start with *16 seconds* and build on it. Don't try to be a high achiever in the first few weeks. Slowly, incrementally, add more time to your practice and don't do too much too soon.

3. **Create a ritual.** Don't pin your meditation to a time on the clock. Use a ritual such as RPM (Rise, Pee, Meditate) or any other ritual that works for you. The afternoon ritual can be RAW (Right After Work) or another ritual that feels comfortable. Allow your 5 to 30 minutes to be sacred.

4. **Don't bring any baggage.** Bring nothing into the meditation other than the object of your attention—your mantra or your breath. Do not have an intention, agenda, or target that you bring into the meditation. Don't force your practice. Let it innocently unfold.

5. **Witness.** Let go of any expectations you may have about the practice. Nothing is *supposed* to happen. Observe whatever flows into you . . . and drift back to the object of your attention.

6. **Let go of meaning.** Don't get distracted with any experiences you have during the meditation. Treat any interruption, sound, old mantra, idea, mood, feeling, expectation, or emotion as you would any other thought. Regardless of what you experience, keep drifting back to the object of your attention.

7. **Surrender.** Follow your breath or repeat the mantra effortlessly, like mist rising off a lake at dawn.

8. **Know that you're doing great.** Whatever happens is perfect! If you fall asleep, have thoughts, experience stillness, or find yourself making lists, do not judge the experience. Every meditation is like a snowflake, unique and never to be repeated.

9. **Enjoy!** Do not get too serious. destressifying is painless and nourishing. This is a lighthearted practice, so enjoy it!

Now you know more about meditation than 95 percent of the planet (and that includes 350 million Buddhists!). If you are willing to follow through on this one practice, destressifying will begin before you even start to meet your needs, heighten your emotional intelligence, communicate consciously, or discover your purpose. You will innocently have mastered your awareness simply by connecting more deeply to the stillness and silence that rests within.

· · · · ·

CHAPTER 6

destressifying by Mastering Your Needs

"A man travels the world over in search
of what he needs and returns home to find it."

— GEORGE A. MOORE

Now that you are well on your way to mastering your awareness, the next step to destressifying is the *mastery of your needs*— identifying, prioritizing, and meeting your vast needs with greater regularity.

Virtually all the stress we experience each day is a direct result of our needs not being met in one capacity or another. Most frequently, the reason our needs aren't met is because we haven't identified or recognized them. In the nonstop go-go-go of life, we rarely take the time for a thorough self-analysis. It's too overwhelming and too complex. But destressifying by *mastering our needs* is really easy, and our exploration of it will shine a spotlight into the darkness.

Since one of the most popular definitions of stress is how we respond when our needs are not met, let's make that our starting point. If we can figure out more effective ways to meet our needs, we will have less stress.

There are two ways to most effectively overcome stress related to unmet needs:

1. *Shift our stress response*—essentially, change what we do and say when our needs are not met

2. *Increase the odds that our needs will be met* by gaining clarity on our expectations, better understanding the situation, taking clear steps to meet our needs, and communicating them to others more consciously

Whether we master one or both of these approaches, simply putting some attention on these solutions will quickly make a difference in how we feel in each moment and ultimately how we feel about our life in general. The deeper work of destressifying— starting here with the mastery of our needs—shifts us internally so that we have fewer unmet needs. Fewer unmet needs equal less stress, which applies directly to our interpretation of life and our perception of stress. So let's start at the very beginning by exploring the concept of our basic needs.

What Are My Needs?

The eight billion people on the planet have eight billion unique interpretations of life, eight billion unique combinations of needs and desires, and eight billion unique expressions of reality through their thoughts, words, and actions. Isn't it amazing how unique you are?

Yet, with all that uniqueness and individuality, all eight billion of us seem to share the same basic categories of needs. In the 1940s, the American psychologist Abraham Maslow wrote *A*

Theory of Human Motivation, in which he outlined five universal categories of human needs that we all share. Maslow taught at Brooklyn College and the Western Behavioral Sciences Institute and was chairman of the Department of Psychology at Brandeis University. From 1967 to 1968 he was president of the American Psychological Association. He has some serious street cred!

It's been said that most of our motivation comes from fear or greed—the old "carrot or stick" punishment-and-reward paradigm. But Maslow took it one step further. He believed that individuals possess a deeper, more core set of motivation systems that are actually *un*related to rewards. And he revealed that these universal needs—bubbling beneath the surface—naturally motivate us toward fulfilling them when they are unmet. Maslow also stressed that the motivation to fulfill these needs will become stronger the longer they are denied. For example, the longer a person goes without water, the thirstier they get; without sleep, the more tired they feel; without food, the hungrier they become.

Prioritizing Your Needs

Maslow prioritized the various categories of universal needs based on the importance each of us organically places on fulfilling them. He demonstrated that they have a hierarchy of their own and that our lower-order needs must be fulfilled before higher-order needs can be realized. Essentially, once a specific level of needs has been reasonably satisfied, we are able to go about fulfilling the next level, and then the next, ultimately reaching the highest tier of fulfillment, which he referred to as *self-actualization.*

That's right. With all of our individual distinctiveness, we each share the exact same hierarchy of needs. You, me, your parents, those you're close to, and everyone with whom you interact—the barista in your local coffee shop, your dentist, your co-workers, your kids, the smartest people you know and the dullest, your boss, your local police officers, the gate agent at the airport, your neighbors, your friends, and even your shrink! We all have the same needs and are motivated to process and fulfill them in the same order.

The Pyramid

An easy way to grasp this concept is to envision a pyramid with five levels. At the base of our needs pyramid are our *Survival Needs*: what we need to stay alive. These are our basic physiological and biological requirements of breathing, drinking, eating, sleeping, peeing, pooping, and having sex. Once we meet those basic biological imperatives, we can aspire to meeting the next set of needs in the pyramid: our *Safety Needs*. We need to be able to have a roof over our head to protect us from the elements; we need to know that we can go to work without being shot at; we need to feel that our possessions are safe; and we need to know that we are protected by some social codes or laws.

Moving up the pyramid to the next level, we find our *Social Needs,* which include belonging, love, the nature of our relationships, and all that comes with that—essentially the needs of our heart. Once this core group of needs is met, we can move up to a more evolutionary grouping known as our *Esteem Needs,* which include personal self-esteem, status, titles, prestige, positions, achievement, and responsibility—even mastery of our chosen field.

Maslow argued that once these four sets of needs are met—survival, safety, social, and esteem—an individual is primed for the fifth and final stage in the hierarchy: *Self-actualization*. This is where our deepest needs of personal growth and purposeful fulfillment are achieved. We are self-actualized when most of our lower needs are consistently met, we master our chosen field, we seek peak experiences, and we help others to meet *their* needs.

MASLOW'S HIERARCHY OF NEEDS
(ORIGINAL FIVE-STAGE MODEL)

SELF-ACTUALIZATION
Personal Growth, Self-Fulfillment

ESTEEM NEEDS
Achievement, Status,
Responsibility, Reputation

BELONGINGNESS AND LOVE NEEDS
Family, Affection, Relationship, Work Group, Etc.

SAFETY NEEDS
Protection, Security, Order, Law, Limits, Stability, Etc.

BIOLOGICAL AND PHYSIOLOGICAL NEEDS
Basic Life Needs — Air, Food, Drink, Shelter, Warmth, Sex, Sleep, Etc.

Maslow stressed that we do not have to rigidly fulfill all the needs in a particular category before we can address higher needs. He claimed that the tiers are interrelated rather than sharply separated, which means we can work at fulfilling multiple levels simultaneously.

Over the past 70 years, many scientists, philosophers, psychologists, and theoreticians have built upon Maslow's framework of needs. His five categories have stood the test of time in bringing clarity to the motivating forces in the lives of most human beings on planet Earth. We are all moving from pure survival to becoming the best version of ourselves. So let's go deeper and explore the universal needs we all have and take some steps to meet them.

Drilling Down to Meet Our Needs

Let's start at the base of the pyramid. We'll begin by taking a look at our Survival Needs, which we share with virtually every living being on earth.

Survival Needs

According to Maslow, our *Survival Needs* include the most basic physiological needs for oxygen, food, water, and warmth. Sexual needs are also included in this category because they are vital to the procreation and survival of our species. But outside of the physical act of having sex or making love, we all need some basic physical nurturing, whether we're being rocked to sleep as a baby, being held as a child, or being cuddled as an adult. So long as our physiological needs remain unsatisfied, they will drive and motivate us to their ultimate fulfillment. And until these requirements are met, it is unlikely we will be focused on higher needs.

For example, if you haven't eaten for a while and your blood sugar is dropping, or if you have to pee really badly, it's unlikely that your primary concern will be whether you've received enough love yet today. Once you've met these basic physiological needs—you've gotten a bite to eat or had the chance to empty your bladder—then you are motivated to meet needs further up in the hierarchy, such as falling in love or boosting self-esteem.

Do you have any unmet Survival Needs? Maybe you have to pee right now. If so, go and do it, because until that need is met, you most probably won't absorb anything.

Okay, I'm guessing you're back now. Don't you feel better? Let's continue . . .

Safety Needs

According to Maslow, our *Safety Needs* include shelter, stability, protection, freedom from fear and anxiety, structure, order, and law. We can witness this need in virtually every animal on the planet—from snakes and lizards to co-workers and family members.

There are currently 32 wars going on across the globe. For people living in one of these war zones, even the most basic of Safety Needs is not being met. They lie in their beds at night listening to the sound of gunfire; the law of the land can change each day based on who is in power at the moment. Even if they do have their Survival Needs met, they often can't get food, water, or even travel to work without fear of being physically or sexually threatened. This is a common mind-set for daily living in such places as Israel, Iraq, and many countries in Africa where the threat of an incoming missile, a marauding gang of machete-wielding troops, contracting Ebola, or being the victim of a suicide bomber weighs in the back of your mind throughout the day, every day, and into your dreams while you sleep.

People in these situations are in a constant state of stress because their most core Safety Need is not being met. Living in the West, far from the blare of air-raid sirens and threats to our physiology, allows us to move through the day mostly without fear of physical threat. This doesn't mean our day is confrontation free (and we'll address meeting this need through *conflict resolution* in Chapter 9), but we are not constantly distracted by the thought of being killed as we wait in the Starbucks line or sit in traffic on the freeway.

Is Your Need for Safety Being Met?

If our Safety Need wasn't met during childhood, it's quite possible that we are still carrying that wound—waiting for someone or something to trigger it. So even though the event that ingrained itself into our being is so far in the past that the details might be fuzzy, our unmet need for safety is crystal clear, lingering in our thoughts throughout the day. Recognizing this rather than denying it is a powerful step toward meeting the need.

Often, people who have survived a devastating natural disaster; an abusive person, parent, or partner; or the "rules" of life being changed on them in some way, will spend their entire lives with a victim mentality. Not only is this mind-set stress creating—it's stress sustaining! Individuals living with this perspective become very fearful. Due to their inner disconnect from perceived structure and order, they become overly insistent on following the rules, often acting righteous about their beliefs or moralistic with those lacking structure or order in their own lives. History is laden with petty dictators and corrupt rulers who have clearly been stuck at this second stage of needs.

People whose Safety Needs are challenged will sometimes construct rules for others to follow. A daily practice of *destressifying* can help us to successfully shift from this constricted world view—and the chronic stress that accompanies it—to an empowered survivor mentality, and ultimately to a stress-free thriver state of mind.

Bottom line, if we are cold, homeless, and afraid without knowing how to get help, or if we're suddenly thrown into an unfamiliar situation, then we operate from the more granular view of solving our basic safety and protection needs. We live from a place of fear and a "less than," high-stress state of consciousness. We worry about the weather, we fret over traffic, and we agonize over things out of our control.

The Price of an Unmet Need

Living from fear, we hesitate to make decisions because we dread being wrong; we struggle with judgments, and we question and regret past actions. We travel through life in an overly cautious way. We may become so indecisive that we get stuck . . . frozen . . . paralyzed by fear of making a mistake. We project into the future and see such dark clouds on the horizon that we become unable to move, and we begin to resent the world around us, as well as resenting others who seem to move through life with grace and ease.

So the key to meeting this need is our orientation to our sense of security or safety. If we can give up our need to control a little bit or start realizing that we really have very little control, our need for security will be more effectively met. Once we "own" the fact that uncertainty and surprises are woven into every moment, we can receive them more positively.

Are You Wasting Energy?

Where do you see yourself right now? Are you struggling, surviving, or thriving in the realm of security? How much of a control freak are you really?

It's important to note that there is no right or wrong. Security has a different definition for each of us. But those who consistently ruminate on their bank balance, whether their car will start, whether they'll have enough to make their monthly payments, whether their job is secure, whether they will get sick and die, and so on, are living in unnecessary pain and setting themselves up for massive stress consequences. Even if it doesn't impact their health, it is emotionally sucking the life out of them—and the time spent on worrying is wasted energy. When we are stuck at this level, it's difficult to be effective at fulfilling our Social Needs, our Esteem Needs, or the needs that will truly actualize us.

Certainty or Clarity—Which Do You Really Crave?

If we can calmly and with a clear head go through a process of identifying our Safety Needs, prioritizing them, releasing what doesn't serve us, and bringing into our life what we truly need, then very quickly this category of needs will be fulfilled at a higher level.

What makes you feel safe, secure, and taken care of? Do any of these resonate?

- A dependable car
- A steady job
- Health insurance
- Money in the bank
- A partner you can trust

- A nest egg for retirement or that rainy day
- Bonding experiences
- Life insurance
- Belief in yourself
- Faith in God
- A house or apartment you are proud of
- Little or no debt
- An alarm or security system or living behind secure walls or gates

There can be deeper levels of Safety Needs, such as finding your birth mother or father, knowing your divorce is final, learning your diagnosis is benign, and the like. And if you can move through the process of gaining greater clarity about your needs with a destressifying mind-set, then when you receive your "answer," it will actually fulfill you.

Sometimes we think we want certainty so we can believe that everything is okay, *but what we really want is clarity:* the ability to receive the news—good or bad—and then understand the steps we need to take to meet the new need. Certainty lasts for only a little while, and then the wind blows and what we thought was carved in stone suddenly shifts or changes like sand under our feet. Clarity can support us over and over in each new situation. I'll choose clarity any day over certainty.

What are *your* unmet Safety Needs? Do you feel a sense of safety regarding your home, your job, and your material world?

Regardless of the past, once we obtain a sense of security of employment, consistent shelter, safety of property, and physical comfort, our Safety Needs become more actualized and we can take a step in the direction of meeting our Social Needs.

Social Needs

According to Maslow, our *Social Needs* include the need for belonging, connection, group involvement, and love. We need to feel that we are a part of the broader collective. Our need to fulfill the core emotional essentials of the heart and our inability to effectively make that happen can keep us forever mired in this category of unmet needs, building up stress on a daily basis as we flail around in the quicksand of our emotions.

We are on a lifelong quest to meet the following needs:

- Intimacy
- Love
- Belonging
- Trust
- Inclusion
- Compassion
- Connection
- Fairness
- Exchange
- Cooperation
- Nurturing
- Communication
- Closeness
- Support
- Community
- Companionship
- Empathy

It seems that all these can be distilled down to a powerful grouping of needs I refer to as the *Four Needs of the Heart.* So let's walk through these four critical needs together since most of us get stuck right here, and this can be ground zero for the development of stress in your life.

The Four Needs of the Heart, also known as the *Four A's*, are attention, affection, appreciation, and acceptance. Fulfilling the Four A's on a daily basis is core to meeting our Social Needs. Appreciation is also vital in fulfilling the next level in the hierarchy—Esteem Needs.

The Four A's

These are the Four Needs of the Heart:

- Attention

- Affection

- Appreciation

- Acceptance

Attention

The first A is our need for *attention*. We all want to be seen. We all want to be looked at. We struggle so hard to receive eye contact, even if it's fleeting. This is where we get validated for simply existing. Everything in our life is based on our attention and our intention. What we place our attention on grows and blossoms in our awareness; what we drift our attention away from diminishes and dies. We know that when someone "pays" attention to us, they are unplugging from their world and redirecting their focus to us. We sense it. We value it. We need it.

Affection

A bit deeper than attention is *affection*. We all want to receive a physical display of that validation—a wink, a nod, a smile, a hug, a kiss, a pat, a pet, a stroke, a squeeze, or a kind word. It distills that distant attention we crave down to a level of closeness, where we experience someone's warmth or fondness for us. Anyone can look at us. Only someone who "cares" about what they are looking at would then take it a step closer and demonstrate affection.

Appreciation

One step deeper than affection is *appreciation*—moving from a kind word to genuine gratitude. We all want to be thanked, recognized, and acknowledged. We all want to feel that we have added value to the task, chore, project, process, vision, initiative, or mission. Appreciation is the public acknowledgment of a good deed, a job well done, an act of generosity, or an important contribution. We intertwine the concept of appreciation with receiving a certain level of respect from someone. While this also feeds deeply into our Esteem Needs (as you'll soon see), meeting this core need of our heart in the social context is critical to living a destressifying life.

Areas of our life where we don't feel appreciated cause us extreme struggle and result in a wide range of emotions. Right now there is probably a gift or a kind word you gave someone for which you did not receive the thanks or gratitude you were expecting . . . and it still haunts you. And this little irritant, resting under the surface of your life, can influence and impact your daily anxiety, anger, or irritation.

Our Need for Validation

Remember being a teenager? We didn't have a clue about what really lay in the years ahead of us, yet we boldly flaunted our newly acquired independence as we announced our individuality to the world. But even with all our uniqueness, we were totally dependent on the feedback of our friends, siblings, parents, and teachers. Every decision was made with the hope of some acknowledgment that we had done something worthy of appreciation.

Every one of us still craves appreciation. It's our external validator that we are connected to others, that our actions are having impact, that we are adding value, that we are making a difference in the lives of others, and that we are on the right path and doing the right thing!

If we don't receive that validation, it can scar us forever. We can take on a bitter persona or demanding expectations, and in that world—which can become a living hell—no one is ever meeting our need of appreciation.

Acceptance

An important need resting at the core of our Social Needs *and* Esteem Needs (and the fourth A) is *acceptance*. Our need for acceptance drives so many of our daily and life decisions. As kids, we based our self-worth on whether we were accepted into various groups, depending on our internal assessment of how cool, relevant, or popular the group was. Whether we were a jock, a nerd, a cheerleader, a bookworm, a prom queen, a hippy, a trust-fund baby, or a mouseburger, we wanted to be accepted by the group we respected. Even if we were making rebellious choices against the grain of society, we desired to be included in the "rebellious" collective. We wanted it then. We need it now. We crave this acceptance.

Our need for support and respect from those *we* respect can be a powerful driving force in our lives. Back then we might even have wanted to be invited to a party we would *never* attend so we could know on some level we were accepted. Nowadays, we seek this through our affiliations with religious groups, sports teams, schools, clubs, political parties, causes, points of view, social collectives, philosophies, neighborhoods, cities, nationalities, ethnicities, and cultures. It's all about being accepted. We have shirts, hats, jackets, bumper stickers, credit cards, rings, necklaces, and Facebook pages that announce our affiliations. Many of us even crave to be accepted by people we *don't* like!

Just Looking to Feel Included

When we don't feel the acceptance, we spend a lot of time stuck at the level of Social Needs, and our internal dialogue starts to reflect this. We can even move into that emotional fight-or-flight mode regarding our lack of acceptance. We respond by feeling "less than." We isolate ourselves (flight), act desperate (reactive), or behave resentfully (fight) regarding our lack of inclusion.

Our natural inclination is to feel accepted. Why not? Aren't we all part of one big global posse? Don't we all feel the same things and live the same challenges and triumphs? Aren't we innately part of the whole? Aren't we all just a singular reflection of the totality of humanity? Albert Einstein summed up the challenge of this category of needs:

> A human being is a part of the whole, called by us "Universe," a part limited in time and space. He experiences himself, his thoughts and feelings as something separated from the rest—a kind of optical delusion of his consciousness.

When we don't receive the attention, affection, appreciation, or acceptance that is our birthright, we feel shame, anger, jealousy, and even vengeance. All these trigger stress responses that will prevail as long as the unmet need does. That's putting a lot of power in the hands of others—depending on *them* to validate *you*.

This is why a core requirement in the category of Social Needs is *self*-acceptance, rather than relying on someone else to "approve" you. Remember, their opinion is based solely on *their* interpretation of you. If it's lower than your interpretation of yourself, then "Houston . . . we have a problem." If it's greater than your self-interpretation, then take as your inspiration Woody Allen's paraphrasing of Groucho Marx: "I would never want to belong to any club that would have someone like me for a member."

Yes, acceptance starts with you! Are you accepting of how you act, speak, and show up? Are you accepting of all you've done in your life, or only the "good" things, while you reject the less positive ones? Do you expect others to accept you for who you are—or are you wearing a mask in certain situations to make yourself more acceptable? We all do this—showing our best side to those we're trying to impress, hoping they'll accept us.

And think of the devastation that can occur when children didn't make the team, weren't included in the cool group, weren't invited to the important party, or were picked last. Those types of stressful traumas can inflict a deep wound that may never heal. As kids, we assume other people know what they are doing by not accepting us, and then we may make a lifelong determination that we are not worthy.

Let Your Voice Be Heard!

An under-the-radar Social Need is that of *being heard*. Some of us are biting our tongue or walking on eggshells; others wait for the right time to speak (some of us are still waiting!); some of us are listened to but don't feel heard; some of us won't shut up. People express themselves through their hair, makeup, clothes, and demeanor; others try to make themselves heard through their professions: songwriters, models, actors, authors, visual and performance artists, hairstylists, painters, designers, sculptors, remodelers, singers, musicians, gardeners. They all want you to hear . . . see . . . feel . . . what they are all about.

Expressing ourselves physically, emotionally, verbally, and intimately are very important needs that require a receptive listener, receiver, or audience. Each of us desperately wants to be heard in some way. Many of us feel the need to compel, convince, persuade, or convert others. It seems to be in our DNA—it completes our sense of self-worth and better defines the relationship we have with another person. Internally, we see it as a win, and chemically we are rewarded with ripples of feel-good hormones.

But not everyone needs a win. Some of us fulfill our Social Need of expression simply by putting ourselves out there to be observed and heard by releasing what has become bottled up inside. We want someone to know how we feel or what something means to us. We want people to see our "real" self at its best. We long for someone to understand us, know us, and connect with us on our own terms.

We all have the need to purr and roar. Choosing your moment can make all the difference, but holding back what needs to come out can lead to extreme chronic stress that gets reinforced over a lifetime. Speak and your life will change forever!

The Need for Relevance

Unmet Social Needs can hold us back from feeling whole, relevant, and included as a member of the tribe. Yes, it goes back that far. Way back in the day, the consequences of being exiled from a tribe and not included in the community often meant dire consequences for our ancestors. And even though most of us aren't at the mercy of the elements, scrounging for food, or battling warring tribes these days, our Social Needs are still very much in place from thousands of years ago! If they're left unmet, our sense of self-worth is constantly challenged, creating ongoing, lifelong chronic stress.

But if we can calmly and with a clear head go through a process of identifying our Social Needs, prioritizing them, releasing what doesn't serve us, and bringing into our life what we truly require, then very quickly this category of needs will be fulfilled at a higher level. Looking at life through a clearer lens will make this possible, and we'll do that process in the next chapter.

But right now ask yourself, *What gives me a sense that my Social Needs are being met?* See if any of these experiences are part of the answer:

- Getting attention from your friends
- Expressing yourself and being "heard"
- Receiving affection from your loved ones
- Being spoken to in a kind way
- Inviting people over to your house
- Forging new relationships
- Creating content, music, or works of art for people to enjoy
- Having a few important or special relationships
- Being seen as the person with the answers
- Connecting people together
- Forgiving someone who has hurt you

- Participating in civil responsibilities or cause-related efforts
- Being treated tenderly and lovingly
- Feeling appreciated at work
- Throwing a party
- Performing random acts of kindness
- Being included in others' intimate conversations
- Making the cut
- Getting a raise
- Being accepted by your core affiliation
- Knowing others are rooting for you
- Being the center of attention
- Giving unexpected gifts
- Forgiving yourself
- Receiving gifts with genuine appreciation
- Being invited to participate in things that matter to you
- Responding with grace, patience, and compassion
- Giving to charity

And what are your unmet Social Needs? Is there anything on the list? Do you mostly feel connected or disconnected? Humans are social beings. Once we experience some bond—either an intimate one, a more formal one, a sense of belonging rooted in family or community, or simply being welcomed or received by a person or group—then the acceptance component of our Social Needs starts to become actualized. When our more basic needs of Survival and Safety have been satisfied, our critical Social Needs begin to play a more prominent role in motivating our behavior. If we build on that, we can take a step in the direction of esteem.

Esteem Needs

According to Maslow, our Esteem Needs include achievement; status; reputation; and the yearning for self-respect, self-esteem, and the esteem of others. Maslow identified two basic forms of Esteem Needs: external and internal. The external form of esteem is the yearning for attention and acceptance *from others* in the form of status, recognition, and prestige. Many of these are unmet Social Needs bubbling up into the esteem realm of the pyramid.

The internal form of esteem, which Maslow felt was the higher form of this category, is our own personal need for self-respect. *This higher form (self-esteem) is nourished by our internal abilities combined with our life experiences and is not based on what anyone else thinks or says about us.*

Mirror, Mirror

When directed at the self, the concept of esteem reflects our emotional evaluation of our own worth—our positive and negative judgments and attitudes regarding our sense of self. And this all hinges on how we interact, transact, communicate, and relate to the social world outside of us. Now you can understand why we are driven to meet our Social Needs before we are motivated to meet our Esteem Needs.

What do you really see when you look in the mirror? Self-esteem encompasses our beliefs about ourselves such as "I am smart," "I am worthy," and "I am attractive." Self-esteem also includes the roller coaster of emotions, such as the pride of winning and the despair and shame associated with losing. Depending on whether we feel that we're winning or losing in a given moment, our self-esteem will range somewhere between triumph and discouragement.

Self-esteem is a mind-set that represents a person's judgments of their own sense of worthiness. You can quickly gauge your self-esteem right now with the answers to these questions:

- *Am I entitled to success?*
- *Am I entitled to be happy?*
- *Am I entitled to a loving relationship?*

If you feel inherently worthy in these aspects of life, then you will have a higher quotient of *self-confidence* and *self-respect,* two characteristics necessary to feel actualized in the realm of Esteem Needs. Going even deeper to the core of your self-assessment are the internal judgments you have regarding your *ability* in areas such as these:

- Facing life's challenges
- Understanding the task at hand
- Feeling competent
- Solving the problem

Esteem Needs are multifaceted. In addition to our own self-esteem, we are looking at life through a lens of comparison to others—essentially an esteem filter through which others see us. As we embark on any journey to accomplish a task, undertake a mission, or achieve a vision, and as we recognize the need to be involved with others, we evaluate our own worth *as an individual in relation to others.*

This is a powerful shift from our lower set of Social Needs, where we are concerned with personally receiving attention and affection as an individual. In the esteem realm, we look at ourselves within the context of being a member of a collective—as a couple, a group, a team, or a department. Often we become so focused on the group needs that we lose sight of our own needs, becoming more concerned with what everyone else thinks about us as we strive to meet the needs of the collective and, in the process, create internal friction and stress. In this environment, where we are so focused on our relationship to the group dynamic, the smallest disagreements can become emotionally charged if we are not communicating consciously. The slightest differences in opinion can devolve into dramatic conflict if we are not in tune with our emotional intelligence and playing well with others.

Is Reality TV Our Reality?

Learning how to work with others and establish appropriate boundaries is part of fulfilling our Social Needs—and it's a crucial component of achieving self-esteem. It also accounts for our great interest as a society in the private lives of celebrities and reality TV programs as we try to figure out our lives by watching how others do it brilliantly or horribly. *The Bachelor, Dancing with the Stars, The Voice, Big Brother,* and the *Real Housewives* franchise are a few popular shows that have captured our attention as we compare ourselves to others who each week place themselves in vulnerable situations—circumstances where we "know" we could do it better.

One of the most enlightening and highly entertaining shows to help us understand self-esteem and the esteem others have for us is Mark Burnett's *Shark Tank,* featuring serial entrepreneur and Dallas Mavericks owner Mark Cuban; Daymond John of FUBU fame; New York City real estate mogul Barbara Corcoran; Kevin "Mr. Wonderful" O'Leary; QVC queen Lori Greiner; and tech security genius and racing enthusiast Robert Herjavec. Each episode, these "sharks" listen to business owners pitch them for investment capital in exchange for a piece of their company.

Most often, after the entrepreneur presents their business and asks for money in exchange for a percentage of the business, they are mocked, abused, debased, ridiculed, or summarily dismissed for overvaluing their vision or coming up with a silly idea or an unprofitable business model. And every once in a while, there is a brilliant deal. But to watch an individual who has poured their life essence into a dream be derided by highly successful individuals they admire is a powerful test of their self-esteem. We can learn a lot from this show about holding our ground, sticking to our guns, leaning in the direction of our dreams, following through on our beliefs, and trusting in ourselves amidst negative feedback.

Are your Esteem Needs being met right now? Are you receiving the acknowledgment you feel you deserve from yourself and from others—your partner, your friends, your co-workers, your boss?

Finding Esteem

Each of us craves appreciation. It's our external validator that we are connected to others . . . that our actions are having impact. In the workplace, lack of appreciation, recognition, and acknowledgment can totally unravel you. If you spend all your time championing how great you are, how hard you work, and the value of your contribution, most likely you will grow to expect a very high standard of appreciation and the acknowledgment that comes with it. The bar gets set pretty high and most likely won't be met.

If you don't receive external appreciation in the form of praise, public recognition, and an increase in pay or rewards at home, then your need will not be met in spite of the brilliant work you are doing. This can lead to you resenting your boss, your job, and even the work your company is doing. And at home it can lead to resenting members of your family or your loved ones. Ultimately, festering in this unmet need can lead to schadenfreude (a German term that literally means "harm-joy"), where you start to root for others to fail or you gloat over their lack of success. It's a horrible emotion to have because it is a direct source of stress. Are you rooting for anyone to fail right now?

Assuming you don't champion your amazingness at home or in the workplace, is anyone noticing your contribution? Have you silently built up bitterness, animus, or resentment because you are not receiving your props?

Once our own sense of confidence, ability, and achievement is firmly interwoven into our self-esteem *and* we feel the recognition of—and the respect for—that achievement from others, that's when our Esteem Needs become actualized.

What Esteem Needs do you have right now? Do you feel any of these qualities internally?

- Worthy or unworthy
- Confident or fearful
- Emotionally strong or vulnerable

- Capable, competent, and skilled or underqualified
- That you are making a contribution or that you are "posing"
- Good about yourself or "less-than"
- Empowered or helpless
- A master of your destiny or victimized
- Proud or ashamed
- Accomplished or struggling
- Superior or inferior
- Independent or needy
- In the zone or out of sorts

Do you feel any of these qualities externally?

- Worthy
- Accepted
- Appreciated
- Respected
- Valued by others
- Championed by others
- Talked about
- Included
- Supported

As you begin to gain clarity in your self-perception and your perception of how others view and treat you, fulfillment will accelerate in the area of your Esteem Needs.

At this point, you have a deeper understanding of your basic needs in four levels of the hierarchy—survival, safety, social, and esteem. You are ready to explore the concept of self-actualization!

Self-Actualization Needs

Once these previous four basic categories of needs have been fulfilled, we can place our attention on another level: our self-actualization or personal growth needs, which include pursuing personal evolution, realizing our ultimate potential, having peak experiences, and finding deeper fulfillment.

According to Maslow, our Self-actualization Needs are essentially about becoming the best version of ourselves and *moving closer* to the ideal version of ourselves. We do this through being honest about our strengths and weaknesses, by risking being vulnerable, by moving through our pain, by building on our capabilities, by seeing each moment as the perfect teacher, and by integrating all the moving parts.

The resulting outcome of these behaviors is that we end up being rewarded at the highest level within each category of lower needs, and we fully destressify. Our relationships thrive, and we deeply connect with a select few in long-term, nourishing relationships. We realize that having experiences fulfills us more deeply than acquiring things, and we are more selective with our bonds to people and objects, cherishing who and what we do bring into our lives. We are secure in our own space and protective of our loved ones, and we value our beliefs and resources. And we realize that we are not in the world . . . the world is in us.

Once we have reached this fifth level, we innately start taking steps to continually improve, understand the bigger picture, reach for peak experiences, and flow our ever-expanding growth back out into the lives of others. destressifying creates the platform for fulfilling these higher-level needs as your lower needs are met with increasing frequency. Your destressified state fuels your evolution and allows this effortless growth to take on a life of its own. Practicing daily destressifying helps you meet your needs of self-actualization as you begin to grow in becoming:

- Calmer, more relaxed, and less reactive

- More introspective and self-confident

- Self-empowered, adventurous, and free
- More organized and uncluttered
- More attractive to yourself and others
- Comfortable leading or guiding others
- In control of your destiny
- More spontaneous, open, and independent
- More "spiritual" or connected to a higher power
- More accepting, tolerant, patient, and compassionate
- Less concerned with success as defined by others
- More focused on having experiences rather than having things
- Free to actually "Be" yourself
- More independent regarding choices and decisions
- Emotionally intelligent
- More comfortable with your goals, meeting them more frequently
- More generous with your sharing, teaching, and allocation of time
- More aware of your purpose
- Skilled at communicating your needs more effectively
- Capable of seeing the bigger picture *and* the more granular details

The destressifying philosophy regarding self-actualization guides us simply to be better than we were five minutes ago—and there are no shortcuts to self-actualization. It's all about meeting our lower needs and then building on that foundation. Coming from a more relaxed, clear, and purposeful space, destressifying allows us to self-actualize effortlessly.

The Path to Self-Actualization

destressifying pushes the envelope of self-actualization by accelerating you to meet your base, middle, and higher needs. *This tier of the pyramid is the most powerful by-product of destressifying.* And as Maslow emphasized right up until his death in 1970, "There are no perfect human beings." Those who choose a path of destressifying experience an ongoing state of self-actualization demonstrated by the following dozen destressifying characteristics:

1. Openness to uncertainty

2. Spontaneity in thought, word, and deed

3. Emotional intelligence

4. Acceptance and appreciation of themselves and others as they are

5. Issue- or challenge-centeredness rather than self-centeredness

6. Purpose in their language and actions

7. Appreciation of humor, seeing life without melodrama or charge

8. Natural creativity, consistently coming up with new ideas

9. Attraction to—and passion for—the welfare of humanity, other beings, and the planet

10. Capacity for deep appreciation of basic life experiences

11. Preference for deeper satisfying interpersonal relationships with select people

12. Tendency to thrive on peak experiences

Before we dive deeper and tie this chapter together with a powerful exercise, just reflect on the following short list of destressifying steps you can take right now to launch your self-realization process:

- Listen to your own feelings in evaluating experiences instead of the voice of conformity

- Embrace being vulnerable—start experiencing life like a child, innocently and fully present

- Give yourself permission to try new things that allow you to veer from conventional paths

- Speak your truth, communicate consciously, and don't play head games with others

- Own your impact—don't run from your decisions; take responsibility

- Identify your areas of resistance and defense and choose to give them up

Since identifying our needs is the first step of need mastery, let's start the ball rolling with this exercise.

Identifying Your Needs

In just seven easy steps, you can unearth your needs and begin to formulate your own personal hierarchy-of-needs process. Use a journal, a notebook, or a separate piece of paper to track your evolution; feel free to repeat the exercise every month or after you've experienced a destressifying shift. Don't overthink the process; practice *16seconds* before taking each step to increase your clarity.

1. Read the following list and write down the needs that are core to you *right now.* Make this personal. Truly connect with what you feel you are lacking at the most primal level.

    - Survival Needs: our biological and physiological requirements of air, food, water, warmth, sex, sleep . . .

    - Safety Needs: protection from elements, shelter, security from physical threats, law, order, structure . . .

- Social Needs: belonging and love, connection, community, family, affection, relationships, attention, appreciation, acceptance, personal expression, interaction . . .

- Esteem Needs: self-esteem, significance, achievement, material success, influence, independence, status, leadership, prestige . . .

- Self-actualization Needs: expanded thinking, purpose, serving others, insight, realizing personal potential, self-fulfillment, having peak experiences . . .

2. Now rank your needs from highest to lowest. What's most critical right now—today? What hurts most? What unmet need is impacting your life the most?

3. Reflect on how you're currently guiding your life and what you are doing to satisfy those needs (choices, decisions, behaviors, habits). Reading this book could be an important step you are taking.

4. What needs could use a little more attention right now?

5. What needs are not being met because you are distracted, overwhelmed, or stressed?

6. What are the needs that have changed since last week? Last month? Last year? Since you were a child? Since you had a defining moment?

7. Read the list over a few times and make refinements and adjustments as your understanding of your core needs evolves (you'll refer to it in the next chapter when we address how to meet your needs).

Identifying Others' Needs

Hopefully going through that basic exercise helped you identify your needs and group them in some way that brings clarity—but what about the people in your life and their needs? So often we try to meet others' needs when we are just guessing what's important to them. It's pretty ironic since we have not yet had clarity on our own needs. Placing attention on your needs (as you have just done for a few minutes) and seeing how you prioritize them suddenly opens up a new horizon to understand others also.

So right now, reflect on your core relationships: your spouse or partner of the moment, your closest friends, your parents, your children, your boss, your co-workers, your teachers, people who report to you, the local barista at your morning coffee place—the people you are closest to and the ones you interact with frequently.

Now pick just one person, and for a few moments think about what their top three needs might be. Remember, you're probably just guessing (or as my dear friend and mentor David Simon referred to it, "ESPing all over yourself"). When was the last time you asked someone what their needs were and if you could help in fulfilling them?

Sharing your needs, their priority, and how they affect your life with the people in your core relationships is another valuable exercise to help you destressify. Whether at home or at work, learning what is important to those you're closest to lessens stress, improves communication, and reduces conflict. In the process, you will most likely meet one of your own needs.

And the next time someone pushes your buttons or irritates you, understanding their needs will enlighten you not to take it personally because *most likely they are acting to fulfill one of their unmet needs.* They may be revealing an even more intimate aspect of themselves to you—not just trying to push your buttons! That would be the perfect time to ask them, "How can I help you meet your needs?"

• • •

Needs assessment and prioritization can be overwhelming at times. That's why there is an easy tool to help you clarify your needs in any given moment and meet them! When we look at our needs through the lens of the *Five Realms of Our Life*, answers effortlessly flow to us. Now that you fully understand the hierarchy of needs, it's time to make it real by going deep into your own needs in each category. So take a breath . . . and let's dive in.

• • • • •

CHAPTER 7

Using the Five Realms to Master Your Needs

"There is something in every one of you that waits, listens for the sound of the genuine in yourself—and if you cannot hear it, you will never find whatever it is for which you are searching . . . if you cannot hear the sound of the genuine in you, you will all of your life spend your days on the ends of strings that somebody else pulls."

—HOWARD THURMAN

So now you are pretty much an expert in the concept of motivational needs, and you've identified and prioritized your most pressing needs. Pretty intense, right? Let's go deeper into destressifying and take clear steps to meet your needs by looking at your life through the lens of the Five Realms.

Let me walk you through this framework. When we look at our life in its totality, there are some parts that overlap and others that are distinct. We've all heard of the concept of work-life balance. But in truth, that separation between work and life is artificial since for many of us our work is our life; others work at home; and for all of us, the behaviors and actions we perform in daily life spill over into work, home, commute, relaxation, meals, the bedroom, and so on.

A more accurate breakdown is to separate our life into the five truest aspects of our existence:

- The physical realm
- The emotional realm
- The material realm
- The relationship realm
- The spiritual realm

This process allows us to move back and forth from the big picture to the more granular aspects, irritants, and blockages of our life. It brings us a single-pointed intention so that we can look at our life under the microscope and make tiny, incremental shifts that have a huge destressifying impact. And by focusing our attention on these five core areas, clarity naturally flows to all our answers.

Stress and the Five Realms

When you look at your life through the lens of the *Five Realms*, you will gain increased clarity, become less stressed, and develop a doable action plan for living your life with greater fulfillment.

Exploring the Physical Realm

The physical realm contains all aspects of our physical being: the balance, nourishment, health, and care of our body, our physiology, and our biology. It's also the realm of all our Survival Needs and the behaviors we use to maintain our physical existence—our diet, health, exercise, rest, sleep, skin, digestion, weight, sexual functions, and overall well-being. This includes the physical habits that nourish us: brushing, flossing, bathing, working out, eating mindfully, eliminating regularly, training, dancing, resting, cuddling, walking, getting a massage, sleeping restfully, and so on. And it includes the habits that don't necessarily serve us, such as nail-biting; smoking; gambling; binge-watching TV; staying up late; driving fast; consuming too much alcohol, sugar, coffee, or dairy; doing mindless online surfing; taking drugs; holding on to excessive weight; and so on.

Identifying aspects of your physical realm should be relatively easy since our culture is so body-centric. If you are stuck, just look in the mirror, look at your body, look at your daily routine, and look at what you physically do that's either nourishing or non-nourishing.

Exploring the Emotional Realm

The emotional realm is how we respond to the world around us, specifically *when our needs are not met*, which includes our patterned reactions, conditioned responses, ability to listen and witness, and our hot buttons. This is our realm of response to all external experiences—our ego or reactive responses; our interpretations of each moment; and our level of defensiveness, fear, anger, patience, compassion, tolerance, acceptance, joy, anxiety, judgment, and constriction. The emotional realm encompasses *how we react* to certain people, situations, and circumstances, especially the words, conversations, and interactions that push our buttons and trigger us.

You can spark the exploration of your emotional realm by reflecting on what experiences, regrets, or grievances you are choosing to retain, hold on to, or define yourself by or what you look or feel like when you respond to the external world. Ask yourself, *Why do I lash out, get red in the face, withdraw, shut someone down, or storm away when they open their mouth? What rests even more deeply within that's making me reactive in certain situations?* Remember this realm is all about you, *not* the other person. Bottom line: *How do you respond when your needs are not met?*

Exploring the Material Realm

This is the realm of wealth consciousness and contains our relationship to money and money energy in all its possible permutations. The material realm is the domain of all our "stuff," our "things." It includes our job, career, title, responsibilities, house, car, clothes, furniture, electronic devices, vacations, bank accounts, retirement fund, insurance, possessions and positions, status, trappings of success, and orientation to abundance in our life.

How we see the material realm is often a reflection of our mind-set about the flow of all things in our life. Some of us are hoarders, while others are very selective in what we choose to bring into our life. Some of us give and give until there's nothing left, while others spend our time thinking about what we can get.

This realm is vast. Exploring it reveals our true orientation to the circulation of wealth in our life. How do we see the material world? Are we looking from a perspective of abundance consciousness (the pie is big and getting bigger!) or poverty consciousness (there's only one slice left—if I don't get it now, there'll be no more!)? Fear and all our emotions regarding money and what it can do are just a reflection of our orientation to life.

Exploring the Relationship Realm

The relationship realm encompasses our links to all the people in our life and includes the connection we have with our self, our core relationships, family members, colleagues, friends, workmates, those we have a grievance against, those we interact with but don't necessarily "know," those we are looking to have a bond with, and those who have died. This realm guides us to take one of four actions with every relationship, especially those in flux: birth it, repair it, shift it, or end it.

Exploring the realm of relationships is mind-blowing when you think about how many diverse connections we all have. And whether you're close with someone, seldom speak to them, or can't stand them, you are holding on to mental, emotional, time-consuming energy regarding the relationship.

But the key to this realm is the relationship you have with *you*. How do you treat yourself? How's your sense of worthiness? Are you arrogant, condescending, and mean to yourself? Or are you loving, forgiving, nurturing, and compassionate? As you expand the circle beyond yourself, ask, *Who's in my front row?* Essentially, who are your die-hard supporters, your cheerleaders, and your champions? Those are the relationships you should be paying attention to. When you stumble or fall down, who is rooting for you to get back up? Who is not rooting for you? Are there people in your front row who don't belong there (those not rooting for you)? Are they just taking up space in your head . . . in your life . . . blocking new champions from taking *their* seats in the front row? Keep widening the circle and identifying tiers of relationships until you've included everyone you can think of.

The Four Paths of Relationships

There are four ways to proceed with a relationship:

1. Birth it: Start new, fresh, unfettered . . . as we were born . . . whole, perfect, pure, and unconditioned. There are infinite possibilities. Don't box yourself in.

2. Repair it: Ask first, *Do I want to keep this damaged or wounded relationship alive?* If the answer is yes, then release the past and commit to soothing the wounds. Let go of grievances and forgive, forgive, forgive. Forgive yourself, forgive them, and make peace. If you've tried and it can't be repaired, then shift it.

3. Shift it: Relationships evolve all the time. If the dynamic has moved in another direction—maybe you are taking a platonic relationship to another level or now you have a work relationship with a friend or you were too close and you need to step back a bit. Whatever the reason, the old way doesn't work in the current environment, but you still want to be connected at a higher or lower level. If a boundary was crossed or the understanding has changed, then new boundaries, new understandings, and new rules of engagement must be established, articulated, agreed upon—and committed to by both parties. If you have given your all, and new terms of engagement can't be agreed upon, then most likely you need to end it.

4. End it: It's time to cut the cord, say good-bye, and every day release one more piece of the relationship. *Truly* let it go if it does not serve you. When you think you have let it go, let more go. Journal . . . share . . . "Sharpie" their name on a rock, charge it with your emotional pain, and throw it into the ocean, a river, or the woods. Write down your grievances and burn them in a ceremonial fire. Why would you let someone into your head that you would never invite into your home? It's in your best interest to stop communication with them on all fronts and remove them from the front row of your life, which will open up a seat for someone else more worthy.

Since nothing on this earth ever really ends, and since energy can't be destroyed, the concept of complete closure is a myth. Energy can be transmuted, however, and we must make peace in our own heart, forgive ourselves, and forgive the other. The key to this is to release, release, release. A note on forgiveness: It has very little to do with the other person. As my mother always encouraged me, "When we forgive, we free ourselves from the ties that bind us to the one who hurt us." So start to loosen your grip on those ties.

Exploring the Spiritual Realm

This is the realm of your connection to something beyond you . . . much bigger than you . . . your connection to the divine creator, God, Spirit, the Holy Ghost, the universe, Jesus, Source, Buddha, Vishnu, Allah, or whomever you determine is your higher power. The spiritual realm contains your deepest beliefs, core values, and interpretations regarding why you are here and what you are here to do. It includes your religious or spiritual practice as well as your underlying belief system and your purpose or meaning in life (which doesn't necessarily have to be your job).

It's often been said that *we are not human beings having the occasional spiritual experience; we are spiritual beings having this unique human experience.* If we can envision an archetype of us that is growing, trying to be better, learning from our missteps . . . a personification that is successful, happy, empowered, compassionate, whole, pure, and peaceful . . . an embodiment of ourselves that spontaneously says and does the perfect thing at the perfect moment . . . that's our spiritual self.

Spirituality is simply the journey we each take from our current version of ourselves to our most divine version—our most self-actualized version—where we touch perfection, glimpse clarity, bask in brilliance, and receive deep insights. But it's not a one-way voyage—it's a round-trip experience; we get to integrate the best version of ourselves back into our day-to-day life and incorporate these transformational life lessons into our thoughts, words, and actions.

A Word about God

Some of us trust in a divine entity or God to help guide us when we show up as human. I am not here to tell you who to pray to or believe in. Use whatever feels right for you. Many people struggle with the concept of God because of their childhood training or because of something that happened in their life. If this is you, then use your higher power, your belief in the universe, your trust in a divine creator, or your belief in your highest self. Whatever it is you have faith in—that is your understanding of Spirit.

The Five Realms of My Life Process

We all stress and suffer from the dysfunctional or non-nourishing aspects of our life. Over time, we often become attached to some object, attitude, behavior, belief, or way of doing something—that is, we become conditioned. But what worked for us 15 years ago will not necessarily work for us now. The resources we relied on, the mind-set we held, the challenges we faced, and the conditioned ways we responded all might have served us then. *But what got us here will not get us to where we need to go.* We need a fresh new paradigm to take us to self-actualization. That's why it's helpful to start every process by releasing something. Nature abhors a vacuum, and once you release anything, a void is created. And after releasing, whatever new thought, word, behavior, or response you conjure will innocently, subtly, and effortlessly fill the empty space.

So let's do an exercise that can change your life forever. But ideally, you want to come from a destressified state of mind when you do this exercise, so don't be in a hurry. To help with that, let's practice *16seconds* before we start . . .

Take a long, slow, deep breath in through your nostrils, and as you do . . . slowly count to four. Observe the air as it moves into your nostrils and to the back of your throat. Watch it as it moves down your chest and deep into your belly. Feel your belly expand. Once your belly is filled, hold that breath in to the count of four. And just witness the breath in your belly as you silently count. One, two, three, four. Now slowly—to the count of four—exhale through your nostrils and again watch your breath as it moves up into your chest, into your throat, into your sinuses, and out through your nostrils. And when the last wisp of air is out of you, hold that breath out to the count of four. Observe it, watch it, witness it . . . as it dissipates into the air.

Let's do that one more time.

Take a long, slow, deep breath in through your nostrils, and as you do . . . slowly count to four. Observe the air as it moves into your nostrils and to the back of your throat. Watch it as it moves down your chest and deep into your belly. Feel your belly expand. Once your belly is filled, hold that breath in to the count of four. And just witness the breath in your belly as you silently count. One, two, three, four. Now slowly—to the count of four—exhale through your nostrils and again watch your breath as it moves up into your chest, into your throat, into your sinuses, and out through your nostrils. And when the last wisp of air is out of you, hold that breath out to the count of four. Observe it, watch it, witness it . . . as it dissipates into the air.

Welcome back! Now you're ready. You should be pretty destressified right now. So settle in a bit more, and just sit in silence with your eyes closed for a few moments before we dive in . . .

Ready? Now let's explore the Five Realms of your life:

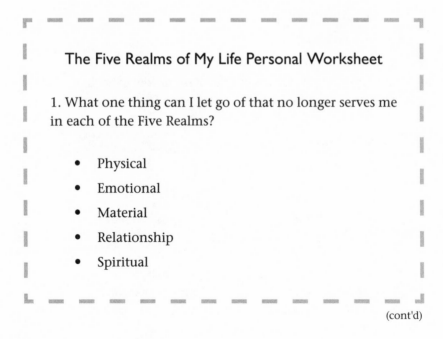

The Five Realms of My Life Personal Worksheet

1. What one thing can I let go of that no longer serves me in each of the Five Realms?

- Physical

- Emotional

- Material

- Relationship

- Spiritual

(cont'd)

2. What one thing can I add to my life to nourish me in each of the Five Realms?

- Physical
- Emotional
- Material
- Relationship
- Spiritual

3. What intention would I like to plant in each of the Five Realms?

- Physical
- Emotional
- Material
- Relationship
- Spiritual

4. What commitment can I make right now in each of the Five Realms to take my life to the next level?

- Physical
- Emotional
- Material
- Relationship
- Spiritual

For deeper insights and greater clarity, visit davidji.com/destressifying to take the process even further through the Five Realms of My Life guided meditation.

So now you *really* understand the Five Realms of existence. Use the worksheet regularly as a tool to help you get clear on your needs in each of the Five Realms. Refer to the worksheet every day, and within a week, you will destressify as you meet your needs more effectively; release what no longer serves or nourishes you; and usher into your life more deeply fulfilling behaviors, people, and experiences.

Conscious Choice Making: The First Step into Clarity

Taking these first powerful steps of destressifying is a bold move, and I commend you for your courage. Your learning will start to accelerate now that you have these tools, and one of the first outcomes will be a renewed sense of clarity.

Our past behaviors and experiences are based at least in part on choices we have made over the course of our lives. Everything flows from the original seeds we planted. Our best choices and our worst decisions have consequences that we are living with today— right now. And some of the haze in our life is from those choices and the ripples they have.

But we are not stuck. As much as we may be tortured by them, our past decisions are not death sentences. That is the beauty of life. We get to recast the moment if we are willing to muster the courage and start anew.

As you proceed, you will be making new, fresh, richly conscious choices. Your journey of destressifying and the outcomes you experience will be based upon the very seeds you plant from this moment forward. So let's explore that.

Fractals—The Seeds of Our Needs

First impressions. They set the tone for how we think, feel, and move forward with situations, circumstances, and relationships. The earliest seeds of these initial impressions are called *fractals,* and they are the foundation for how the next moment will unfold while setting the stage for how the longer-term aspects of a relationship or scenario will evolve. Fractals set the tone and establish the trajectory of everything.

In science, a *fractal* is a natural phenomenon or a mathematical set that exhibits a repeating pattern that has the same statistical character as the whole. The most common examples in our world include snowflakes, waves in the ocean, nautilus shells, ferns, crystals, leaves, blood vessels, broccoli, DNA, our heartbeat, the eye of a hurricane, even Elliott wave theory in stock market technical analysis. We can predict the evolving future of something based on its first few moments. And then it grows exponentially, often through the golden ratios of life.

Fractals appear everywhere, and they are inherently embedded in everything we do. Yet so often we find ourselves being stunned when a friend, lover, boss, colleague, teacher, mentor, or loved one acts in a way "we didn't see coming." Or perhaps a situation starts to unfold in a way that shocks or surprises us.

If we could turn back the clock to the fractal of that interaction or that decision, we'd see there were signs . . . there were clues . . . there was evidence we ignored because we were acting out of infatuation, attachment, emotion, reactivity, denial, or a conditioned behavior.

The fractal holds the key. These are the moments that are critical to us living life with less melodrama, less pain, less confusion, greater clarity, and greater fulfillment.

So how do we identify those fractal moments? Our fractals make themselves known through our deeper awareness of our needs and emotions . . . through the quietude we establish in our daily destressifying techniques . . . through our heightened attention . . . and through our exploration of the Five Realms of our life. Once we've identified them, we don't have to accept that this is the way life must continue—we just need to know that:

- **If we do nothing,** we will get more of the same.

- **If we make more conscious choices,** we can shift the trajectory that was put in place. *It all starts with the fractal moment.*

What's done is carved in stone, but we can always take action in the now to alter, shift, change, or transform the direction things are headed. If we breathe before we act, we will make more conscious choices. And we often have a few moments of potential clarity right before we make a decision to ask ourselves five simple questions that can have a profound impact on whether, and how, we proceed:

Making the Best New Choices

1. First ask, "What need is being fulfilled by me taking this step?"

2. Next ask, "What are the consequences of this choice I am about to make?"

3. Then ask, "Who will be impacted by my decision?"

4. Then ask, "What compromise am I about to make right now?" (*This* is your fractal moment.)

5. And lastly, ask, "What am I not seeing in this moment?"

If we choose to be even more patient with our choice-making process, we can take it one step further. We can close our eyes and place our hand on our heart . . . get really quiet (by gently following our breath) . . . and one by one, ask and answer these five timeless questions. When we are coming from a place of stillness, our heart will signal pain or pleasure, comfort or discomfort. We will see the fractals in our life, choose more wisely and in a more nourishing way, and recognize the bigger picture. We will be happier with our choices, make more conscious decisions, and have fewer surprises of our own making. We will definitely have less struggle and less stress. This will allow our lives to flow with greater grace and ease.

• • •

You are well on your way to destressifying through your mastery of awareness, a better understanding of what you really need, and your immersion into the Five Realms of your life. On top of that, you have several daily destressifying tools to help you meet your needs more effectively. If you can drill more deeply into the way you respond to the world around you, then you will transform in an evolutionary way. So let's cultivate the next step in destressifying: *mastering your emotions.*

• • • • •

destressifying by Mastering Your Emotions

*"I've learned that people will forget what you said,
people will forget what you did, but people will
never forget how you made them feel."*

— ATTRIBUTED TO MAYA ANGELOU

We live each moment of our life through the ebb and flow of emotions. It's almost as if each beat of our heart and every breath we take move us in one direction or another. The phone rings and a feeling sparks, a thought pours in; someone says something to us and suddenly our mood shifts and our face changes; we feel the sun on our cheek and the wind in our hair, and as memories awaken, a sensation ripples through us. We are a bundle of conditioned emotions that are primed to respond to the momentary assessment of whether our needs have been met or not.

As we better understand our needs and begin fulfilling them on a more consistent basis, moving through the world each day becomes more satisfying as many of the blockages and constrictions from our previously stressful life fall away. In the process, we become more in touch with our emotions, learning to differentiate knee-jerk and conditioned reactions from more desirable and effective responses. This doesn't make us softer or less effective; it makes us even *more* effective—*allowing us to rule our emotions rather than them ruling us.*

By *mastering our emotions*, we start to live each day, each thought, each conversation, each interaction, and each decision from a calmer, more grounded, more centered perspective with less reactivity and greater intuition. Very quickly, our thinking becomes crystalline, our problem-solving skills start to expand, our decision making becomes purposeful, and the fruits of our enhanced emotional awareness elevate us beyond being ruled by our amygdala.

What Are Emotions?

Simply put, emotions are subjective, conscious experiences that link our interpretation of a given moment to a biological reaction, creating a particular mental state. We may hear a voice down the hall or receive a text and—based on our perception of the owner of that voice or message, our interpretation of the content, and the wiring of our neurocircuitry—*boom!* In an instant we may grimace or smile. In the process, as we interpret the experience negatively or positively, our body and mind react accordingly.

Have you ever yelled at someone after having a tough time or a difficult encounter, even though it had nothing to do with them? Psychologists refer to this misdirection as "emotional leakage." Suppressing emotions is as difficult as holding a balloon underwater. Instead of keeping them hidden, you're likely to express them inadvertently by being snide, sarcastic, snarky, retaliatory, biting, harsh, or downright mean to people who had nothing to do with your initial frustration. Suppressing your feelings—and the associated stress—is now scientifically proven to lead to poor memory, relationship challenges, and deeper health issues as your body is influenced strongly by your subjective conscious experiences.

We have these subjective, conscious experiences (emotions) every time we smell an aroma, receive news, step in the shower, log online, sit in traffic, see a mosquito, watch a movie, attend a meeting, have a thought, hear a sound, reflect on words we said or didn't say . . . In every moment, thousands of subjective conscious experiences are rippling through us.

Emotional Awareness

Right now think of something that makes you smile, like the last time you were on vacation or your most recent celebration. Witness your emotions as they flow through you. What does it feel like? How does your body respond?

Now place your awareness on another experience from the past week—something a little more complex than your vacation. Place your hand on your heart or your solar plexus. Take a deep breath in. Conjure the experience in your mind's eye. How does it make you feel? What emotions are arising? See if you can sit with it for a few moments and give names to the various ways it makes you feel. Take your time.

Now do this again—but this time with your eyes closed. Take ten seconds now . . .

What emotions were you aware of in this exercise? Many psychologists have claimed that certain emotions are more basic than others; in fact, Dr. Robert Plutchik, psychologist and professor emeritus at the Albert Einstein College of Medicine, identified eight core emotions we all share—anger, fear, sadness, disgust, surprise, anticipation, trust, and joy—which he hypothesized are the foundation for *all* other emotions.

Read the broader list on the following page and identify a moment where you have experienced each one. Familiarizing yourself with the vast range of your emotional expression is paramount to cultivating your emotional intelligence.

Affection Anger Angst Anguish Annoyance Anxiety Apathy Arousal Awe Boredom Confidence Contempt Contentment Courage Curiosity Depression Desire Despair Disappointment Disgust Distrust Dread Ecstasy Embarrassment Envy Euphoria Excitement Fear Frustration Gratitude Grief Guilt Happiness Hatred Hope Horror Hostility Hurt Hysteria Indifference Interest Jealousy Joy Loathing Loneliness Love Lust Outrage Panic Passion Pity Pleasure Pride Rage Regret Relief Remorse Sadness Satisfaction Schadenfreude Self-confidence Shame Shock Shyness Sorrow Suffering Surprise Terror Trust Wonder Worry Zeal Zest

Can you imagine all the chemicals, hormones, and neurotransmitters that are surging through you as you read each word?

Interpreting the Moment

Emotions are an extremely complex state of feelings that result in physical and psychological changes that powerfully influence our behavior. And it's all based on our interpretation of the moment, in the context of every other moment we've ever experienced.

For example, right now imagine that some random stranger rushes up to you and starts *yelling unintelligible words right in your face!* You might interpret it as a scary, potentially violent threat. And you'd have all the emotions that go along with that threat: surprise, fear, shock, terror, perhaps even anger. Picture the scenario and how you think you'd feel. Most likely your conditioned fight-or-flight response would kick in with all those chemical surges and amygdala stress-based reactions like sweating, racing heart, rapid breathing, and suppression of your immune system.

Now imagine that you see the stranger a little ways off and hear him scream, "My wife just died! I am so distraught!" Then he rushes up to you and starts yelling those same unintelligible words right in your face. You'd have a completely different set of emotions. Picture that moment in your mind's eye. The sense of a threat and all its associated physiological and emotional responses would be replaced by sympathy and sadness. Fight-or-flight reactions would not be triggered, nor would any of the usual stress hormones or reptilian-brain responses. You might even feel grateful for everything you have in that moment, causing a little rush of dopamine and inspiring an even more tender response like compassion, which is a far cry from anger.

Opposite Sides of the Same Coin

With that sliver of a difference between the first scenario and the second, you can experience two widely divergent interpretations of the situation. What were your emotions upon reading that a random stranger rushed up to you and started yelling unintelligible words in your face? Did you feel the physical response anywhere in your body? Place your hand on it. Become aware of it. What were the thoughts you conjured? Did your random stranger have a face? Did you feel any emotional constrictions? Did it remind you of another fearful moment in your life?

Once you understood that the stranger was in emotional pain, how did your interpretation of the situation change? Did you feel a physical shift? An emotional shift? Did you notice anything more about your own feelings? Did you become more sensitive to the stranger's needs?

That was one set of circumstances with two very different biological and emotional responses—and two *extremely* different states of mind. Notice how the slightest shift in your knowledge of the external situation and your reading of the nuance between the scenarios created *two distinct emotional responses*—shaped by (1) your discernment of the rough description of the situation, and (2) your feelings about these four phrases, individually and in combination:

- Random stranger
- Yelling
- Unintelligible words
- In your face

Your assessment, your feelings about the words, and your physical and emotional responses to all the aspects of the experience become the fabric of your life.

Emotional Intelligence

The scenario you just went through should give you an introductory understanding of *emotional intelligence,* known as "EI" in many leadership, psychology, and philosophy circles. EI is essentially our ability to "own" these four capabilities:

1. Correctly perceive emotions
2. Retrieve and produce emotions to assist thought
3. Comprehend emotions and understand them
4. Effectively adjust emotions to promote personal development and growth

These are all aspects of emotional awareness. If you don't know how you feel or why you feel a certain way, you will experience emotional overwhelm or confusion and won't be able to communicate effectively, meet your needs, or resolve disagreements. But if you master your emotional intelligence, you will flow through the world with less stress, more grace, and greater ease. And the more successful you are at heightening this core skill set, the happier and more fulfilled you will be.

The Skinny on EI

The first formal mention of emotional intelligence occurred in the mid-1960s. Twenty years later, American developmental psychologist Howard Gardner introduced the concept that *interpersonal intelligence* (the capacity to understand the intentions, motivations, and desires of *other* people) and *intrapersonal intelligence* (the capacity to understand our self and to appreciate our feelings, fears, and motivations) rest more deeply at the core of our life choices than our IQ.

In the 50 years since the first mention of emotional intelligence, many have used the term *EI,* expanded upon it, and refined its meaning. And it was the author, psychologist, and science journalist Daniel Jay Goleman who took the concept to the next level and truly integrated emotional intelligence into our social and business culture through his many articles, interviews, and books. *Harvard Business Review* reinforced Goleman's findings by reviewing emotional intelligence as "a ground-breaking, paradigm-shattering idea," one of the most influential business ideas of the decade. Goleman is a two-time Pulitzer Prize nominee and the author of more than 14 books, including the 1995 *Emotional Intelligence: Why It Can Matter More Than IQ; Healing Emotions: Conversations with the Dalai Lama on Mindfulness, Emotions, and Health; Primal Leadership: Unleashing the Power of Emotional Intelligence,* with co-authors Richard Boyatzis and Annie McKee; *The Brain and Emotional Intelligence: New Insights;* and his 2013 masterpiece, *Focus: The Hidden Driver of Excellence.*

You can probably tell that I am a big fan of Goleman. I have been reading his words and immersing myself in his lessons for decades. He's brilliant, self-actualized, destressified, and generous with his teachings. I encourage you to seek out his writings (start with *Primal Leadership*—it's quickly relatable to your life, success, and destressifying), his audio interviews, and his YouTube videos.

The Power of Social Emotional Learning

Another profound integration of EI into our current culture is due in great part to the work of Roger Weissberg, chief knowledge officer of the Collaborative for Academic, Social, and Emotional Learning at the University of Illinois at Chicago, the organization that has led the way in bringing Social Emotional Learning (SEL) into schools worldwide.

In Illinois, right in Weissberg's own backyard, SEL learning standards have been established as part of the curriculum for every grade from kindergarten through the last year of high school. In their early elementary years, students are taught to recognize and accurately label their emotions and how the feelings lead them to act. By the late elementary years, lessons in empathy help make kids able to identify the nonverbal clues to how someone else feels; in junior high, adolescents learn to analyze what creates stress for them and what motivates their best performance.

In high school, the SEL curriculum teaches *listening* (what a concept!), *talking* in ways that resolve conflicts instead of escalating them, and *negotiating* for win-win solutions. This has proven a powerful tool to diffuse bullying, build teamwork, create tolerance for others, and raise everyone's standards of interaction as they move out into the real world. And yes, students trained in SEL get along better with their peers, score higher grades, and are more emotionally intelligent.

Can you imagine if this was taught to every child growing up? (You can start with your kids now.) We'd be so much more evolved by the time we hit our 20s. Every training and development program throughout the corporate world should be launching into this skill set even before they teach people the technical skills of their business. There would be a lot less stress, a lot more satisfaction, and a lot more profitability!

The Five Elements of Emotional Intelligence

In addition to the other magnificent work that Goleman has done, he is credited with developing a framework of five elements that define emotional intelligence:

- Self-awareness
- Self-regulation
- Motivation
- Empathy
- Social skills

Let's explore how these core elements are expressed in your EI:

Self-awareness: People with high emotional intelligence are usually very self-aware. They understand their emotions, so they don't let their feelings rule them. They're confident, trust their intuition, and rarely let their emotions get out of control. They practice self-reflection and are willing to look at themselves honestly and objectively. This gives them a greater understanding of their strengths and weaknesses, motivating them to honestly work on their deficiencies so that they can perform better. Many people believe that self-awareness is the most important part of emotional intelligence. I believe that everything in life starts and ends with awareness, which is why mastering awareness is the first step in destressifying. *How aware are you?*

Self-regulation: This is the ability to control emotions and impulses. People who self-regulate typically don't allow themselves to become too angry or jealous; and they don't make impulsive, knee-jerk, or careless decisions. They think before they act. Four key characteristics of self-regulation are thoughtfulness, comfort with change, integrity, and maintaining boundaries (the ability to comfortably say "no"). *How's your self-regulation?*

Motivation: People with a high quotient of emotional intelligence are often motivated individuals capable of deferring immediate results for longer-term success. They're highly productive, love a challenge, and are usually effective in whatever they put their attention on. *How motivated are you?*

Empathy: A key factor in EI is your ability to identify with *and* understand the wants, needs, and viewpoints of those around you. This can happen only if you are a good listener, manage your relationships, and relate to others. People with strong empathy are adept at recognizing the feelings of others, even when those feelings are subtle. They avoid stereotyping and judging too quickly, and they live their lives in an open, honest way. *How empathetic are you?*

Social skills: We get along more easily with people who have solid social skills. More often than not, they are team players. They elevate others and help them succeed rather than get greedy and try to take all the glory. They can effectively manage disputes, are excellent communicators, and are masterful at building and maintaining relationships. *How are your social skills?*

Mastering your emotional intelligence is not simply an important key to destressifying; it can be a key to success in every aspect of your life—especially in your career. If you have ever felt as if you were being controlled by sadness, anxiety, or anger; that out of nowhere you were acting impulsively; that you sensed a disconnection from your emotions, an unfamiliarity with your sentiments, or a numbness regarding your feelings; or that you were riding an emotional roller coaster with highs and lows more frequent than usual, then most likely you were experiencing a breakdown in your EI. Developing and using your emotional intelligence can be a good way to show others the leader inside of you—at work, at home, and in all your relationships.

Emotional Intelligence Can Be Cultivated

The beauty of EI is that it's not a function of simply being born with a high "EQ." Emotional intelligence can be learned, developed, and mastered. Although conventional intelligence is important to succeeding in life, emotional intelligence is key to achieving your goals. Remember, EI is an awareness of your actions and feelings and how they affect those around you. It also means that you value others, listen to their wants and needs, and are able to empathize or identify with them on many different levels. And, in this process, *you will meet more of your own needs!*

Learning to SWEEP

After teaching people the secrets of emotional awareness, I began developing a methodology to awaken EI in anyone willing to play along. Over the past decade, my SWEEP Process for Emotional Awakening has been integrated into the management, leadership training, and employee development manuals of many Fortune 500 companies in the United States and Canada. Let me share it with you. SWEEP stands for:

- Self-assess
- Witness
- Examine
- Empathize
- Practice humility

Here are the steps to mastering your emotional awareness through the SWEEP Process:

Self-assess: *Ask yourself some deep questions about your life and answer honestly.* Start with, *What are my top ten weaknesses?* Be willing to accept that you're not perfect and that you could work on some areas to make yourself a better person. So what *are* your top ten weaknesses? Don't be afraid. This is just a simple starting point to connecting with how you really feel. Remember, third graders in Illinois are learning to do this!

Witness: *Observe how you interact with—and react to—people.* Do you rush to judgment before you know all the facts? Are you a good listener? Do you begin speaking before someone finishes telling you the problem? Do you stereotype? Do you blame others or become angry with them, even when the solution is out of their control? Do you examine how your decisions and actions will affect others? Do you ask yourself how they will feel? Do you explore the consequences of your words and actions before they become a reality—or afterward? If we can cultivate our ability to listen and observe, and then look at potential consequences before we speak or act, at least we're moving forward with eyes wide open rather than blind to the outcome.

Examine: *How do you react to stressful situations?* What do you do in the moment when your daily needs aren't met? Do you become upset when there's a delay, hiccup, speed bump, or roadblock? When something doesn't happen the way you want, what's your first reaction? The ability to stay calm and in control in difficult situations is an amazing gift you can give yourself by taking a long, slow, deep breath in at the first sign of an unmet need.

Empathize: *Put yourself in the shoes of others.* Ask them what their needs are. Try this powerful practice with your spouse, partner, workmates, boss, and employees. Starting today—yes, right now—approach people in your life and ask them, "What do you need?" And, "How can I help?" Remember that they will have to take some time to explore and understand their own needs also. But I can assure you that the dynamic between you and them will transform and elevate. If there was once discord or stress, it will be replaced by appreciation and gratitude.

Practice humility: *Let go of the need to defend your actions or sing your own praises.* This concept is so often misunderstood. When you practice humility, you are essentially saying, "I know what I have done. I have confidence in my work or actions. I am comfortable with my level of self-esteem." Right now, are you seeking attention for your accomplishments? Get over it! It's so draining and disempowering when we shift the solution onto someone else's plate to validate our magnificence. Instead, dedicate yourself to singing the praises of others and shine the light on them. Be one of the people in their front row! But also take full responsibility for your actions. Own your impact. And if you've hurt someone, apologize. Close the loop.

By practicing *SWEEP* on a daily basis—at least making a commitment to practice one component each day—you can shift your stress response in less than a week, elevate your emotional awareness to a new level of brilliance, and effortlessly start to destressify.

In-the-Moment EI

It's no secret that our best leaders, high achievers, and self-actualizers have a higher quotient of emotional intelligence than most people. Since EI is essentially *the ability to read emotions*—your own and those with whom you interact—and *to manage your feelings and sensations* in order to remain calm, it quickly assimilates into your thoughts, then your words, and then your actions. We can refer to it as poise, chill, being unflappable, or keeping our cool. Some people are born that way; but through the practice of destressifying, we all can evolve to this state in a very short time.

Those who demonstrate higher EI use in-the-moment tools to destressify, as well as longer-lasting, proactive daily practices. They understand the value of awareness, which can be achieved only in a destressified state of mind. They know the path to self-realization is in mastering their emotions: *rapidly reducing stress in the moment, identifying the emotions that come up, learning which unmet need is creating the turbulence,* and *resolving the conflicts that arise within them and with others.* If we can master this life skill, we will be light-years beyond where we are now and much closer to living a destressified, self-actualized existence.

You may be worried that once you reconnect to the emotions you put on hold through techniques such as *Reaching for SODA*, you'll be stuck with them forever, but that's not so. As you practice the *Reaching for SODA* pattern interrupt more frequently and pay attention to your emotional intelligence, even the most painful and difficult feelings will subside and lose their power to control your attention. This is a fact of life.

So What Keeps Us Stuck?

Our least conscious behaviors are rooted in our inability to take emotionally stressful situations in stride. Either we haven't learned the tools to interpret, absorb, and integrate stress in a healthy way, or we are new to the journey of personal development. Whatever may be holding you back from achieving emotional freedom, let's eliminate some of the more common roadblocks that stand in the way of us becoming more emotionally aware.

A stressful situation appears in the form of a conversation or interaction. An emotion pops up and you . . .

- **Shut down or shut it out:** Think of the kid sticking his fingers in his ears and saying, "La la la la la la la! I can't hear you!" Many of us adults run away from our feelings, numb ourselves in more subtle ways, or deflect it all by making a joke. But these responses ultimately lead to us being disconnected from—and immune to—our emotions. In this response, we are distinctly not at our best.

- **Distract, distract, distract:** Obsessive game playing, circular internal conversations, mindless entertainment, spending hours on Facebook, binge-watching TV shows, online surfing, and getting drunk or high are common ways we escape from dealing with our feelings. We run from them! As painful as that first moment is when the feeling etches itself into our body, we need to own our emotions, feel them, name them . . . sit with them for a bit . . . and allow them to fully emerge, if we are ever to understand and ultimately release them. Distraction only pauses *you* from experiencing your emotions. *It doesn't pause them, as they continue to fester beneath the surface.*

- **Respond in a conditioned way:** Many of us developed coping mechanisms as children. We practiced and prepared always having a quip, automatic response, joke, or phrase to protect our hearts from being wounded and avoid feeling sad. It may have worked brilliantly when we were kids. But it's been a few years, and that no longer serves us—in fact, it's detrimental to cultivating our emotional awareness. Sticking with one emotional response that we feel comfortable with—no matter what the situation—limits our personal development, our growth as a member of a relationship, and our emotional understanding.

Breathing to Awaken Your Emotions

Awareness of your breathing brings you into the present moment, which is where you have the truest awareness of your emotions. Here are six powerful destressifying breathing practices to take you out of the past and into the present moment. One by one, let's walk through each of them:

- **Quiet continuous breathing:** *Slowly breathe in through your nostrils as quietly as you can, and then slowly breathe out through them with the same silence. At the end of each inhale, gently, quietly turn the breath around and release it back out. Silence is key. Make believe you are trying to create the quietest process you know how. Do this for just a few minutes, and you will feel your body and mind slow down to a place of calm.*

- **Sipping breath:** *Purse your lips as if you're sipping a hot cup of tea. Take long, slow, deep breaths in through your pursed lips. This will totally release tension and help you transcend any anxiety of the moment. To add more force to the practice, as you breathe in, clench your fists and arms and bring them to the side of your face. As you exhale, release the tension in your hands and arms and gently let them rest by your side.*

- **Gargling breath:** *Open your mouth as wide as you can—as if gargling—and take a long, slow, deep breath in and count until your chest fully expands. As you exhale, make sure that your out-breath lasts one second longer than your inhale. Practice this for a minute. If at any time you get light-headed, stop, take a seat, and just breathe normally.*

- **Ocean breath:** In this meditation we re-create the powerful physical and emotional nourishment of swimming underwater. The ideal way to practice this meditation is to *fill your bathtub with four inches of water . . . then lie down on your back until your ears are totally submerged underwater. Just lie there and breathe through your nose for a few minutes, and you will experience what it's like to go scuba diving.* Obviously, you can't carry your bathtub around with you. But you can *simulate the powerful bodymind benefits of ocean breathing by simply placing your palms over your ears and taking long, slow breaths in and out of your nose.*

- **Alternate-nostril breathing:** This is a very calming and centering practice that actually aligns the right and left hemispheres of your brain in only a few moments. You can use it as a relaxing tool before beginning your meditation; when you find yourself overwhelmed in the middle of the day; or to ease mental chatter, anxiety, or emotional turbulence before going to bed. Known in Sanskrit as *Nadi Shodhana,* or "clearing the channels," *alternate-nostril breathing* is best done with your eyes closed. Here's how it works:

    Gently rest your right pointer finger against the bridge of your nose as if you were about to sneeze. Then hold your right thumb over your right nostril, pressing it closed, and inhale deeply through your left nostril. When you have inhaled as far as you can, close off your left nostril with your middle finger, release your right thumb from your right nostril, and then exhale smoothly through your right nostril. After a full exhalation, inhale through your right nostril, and then close it off with your right thumb at the peak of your inhalation. Release the pressure on your left nostril, and exhale through the left. Then inhale through the left nostril, and at the peak of the inhale . . . close it off again with your middle finger. Release your thumb's pressure on the right nostril, and exhale through the right nostril. Repeat the alternating pattern as long as you like—ideally for three minutes or more—breathing out and in through the open nostril, and then closing it with your thumb or middle finger as you breathe out and in through the alternate open nostril. Your breathing should be effortless, as your attention stays on the gentle inflow and outflow.

- **Metta meditation,** the most powerful emotional-shift meditation: *Start by placing your hand on your heart, taking a long inhale, and bringing* <u>metta</u> *(an ancient Pali word for unconditional loving-kindness) into your heart, and then, as you exhale, radiate it out. You do this by sitting for five minutes and focusing your attention on loving thoughts and feelings. Use deep inhales to fill yourself up with loving thoughts, and then let that love flow through you and out of you in a long exhale.*

  Begin the metta meditation by taking a long, slow, deep breath in and feeling the metta of the universe come into your heart. As you exhale, radiate the metta back out. First radiate metta to your loved ones . . . then inhale the unconditional love of the universe and radiate metta to your friends . . . then inhale the unconditional love of the universe and radiate metta to your acquaintances . . . then inhale the unconditional love of the universe and radiate metta to those who are suffering . . . then inhale the unconditional love of the universe and radiate metta to those with whom you have a grievance . . .

*then inhale the unconditional love of the universe
and radiate metta to those you'll never meet . . .
then inhale the unconditional love of the universe and
radiate metta to all sentient beings . . . then inhale
the unconditional love of the universe and radiate
metta to every corner of the galaxy. Then breathe in the
unconditional love of the universe from every corner of the
galaxy into your heart and sit with that gratitude.*

When you do this in a group: *At the end, after
you've inhaled the metta from every corner of the galaxy,
radiate it out to everyone in the room with your final
exhale and just sit with that for a minute as you feel
metta pour into you from everyone in the space.*

Breathing is key to destressifying. And it comes naturally—you may just have gotten out of practice. By maintaining awareness of your breathing throughout the day, you will naturally destressify. Which technique resonated with you most? Which had the deepest impact? Do you notice a more profound connection to your emotions? Which ones arose? If you regularly practice these six breathing techniques, you'll get comfortable with each of them, and you will find that you can invoke them in the moment—any moment—to shift your emotional energy.

Mastering Your Emotional Awareness

Now you are pretty well versed in emotional intelligence, and you have some powerful tools for mastering your emotional awareness. You are probably even feeling more confident in your ability to fully destressify. Yay! Of course, as you move through each day, you'll realize that other people's emotions are projected to you more subtly than your own, and they become more difficult for you to read. (Whether people are extroverted or introverted will determine how prone they are to publicly expressing their emotions or concealing them.) But mastering your own emotions will lay some fertile groundwork for you to detect the nuanced emotional expressions of others.

Remember that when you are calm and relaxed, you have a much better handle on your own emotions than when you're agitated, anxious, angry, or stressed. Imagine how blind some people are to their own and others' emotions when they are living in states of chronic stress. Think back to your last stressful moment. Do you remember how oblivious you were to your own emotions at the time? You were probably at an emotionally intelligent low—and were not even thinking about anyone else's emotions.

Remember, it's not the event—*it's our interpretation of the event* that triggers emotion. For example, the emotion of fear usually occurs in response to a threat, real or imagined. Our understanding and internal labeling of the concept of "being in danger" (based on our interpretations of the past and our interpretation of the moment) is the trigger that arouses our autonomic nervous system.

So if you don't view a person or experience as "dangerous" or "threatening," your bodymind will treat it as a non-threat. Having faith that the next moment will be better can quickly shift your mind-set regarding the true danger right now. That's why your belief that there will be another moment in the future where the pain subsides is critical. You just have to know . . . to realize . . . to truly understand that unless someone is about to kill you, the stress of the moment is probably noncritical.

Owning Your Emotions

In order to destressify, we have to be able to recognize the first spark of emotion before it devolves into emotional overload, which actually disconnects us from our feelings. Without an awareness of what we're feeling, it's impossible to fully understand our own behavior, appropriately manage our emotions and actions, and accurately "read" the wants and needs of others.

Moment-to-moment awareness of the influence our emotions have on our thoughts and actions is key to destressifying.

Many people are disconnected from their feelings—especially strong core emotions such as anger, sadness, fear, frustration, and resentment. This may be the result of negative childhood experiences that conditioned us to lash out or shut down. But although we can distort, deny, or numb our feelings, we can't eliminate them. They're still there, *whether we're aware of them or not.* And without emotional awareness, we are unable to release those feelings, manage our stress, fully understand our own motivations and needs, or communicate effectively with others.

Through the power of enhanced emotional awareness, you are able to do all this:

- Recognize and rein in your emotional stress

- Understand and empathize with others

- Communicate clearly and effectively

- Make wiser decisions based on the things that are most important to you

- Get motivated and take action to meet goals

- Build strong, healthy, and rewarding relationships

The Good in the "Bad"

All emotions are good for us . . . if we listen to the message. The benefits of "negative" emotions are that they are telling us something or advising us on our next step. If we don't absorb their messages, we are wallowing in our negative, painful emotions for no reason and suffering unnecessarily. Fear can put a stranglehold on us, preventing us from moving in any direction. But it also wakes us up to the possibilities around us. If we use it as a *tool* rather than as a noose, it can enlighten us about where we stand in a given moment. Fear is a symptom, just like sadness is a symptom—a symptom that somewhere you have leaned away from balance.

When you sense fear, pay attention, but don't stay frozen. Learn from it, and either summon courage to confront it or choose another path. Anger obviously has its downside when it's unfocused rage. But it has a deeper, more powerful, positive upside. Anger can be the spark that kicks us in the butt, the inspiration we need to leap out of self-pity or less-than thinking and take action.

Sadness also has an upside. I've often said that visiting the land of hurts and wounds is healthy and soothing once in a while, but no one benefits long-term by living there. Chronic sadness can devolve into depression. But in-the-moment sadness is a healthy message to pay attention to how we feel. Sadness encourages us to take some time, slow down, and accept our vulnerability rather than creating a hard, false, protective shell. Sadness allows us to grieve, survive, and ultimately thrive after a loss.

Your Emotions in the Real World

Here's an effective exercise to bring you greater clarity on your personal emotional intelligence:

1. Make a list of your top ten "negative" or uncomfortable emotions, including fear, anger, and sadness.

2. Write down the benefits that might come to you right now in a real-world situation with each emotion. To ignite your creative thinking here, ask yourself, *What is this emotion telling or teaching me about myself or my situation? What did I just learn about myself?*

Remember, everyone has these emotions—every sentient being on the planet. Every successful person, every great scientist, every guru and swami, every CEO, every Oscar winner, homeless person, and flight attendant. No one is immune—but perhaps they've done some work on themselves. You can, too. This exercise alone will destressify you as you actually learn more about who you are and how you respond to the world around you.

Cultivating your emotional intelligence will help you fulfill your Social Needs of compassion and empathy, your Esteem Needs of self-esteem and self-awareness, and your Self-actualized Need of flexibility—all important contributors to success in your life.

• • •

The next step in destressifying is mastering your capacity for conscious communication—the all-important way you share and receive information with others and yourself. Like fulfilling needs and mastering emotional intelligence, communication is a process that seems inherent but is actually a learned skill and requires cultivation to truly master. Once you understand how to communicate nonviolently, nonverbally, and consciously, then destressifying will take hold. And as long as you continue the practice, your needs will be fulfilled, your relationships will flourish, and your life will unfold more gracefully and effortlessly. So let's continue.

• • • • •

destressifying by Mastering Your Communication

"I meant what I said and I said what I meant.
An elephant's faithful one hundred percent."

— DR. SEUSS

Everyone thinks they can dance, everyone thinks they can sing, and everyone thinks they can communicate—but all three are skill sets that require attention, understanding, and practice in order for someone to become proficient (and it also helps to have some God-given talent). But as we know from the long line of pop stars with very little talent but brilliant marketing, success is not always contingent upon genius.

Mastery, however, requires a deeper capacity. When we've mastered something, we are no longer thinking about how to do it. It becomes us. It weaves its nuances into every fiber of our being. It inhabits every cell in our body and every thought that flows through us. It becomes embedded into our words, our relationships, and our behaviors. Ultimately, we grow into our new skin, and it defines us.

Our language does not simply describe our reality; the language we use creates its own reality! The language we choose defines us, and through *mastering conscious communication*, you will evolve as a person. You will respond in difficult situations with grace; you will suddenly start speaking the perfect words in the perfect moment. Your timing and impeccability will merge, and your interactions will take on a higher level of meaning. This is where you really start to flow destressifying into the world.

Un-Conditioning Our Communication

Mastering the art and science of conscious communication requires only one foundational element: a willingness to let go of the habitual way you've communicated up until now. This means that you will need to replace the lifetime of conditioning and reinforcement with a new, more expansive paradigm that incorporates new ways of being. So much of the pain and drama of life occurs from downright poor communication—not because the words weren't impeccably chosen, but because they didn't convey what was meant in a thoughtful way.

We've all misspoken. We will again. We've all said words we don't mean—even when we were trying very hard to convey a particular message. We've all sent the scathing e-mail or reactive text laden with emotional charge that didn't accomplish our goal. We've all assumed that people understand exactly what we mean when we say something that seems so obvious to us. We've all shut down and walked away, either physically or verbally. Most of us are actually skilled at *un*conscious communication.

We've all heard the story of the American tourist who goes to Japan and asks in English for directions to a restaurant, but no one understands him, so he speaks louder—so they can hear him better. We are always assuming that people "get" us—that they think what we are thinking, understand the motivation behind the words we say, and comprehend the nuance of our phrasing.

The reality is that 90 percent of all our issues with others are due to poor, confusing, or violent communication. Even if you are a brilliant communicator, as soon as stress takes over your mind, you are no longer at your best.

Previously, we discussed how small spurts of stress can increase your performance under pressure. But when that stress becomes prolonged and doesn't wind down quickly, one of the first skills to suffer is your communication. You start to become constricted as you enter reactive or ego stress-response mode—forgetting the real goal of the moment and losing the bigger picture. As the blood leaves your brain and flows into your extremities—and waves of adrenaline and cortisol wash through you—clarity, creativity, intuition, and connection are replaced by overwhelm, fogginess, fearful choice making, and defensiveness.

The Truth about Our Communication

So what *is* conscious communication? Let's start with the basics: where we are and where we came from. The English word *communication* comes from the Latin word *communicare,* which means "to share"—yet that's not what we always do. Most often we talk *at* someone; and if they speak, we are rarely engaged in what they have to say. We are waiting for them to stop so that we can talk again. Even if our intention is to share what's in our heart, we often fumble through some Hallmark card as our guide rather than speaking from a space of true vulnerability. If we are trying to convey our need to someone, it usually is coming from a place of frustration or irritation, and our communication can be laced with emotional charge topped off with quick phrases such as "You're always late!"; "Don't drive so fast!"; and "You never compliment me!" If we are trying to convince someone to do something, we reach back to memories of all the authority figures who have convinced *us* of something, and we use them as a model. We have built our entire communication foundation on *a conditioned framework* we learned, cultivated, and "mastered" when we were children—physically, emotionally, and verbally.

But the ways we respond to life right now are different from when we were nine years old, and our world has gotten a bit more complex. Think about it: From the moment we left the womb through our first few years, our earliest conversations were with our parents or caregivers. We figured out that people paid attention to us when we cried; and they responded by either feeding us, holding us, or cleaning us. That was a pretty effective way to meet our basic Survival Needs as a baby.

Working the Crowd

As the months unfolded in our babyhood, we realized that positive responses came to us when we smiled, laughed, giggled, or cooed. This helped to meet our Social Needs of love and belonging, and certainly met our needs of attention and affection. This was before we could actually form a word or sentence. We were verbal but inarticulate, so we acted cute. We mastered nonverbal communication as well, since we didn't have the vocabulary to get our point across. We clapped, danced, wriggled, squirmed, made facial expressions, and moved our bodies to "speak" to the world around us.

As the years unfolded, we reinforced those behaviors with the few words we learned, and then our internal dictionary started to expand as we went to school. But we remembered very well how people responded to us in certain circumstances and regarding certain needs, so we reinforced those behaviors . . . and here we are.

But between third grade and now, no one has evaluated our communication skill set. When we were little, we got really good feedback from our parents and teachers regarding what we should say and what we shouldn't . . . what worked and what didn't . . . and we followed their lead. At that point we were building our life structure based on the guidance of a few well-intentioned (but clueless) 20-somethings. It's a bit scary to think about how we made it this far with that type of direction and leadership. But we did. Actually, they did an amazing job. It got us to this moment.

But for us to get to the next moment—and fulfill the needs that we have right now—we need more effective and longer-lasting tools. The commitment we make to heightening our emotional intelligence and communicating consciously will have lasting and powerful effects.

Awareness of Our Words

Being "conscious" about our communication simply means we are aware of it, just as emotional intelligence involves an awareness of our own and others' emotions. Conscious communication is an awareness of our words, as well as the words of others; the circumstance and the emotional space of the other person; our tone, speed, and cadence and their impact; our body language, physical movements, and eye contact and their subtle messages; and our ability to communicate from a place of calm, clear intent with appropriate timing so that those on the receiving end *want* to hear the message, want to respond, want to be engaged with us, and want to help us meet our needs. (It always comes back to meeting our needs!)

When we were babies, virtually all our communication was about meeting Survival and Safety Needs. And most of our requests to others came from biological stress responses. We were hungry—we cried. We needed our diaper changed—we cried. We needed to be held—we cried. And it worked out perfectly! As we grew, our Social Needs of love and belonging were met with our very limited vocabulary, but still we were using the same conditioned or constricted reactions to help us meet those needs.

Fast-forward to the present moment . . . now those same techniques don't work as effectively with our partner, our co-workers, our boss, or anyone else we encounter throughout the day. Now we are old enough and smart enough to understand and cultivate a more advanced communication process, using:

- Methods that will help us meet our more advanced needs

- Emotional intelligence to help us communicate more clearly and more successfully

- Language that will create lasting fulfillment for us and everyone connected to us

The art and science of communication need to be married within us so that we flow words from an unconstricted place, meaning they are not the result of a knee-jerk reaction, a conditioned response, or a familiar pattern. Understanding the emotion behind the words others speak and behind our own words can make the difference between successful and unsuccessful communication. It's also the difference between a stressful experience and a destressifying experience—one that lowers the stress quotient of everyone involved in the exchange.

Being conscious helps us better understand a person or situation and enables us to resolve differences; build trust and respect; and create environments where creative ideas, problem solving, affection, and caring can flourish. As simple as communication seems, much of what we try to communicate to others—and what others try to communicate to us—gets put through all our conditioned filters, which can cause conflict and frustration in our personal and professional relationships.

By learning the core skills of conscious communication, you will better connect with everyone in your life from this day forward.

The Three Gates

We all say or write things we wish we hadn't, and it causes stress. And we often speak words that ultimately hurt others or weave their way into our minds and stress us for longer than we anticipated. There's an age-old filtering practice I'd like to share with you. I've been told that Socrates referred to it as the Three Questions, that Quakers call it the Test of Three, and that it's known in some cultures as the Three Sieves (like sifting flour). David Simon taught it to me as *The Three Gates.*

We are constantly absorbing information through our five senses, our imagination, and our intellect. We hear words or have an interaction and it triggers thought, which touches on a memory, sparking an emotion, which then weaves its way through our conditioned response mechanism, and a whole unconscious process begins . . . often ending with us saying something that doesn't necessarily add value to our life or anyone else's.

The premise of The Three Gates is that just because you think something, that doesn't mean you have to say it. In fact, before you say something . . . anything . . . you should pass your words through three gates to see if those words are worthy of making it into the tangible world. The process takes only a few seconds and may save you much heartache, regret, and stress.

Here's how it works: As a thought pops into your head, first ask the question, *Is it true?* Did you read it, watch it, or hear it? Is it rumor or from a credible source? Is it fact or gossip? Is someone telling you something filled with emotional charge? Are they providing all the information? Do you know the backstory? Is there a way for you to verify before you act? If it's not valid, it does not pass the test, and it does not proceed to the next gate. You don't repeat it. It dies right there. And by placing no more attention on it, its power diminishes, as does its impact on stress in your life. (When you start adding more emotional charge to something that's not even true or that you can't determine is true, that's a lot of effort and energy applied in a direction that does not serve you.) However, if it does ring true, you proceed to the next gate.

At the next gate, you ask the question, *Is it kind?* Conscious communication teaches us that our words should be kind. No one benefits from harsh words or ones that are carrying emotional charge. The message gets clouded—the words take on unintended meanings—and the damage can last in perpetuity. Of course, there are often messages that we need to express that are not in fact kind, such as firing someone, correcting someone's behavior, or telling someone bad news. Whatever the message might be, in all those instances we can opt to speak it in a kind way. Wouldn't you want to be fired with compassion? Wouldn't you prefer to be corrected in a benevolent way rather than with a smack? Wouldn't you rather someone break up with you in a kind way?

If it's true and it's kind, proceed to the third gate, which asks, *Is it necessary?* or as Socrates said, *Is it useful?* Something might be true, and it might even be kind, but if it's unnecessary, then it should die right there. Why put time, effort, and emotional investment into introducing unnecessary or useless information into the world? If you are still not sure, ask, *How important is it?* or *Will it improve upon the silence?* How necessary is it for you to flow this information out into the world? If after applying the third filter, you determine that it's simply not necessary to bring it up, or it adds no value to the tangible world, then let it go. Let the whole flow of thought conclude and just move on. (We could do this with 50 percent of what we think.) But if it meets all three criteria—*true, kind, and necessary*—then rock on! Flow those words! And pass on the power of *The Three Gates.*

The Value of Being a Conscious Communicator

Every day, we have to send, receive, and process huge numbers of messages. But conscious communication is about more than just exchanging information. It's also about understanding the emotion behind the information and the feelings of the receivers of the information, about understanding how changing just one word in a sentence can make the difference between success in the moment or pain for years to come. Conscious communication can improve relationships at home, at work, and in social situations by deepening your connections to others and improving teamwork, decision making, and problem solving. It enables you to convey even negative or difficult messages without creating conflict or destroying trust. This technique combines a set of skills that includes attentive listening, compassionate communication, nonverbal communication, mastering your needs, the ability to manage stress in the moment, and the capacity to recognize and understand your own emotions and those of the person you're communicating with.

While conscious communication is a learned skill, it is more effective when it's spontaneous rather than coming from an instruction manual in the back of your mind. Canned speech rarely has the same impact as spontaneous speech. Learning these powerful destressifying tools is an evolutionary process; and the more you practice, the more instinctive and spontaneous your communication skills will become. But most important, conscious communication is the doorway to meeting all your needs. Are you ready to walk through it?

In every interaction, every conversation, and every thought, we have a choice to promote peace or perpetuate violence. You may be thinking, *Wow, that sounds pretty extreme.* But your words have extreme power. They live on long after you speak them. Right now in your head, you are holding on to conversations that may have taken place 20 years ago! That sounds pretty extreme to me.

The language we use is a major determinant of what follows next. Did we say what we really felt? Did we say it impeccably? Was it even true? Will it have the short- and long-term effect we envisioned? Will it be misinterpreted? Will it help us meet our needs? And will it support the next words exchanged?

Understanding and integrating conscious communication into our lives is a huge step toward meeting our needs, lessening anxiety, reducing tension, healing pain, and resolving a pattern of conflicts. We do this by cultivating a more inner peaceful-ness in the language we use each day. (Don't think I'm getting all woo-woo on you. We all want to live lives of greater peace in a world filled with peace.) Whenever we feel that our personal boundaries have been crossed, it can trigger a strong emotional response. Whether intentionally or not, the words we hear can wound us, creating emotional charge and defensiveness. When we react with anger, hostility, blame, or by shutting down, we create a ripple of negative energy that takes on a life of its own.

Many issues we're struggling with right now regarding another person—such as holding a grudge, being passive aggressive, not feeling treated well, delaying a difficult conversation, having schadenfreude, being in a fight, giving them the silent treatment, and so on—can be destressified by having a conscious conversa-tion. By mastering this core destressifying practice, we can more clearly express our boundaries, feelings, and needs, creating a greater likelihood that they will be understood, honored, and fulfilled.

Nonviolent Communication

Let's take this deeper with some advanced techniques, starting with the teachings of Marshall Rosenberg, Ph.D., an American psychologist and creator of the technique known as Nonviolent Communication (NVC), a communication process that helps people to exchange the information necessary to resolve conflicts and differences peacefully. NVC contains four fundamental steps to more consciously communicate our desires whenever we find ourselves at odds with another person. When one of our buttons has been pushed, NVC can be the powerful language tool for us to express how we genuinely feel, what we need in the moment, and how to request it.

Upon recognizing that a boundary has been crossed or one of your needs is not being met, follow these four steps:

1. Ask yourself, **What just happened?** Answer objectively rather than subjectively or emotionally.

2. Communicate to the other person exactly **how it makes you feel,** sharing your emotions—not your interpretations of what they were thinking.

3. **Communicate the need** you have that is not being met or a need you'd like to have met.

4. **Request** a behavior or action from the person to help you meet your need.

I know. It sounds so easy. And once you get into the groove, it will flow effortlessly. But most times, we are swept up into the moment—trapped in the clutches of acute stress and transported back to our most primitive reactions. In that moment, we are not the best version of ourselves. But NVC can tamp down the drama and bring us to a place of clarity by settling our mind into the four-part structure and offering up the framework for successful, stress-free dialogue.

NVC in Action

Let's take the following three scenarios and explore Nonviolent Communication in action.

When Your Needs Are Not Met

Say, for example, you go to a party with your spouse or partner. He or she spends most of the time with an attractive person you've never met, and you start to get jealous. Of course you start asking yourself, *Have they ever met before? Why are they smiling so intently at each other? I'm here all alone. Why doesn't he or she smile so much with me? Are they having an affair?* The thoughts (one every 1.2 seconds) are pouring in, destabilizing your needs of basic security and your needs of the heart—attention, affection, appreciation, and acceptance.

Or maybe you've just come home after a long day, and there are dishes in the sink, and everyone is off having fun. The expectation is that you should wash them, but you're exhausted and looking to have your own dinner. And you're thinking, *Am I the maid in this house? Why can't everyone take care of themselves and do the right thing?*

Or maybe you were supposed to meet a friend for lunch at noon and they arrive 30 minutes late (as always). And you feel irritated, angry, annoyed, and hungry.

Unconscious Communication

We could go on and on, as there are between 8 and 15 of these moments every day in which your needs are not met and you need to tell someone, so they can either meet them or so you can share how you're feeling. In the first example, after the party as you're driving home, we know a fight is about to break out. Emotional fight-or-flight reactions have been simmering for the whole party. You might even say, "Jeez, I thought you were going to flirt all night long!" or "Why did you ignore me for three hours?" or "You are so selfish—didn't you see me sitting there all alone?" Or in the most extreme case, you might burst out, "We should probably get divorced!"

In the second instance, you might approach the person who put their dirty dishes in the sink and say, "You are so unappreciative. You are so lazy. I worked all day long to put food on this table, and you can't even wash your own dishes?" or "What am I? Your maid?"

And in the third instance, you might say to your friend as they finally arrive, "You are always late!" or "You are so selfish! So inconsiderate!" or maybe, "Why don't you have any respect for people?"

Examples like these are woven into every day of your life and have been for many years. Their impact can twine itself through your thoughts, words, and actions for decades to come. You may even lie awake at night for months, unable to sleep as you replay the situation over and over. You may reinforce your feelings of anger, irritation, and contempt by telling the story to others and trying to get their buy-in on your emotional response (which we know is being driven by stress simply caused by your needs not being met). You may even use this one event as the jumping-off point for changing the nature of the relationship.

In all three cases, chances are that an argument will ensue, tempers will flare, feelings will be hurt, harsh words will be said, and emotional turbulence will be created. The ripples from an innocent "communication" can have devastating results that linger long after the experience. We may even end friendships and marriages over the power of one such situation.

Ruled by Your Primitive Brain

But the reality is that in the very moment you began to have feelings of discomfort, you were being guided by your most primitive brain. Hormones were surging into you as you reacted internally to your unmet need, your immune system was suppressed as you interpreted a threat, the platelets in your bloodstream started plumping up and clotting as your boundaries felt pushed—and what came out of your mouth next was the same as if an angry, reactive, threatened reptile had possessed you, bringing you to your most primal urges. You were light-years from a destressified response because your fight-or-flight process had kicked in and you were in full-on reactive or ego-response mode, ready to emotionally attack or shut down.

You could *Reach for SODA* in that moment or dive into *16seconds* to save the day, and either choice would treat the symptom (your reactivity) by introducing a momentary pattern interrupt, perhaps destressifying you for a few minutes. But they won't solve the problem that rests at the core of the relationship . . . and what about the next time? And the next . . . and the next . . .

But if we can introduce Dr. Rosenberg's easy four-step process into the equation—*poof!* The emotional charge goes away . . . the threat dissipates . . . clearer heads prevail . . . and in all likelihood, you will fulfill the unmet need that pushed you to the brink of breakup, divorce, quitting, tantrum, violence, or withdrawal.

Walking Through the Steps to Nonviolent Communication

First, let's get clear by practicing *16seconds*. Go ahead. I'll wait here . . .

Now, think of a recent situation that has been bothering you, and write down a sentence or two that describes what happened. Take your time and be as clear as possible with what actually happened. Once you are finished writing, let's walk it through the four steps:

1. What happened? Separate your observation from your evaluation. When you describe what happened, pretend that you are an objective reporter and outline the observable facts. For example, "You are such a flirt," "You don't respect me," and "My friend is never on time" are all evaluations. The corresponding observations are "We went to the party, and you only spent 15 minutes with me"; "There are dishes in the sink, and you are sitting on the couch watching TV"; and "My friend said she would meet me for lunch at 12, and she arrived at 12:30." Do you see the difference? Observations simply state observable facts. Evaluations are interpretations and take into account past behaviors, deeply rooted beliefs, emotional slants, and your internal filter. You might as well don the boxing gloves and get ready to rumble!

Using words such as *always, never, repeatedly, frequently,* and other absolutes are often a sign that we are evaluating and generalizing rather than observing. They won't solve what's going on right now—they will only inflame it. And in actuality, saying someone is "always" one thing or another is probably not true anyway and brings in all your *past laden emotional turbulence,* which is like pouring lighter fluid on the fire.

Borrowing a Jack

When I was a child, my mother used to tell me the story of "borrowing a jack."

A man is driving on a country road late at night. He's lost, his phone doesn't work, and he gets a flat tire. He opens the trunk and realizes he has a spare but no jack to lift up the car, so he can't change the tire. He starts to feel a bit nervous because he hasn't passed another car for hours, so the chances of being helped are minimal.

He stands on the side of the road for an hour, hoping someone will drive by; but he is out in the boonies and it's late, so no one passes. He looks at his watch. It's two in the morning. Then far in the distance, he spots a farmhouse. He begins the long walk to the farmhouse in the hopes of borrowing a jack from the owner.

Already scared and in an agitated state, he starts to ruminate on how this potential interaction will unfold. First, he assumes that he will have to wake the farmer, because it's two in the morning, after all. A little bit of nervousness starts to run through his mind. *What if the farmer gets angry at being woken and refuses to help? What if he doesn't believe me and thinks I'm a con artist or a robber?* he worries. He keeps walking through the tall grass, and his heart begins to pound as his breathing becomes more labored.

He keeps moving, perspiration dripping down his face, thinking about what's to come: *And what if he makes me pay to rent the jack—how much is it worth? $5 or $50? That would be pretty extortive if he made me pay $50 just to borrow his jack! That's pretty greedy.*

Then he thinks, *Maybe he won't answer at all because he doesn't know me. Maybe he'll hide in the house. I bet he's locking all the doors right now as he sees me getting closer. What if he's away and he gave his wife instructions to not open the door? Or what if they're all peering at me approaching through the windows? I wonder if they're making fun of me.*

The driver has walked about half a mile, and he's getting closer; but he is tired, agitated, frustrated, irritated, angry, worried, scared, and overheated. As he strides more aggressively toward the house, he starts to brace for an encounter. *After all, the farmer has all the comforts of home right now—and here I am lost, in need, dripping sweat, out of breath, and struggling.* He works himself into a lather as he plays out the conversation that will ensue.

He calculates that if the farmer won't help him, he'll break into the house, get the keys to the farmer's car, pop the trunk, and steal the jack. Then he wonders, *What if he has a dog that he sets loose on me? What if the dog bites me and I get rabies? What if I have to hit the dog with the stolen jack? Then he'll come after me with a gun. What do I do then?*

After about an hour of walking through the tall grass and mud, the man gets to the door. He is absolutely livid. He feels entitled to the jack. At this point, he's even attached to it. But that "selfish" farmer stands between him and his driving off with an inflated new tire. He's exhausted and scared. His pants are covered in mud. His clothes are all disheveled. He's dripping sweat.

And he knocks on the door.

You can fill in the rest. In the story as my mother related it, as the door opens, the man punches the farmer in the face, a fight ensues, and as they roll around on the floor, he yells at the farmer, "Give me my jack!" And then suddenly he realizes that he made up the whole scenario in his mind, and he probably could have just explained his situation and requested a little help.

What's the lesson here? Oh, there are probably a hundred. But for our purposes, it's the difference between an evaluation and an observation. What's the observation? There's a farmhouse in the distance. What's the evaluation, or interpretation? That a selfish, greedy, uncompassionate farmer couldn't care less about the needs of an innocent, hardworking, unfortunate, scared, lost traveler and is conspiring to bring him more misery rather than simply helping him out.

Have *you* "borrowed a jack" recently?

Observations, Not Evaluations

In making an observation, it's important to be specific and avoid verbs that evaluate another person's intentions, such as *undermine, manipulate, threaten, victimize, conspire, punish,* and *betray.* These are not observations. Instead, we have crept inside the head of the other person and interpreted their motivations. But as we saw, it's pretty easy to do this and be wrong. In this first step of the four-step process, describe only what you can observe through your five senses, without filtering the facts through the lens of evaluation. When we evaluate or mix observation with evaluation, it's easy for the other person to resist or hear criticism in our innocent words.

Whenever you find yourself reacting emotionally, *Reach for SODA*, and during that observation phase, truly bring your most objective self to the situation. Doing this means that when you step back during the "detach" phase of SODA, you have an extra second to destressify and observe more effectively. Observations are empowering because they allow you to recognize how much of your typical response is based on interpretation. From this more enlightened place, you can shift how you would otherwise respond.

So now look at what you've written down, and ask yourself, *What actually happened?* And under your first entry, make your answer an observation rather than an evaluation. Once you are clear on your observation, move on to step 2.

2. How does it make me feel? We've spent a lot of time on understanding emotions, so you are probably a bit more skilled right now in describing your feelings regarding a particular situation. Use only words that express your core emotions or sensations—not thoughts, beliefs, or stories. To help with the process, feel free to use the list of emotions in Chapter 8, under "Emotional Awareness"; there are more than 70 different emotions to choose from. Plug in any of those or others that come to mind: I feel *sad, lonely, irritated, scared, jealous, angry,* and so on. "I feel that you are a jerk" is a thought, *not* an emotion. Whenever you say, "I feel that . . ." or "I feel as if . . . ," these are not actually feelings; they are thoughts. We want to convey only our true emotions—not thoughts about things. For this process to work, we have to make sure we are not meting out judgment, criticism, blame, or revenge. The latter will thwart your efforts for a conscious conversation.

Don't Play the Victim

Avoid using words that describe how you interpret other people's actions, such as *disrespected, unsupported, abandoned, betrayed,* or *ignored.* These kinds of words reinforce a sense of victimization, and then you are just venting, complaining, or accusing. For example, when you say, "I feel betrayed," this is actually not a feeling, but an interpretation misdiagnosed as a feeling. You may have in reality been betrayed by someone, but feeling betrayed is not an emotion. You can *feel* hurt, but *betrayal* is an interpretation based on an analysis.

Here are a few more examples of words *not to use* when expressing your feelings:

- Manipulated
- Cheated
- Taken for granted
- Deceived
- Neglected
- Patronized
- Coerced
- Let down
- Attacked

As you develop a broad and accurate vocabulary of feelings, it will become easier for you to connect with yourself and others. Remember, feelings reflect whether your needs are being met or not. Let's keep the emotional charge out of the process. Allowing yourself to be vulnerable in expressing your feelings can also help you resolve conflicts in ways that elevate the process. So how does your situation make you feel?

3. What do I need? During our early years, we know that all our needs were met by our parents and caregivers. And that conditioning lives on in our adult years as we expect those close to us to read our mind and figure out what we need. But realistically, until we immersed ourselves into the hierarchy of needs, even we weren't clear on what we needed—so how in the world can anyone else guess it?

We are much more likely to have our needs met if we can identify them, whether in the moment or in advance by proactively using a tool such as the Five Realms of My Life Personal Worksheet, and then communicate them clearly. Ask yourself, *What do I need in this situation?* You wouldn't be having strong feelings if all your needs were being met. Identify the unmet need behind your feelings, being as specific as possible.

For example, you might say to your spouse or partner, "I felt jealous when you were talking to that other person for so long because I felt insecure and unloved. I need to feel secure and loved in our relationship, and I need to feel that we are connected." You could tell your family member or housemate, "I felt tired and frustrated when I came home after a long day and those dishes were in the sink. I need to feel nourished in our house. I need to feel supported." You could say to your friend, "I felt worried when you hadn't arrived within 30 minutes of our agreed-on lunch time. And then I felt irritated when you arrived. I need to feel celebratory about our time together; I need to feel stress-free about meeting you."

Regarding *your* situation, what do you need?

4. Ask for what I want. Once you have identified the observation, your feeling, and your need, the final step is to make a request for specific behaviors or actions that will help fulfill your needs. If you ask for a state of mind like "I request that you love me more," it's impossible to measure or quantify. Instead, ask for a specific behavior, perhaps "When we go to a party, I request that we spend the first 30 minutes together and then check in with each other every 30 minutes," or "I request that you put any dishes you use into the dishwasher before I get home," or "If you're going to be more than ten minutes late, will you text me so that I don't worry?" If you want more time or attention from your partner, be specific. Ask to take a walk together after dinner or to go to a movie on Saturday night. Express your need in the form of a request rather than a demand. Remember, we always get more with honey than vinegar. And what's one of the first words we ever learned? *Please.* It goes a long way.

When you make a demand, you back the other person into a corner. When you make a request, you invite them in to participate in a solution. It creates a world of difference. You can tell that you are making a demand if you try to blame, punish, or lay a guilt trip on someone if they decline to do what you want. When you make a genuine request, you're able to demonstrate that you understand what might prevent them from fulfilling your request.

So regarding *your* situation, what's your request?

The Essence of the Four Steps

The four-step process doesn't guarantee that you will always get your needs met. It creates the platform for you to express yourself with less emotional charge, a greater chance of impeccability, and more honesty. Using this practice—even just once a day— creates a higher probability that you will indeed meet your needs with more consistency. And it will have a profound impact on destressifying your relationships because the agenda is peace.

What's also happening is that throughout all four steps, you never backed the other person into a corner, you never put a gun to their head, you never accused them of anything—you actually never made it personal. Think about it.

In step 1, you made an observation. (If you make an evaluation, then you poke them or accuse them.) It is simply what you observed.

In step 2, you solely shared your feelings. That's why you need to make sure they are true feelings and not interpretations. It isn't about the other person. It is distinctly about *your* feelings, and no one can really ever tell you, "No. You don't feel that way!" They can tell you that you shouldn't feel a certain way; but if you already do, then they can't claim you don't. Once more, that's why it must be a true feeling and carry no interpretation or opinion. Remember, you are actually trying to solve an issue, not prove you are right about something.

In step 3, you shared your need. Again, these are your needs and no one can say, "No. You don't have that need." That's why it is so important to be impeccable with your words. Take your time. Get clear on the real need that isn't met. At this point, you haven't given the other person a reason to act or feel defensive. You haven't made it about them. It is *your* observation, *your* feelings, and *your* need.

And in step 4, you made a simple, straightforward request—not a demand. You asked for a specific behavior from the other person to help meet your need. *Demands* are harsh. They are in your face; they lack buy-in; and even if they are complied with, the action isn't really voluntary. *Requests* are calls for engagement. They extend the olive branch beyond any past issues. This is where the rubber meets the road.

There are three ways someone can respond to your request:

1. *"Yes, of course I want to meet your need. I'll respect and honor your request with the requested action. I look forward to helping you meet your need."*

2. *"I'd love to meet your need, but I can't. Something outside of me prevents me from meeting your need. But I have an alternative or a compromise. Will this meet your need?"* We can work with that. At least a loving dialogue has begun, and we are working toward a solution.

3. *"No. I do not honor your request. I will not meet your need."* This requires a much longer, deeper exploration of either your request or the relationship in general. If someone does not want to help you in meeting your need, this calls for a full review of whether your request is unreasonable or whether the relationship is really in your best interest.

Remember, as you learned in Chapter 7, on the *Five Realms*, there are four things you can do with a relationship: birth it, repair it, shift it, or end it. Most likely you were trying to shift or repair a relationship in your personal example. If you thought that wasn't going to happen based on past attempts, give it another shot because now you may be able to empathize with what is preventing the other person from saying yes. But after another attempt or an open, charge-free dialogue, if the response still isn't nourishing or supportive, you should consider viewing the relationship in another light.

Not So Smart

Smartphones and other devices coming onto the scene in the late '90s changed everything for the fate of communication on the planet. In the 2000s, it became normal to check messages in the middle of a conversation, to text others while you were in active dialogue, and even to leave your phone on the table during dinner. In 2011, it became acceptable to dine with one hand on your fork and the other on your phone; to only accept texts rather than phone calls; and to use computers, tablets, and phones on planes. Society has not yet felt the impact of the deep wound from its unconsidered communication choices. But needless to say, being wired is a massive stress creator. There's no break in the action . . . no downtime . . . no breathing room. You are on call for the universe from the moment you wake until the moment you pass out at night—and even while you're sleeping!

Ultimately, we'll all have chips in our head like Johnny Mnemonic. But until then, make the rule that your phone does not enter your dinner table (at home, in a restaurant, or in someone else's home), does not cross the line between your night table and your bed, and never touches your hands while you drive. Those three simple shifts will accelerate you meeting your Social Needs. It's simply called *having nourishing boundaries*.

Evolving Relationships Through Conscious Communication

Now you understand the fundamental practice of NVC—four simple steps. Mastering nonviolent communication will immediately empower you. Moving forward, you can have the "difficult" conversations, knowing that you are truly expressing yourself without inflaming the situation. Try this with three relationships or situations in your life right now. Sit down for a bit, write out the four steps for each of the relationships or situations that are causing stress, and then either make the call or meet in person.

Do not start by writing or texting the other party. Without an active dialogue (which texts and e-mails don't offer us), you will only back the person into a corner, making it more difficult when you do ultimately speak. What you want to create is a bridge of empathy through which both of you understand what's in each other's hearts rather than what's in your heads. Don't confuse this with sympathy. You feel empathy when you've "been there"—truly to the depths of their heart—and sympathy when you haven't "been there" and are mentally trying to understand the other person.

Conscious communication skills emphasize *emotional awareness*—seeing with new destressified eyes and without melodrama; *listening*—to ourselves and others, really hearing what is being said; and *owning our impact*—taking personal responsibility for our feelings, our actions, the choices we have made in our life, and the nature of our relationships.

When you place your attention on distilling what is being observed, felt, needed, and wanted, rather than on diagnosing and judging, you awaken the depth of your own compassion. This will help you become more self-empathetic (meeting an important Esteem Need) and *receive* more empathetically (meeting an important Social Need).

To find out more about Nonviolent Communication and the work of Marshall Rosenberg, visit nonviolentcommunication .com and cnvc.org, the website of the Center for Nonviolent Communication. The bible of these teachings is the book *Nonviolent*

Communication: A Language of Life, by Marshall B. Rosenberg, Ph.D. I highly recommend buying at least a couple of copies—one for you and one for the closest person in your life.

destressifying Through Nonverbal Communication

Cultivating your nonverbal communication skills can help create a destressified environment. People engaged in conversation unconsciously mirror each other's body language. If you can set a relaxed tone with your body language as well as your words, then you can remotely destressify everyone around you.

Successful nonverbal communication depends on your ability to manage stress, recognize your own emotions, and understand the signals you're sending and receiving. Do the following whenever you are engaged in a conversation:

- **Make eye contact.** Our eyes are the windows to the soul. Maintaining eye contact can help keep you both in the present moment. Eye contact can communicate interest, maintain the flow of a conversation, and help keep you connected to the other person's response.

- **Stay tethered to the other person.** If you are planning what you're going to say next, daydreaming, or thinking about something else, you are likely to miss nonverbal cues and other subtleties in the conversation. Don't play with your phone or check your watch. Stay present and breathe.

- **Watch for nonverbal cues.** Remember, conversation is a two-way flow. Pay attention to the other nonverbal signals you're sending and receiving, such as facial expression, tone of voice, posture and gestures, touch, and the timing and pace of the conversation.

What Is Your Body Saying?

Facial expressions, physical gestures, vocal tone, verbal pacing, voice volume, cadence, eye movement, head tilting, eye contact, posture, arm and hand positions, activity of the lips, touching the face, and even breathing can transform a stressful moment into a destressified one. You set the tone by whether your arms and legs are crossed or relaxed and open. Crossed arms and legs usually indicate resistance, protection, and defensiveness. Open yours and the room will open. Sitting back in your chair can be off-putting, sending messages of smugness or arrogance. Slide to the front of your chair and lean in. Slow the pace of your delivery and make eye contact, and attention span will rise whether you are in a one-on-one conversation or addressing a whole room of people.

If you pay close attention to your audience, they will provide you feedback on how conscious your communication actually is. Listen and watch, and speak from your heart rather than your emotions or your head, and you will commune with your audience.

Eight Quick destressifying Steps for Conscious Communication

The easiest way to slow down the swirl outside of you is to slow *you* down. Here are eight ways to sloooooow down in the middle of a conversation or a presentation to a larger group.

As you start to feel the physical signs that stress is taking over, identify where in your body the constriction is located and take action:

1. Immediately start *Reaching for SODA*: Stop, Observe, Detach, and Awaken. This will introduce a quick pattern interrupt that will allow you to reset the energy of the situation. As soon as you finish the last step, *Awakening to Your Best Version*, move to step 2 on this list.

2. Practice a quick *16seconds.* Literally in less than a
    minute, you will have recalibrated the intensity of the
    moment and regulated your emotions by becoming
    present, calm, emotionally aware, and reengaged—
    but with less stress. Remember that in stressful
    situations, we often forget to breathe.

3. Practice quiet continuous breathing. Keep long,
    slow, deep, silent breaths flowing in and out of your
    nostrils.

4. Look around for any blue or green in your field
    of vision. These colors have soothing, calming
    properties, as do pastels, earth tones, and white.
    Don't allow your gaze to settle on red, orange, or
    yellow. Like fire, these colors will re-inflame you,
    squirting lighter fluid on the burning coals. If there
    is no blue or green around you, envision it in your
    mind's eye . . . imagine the blue or green, and melt
    into it!

5. Squeeze your hands tightly into fists for five seconds
    and release. This mini version of *squeeze&release* will
    start to release any tension that's building up.

6. Feel free to crack a joke, tell a funny story, or make a
    lighthearted comment that will shift you and anyone
    else into a less serious mind-set.

7. If you are trying to convince or compel another
    person, pull back from your position for a moment.
    Stop "selling" and actually step back and create a
    little breathing room . . . a little space . . . and ask a
    few questions. This will bring the person more deeply
    into your dialogue.

8. If you find yourself in a toxic situation or if the heat
    is still too extreme within you or those around you,
    suggest a break. Call a time-out—sort of like a big
    version of the mini pattern interrupts we've been

cultivating. Step outside and breathe, step into the bathroom and splash some water on your face, or go for a quick walk around the block. Pull up a song on your phone that soothes you and just listen to it for a bit. Remind yourself of a sweet moment in your life over the past few days. The intensity of the energy will break and you can reengage at a higher level. When you come back into the room, try to be in listening mode. Look around, take deep breaths, and let it all soak in before you speak. This will heighten your emotional intelligence in the moment.

Flashing Our Emotions

In every moment, our biosignals reveal our true emotional state; it's as if our mind sends signals to our body, which then reacts spontaneously, creating the perfect feedback loop. We wear our emotions *on* our bodies as well as in our bodies. Yet very few people around us are adept at seeing them. When we are destressified, however, we are usually the calmest, most composed person in the room, so even the subtlest micro-expression (small visual clue) is picked up by our expanded emotional awareness.

There are even those who specialize in the study of human emotions by interpreting facial expressions. The foremost global expert in the field is the American psychologist and facial-emotion pioneer Paul Ekman, who can determine with near certainty whether a person is lying based on their micro-expressions. Ekman established that the face has 43 distinct and involuntary muscle movements that create thousands of expressions of emotion. Ekman's work was the inspiration for the critically acclaimed TV show *Lie to Me*, starring Tim Roth as the micro-expression expert Dr. Cal Lightman.

Mastering micro-expressions requires intense study and consistent practice. But if you want to learn more about this fascinating school of psychology employed by law enforcement throughout the world, visit paulekman.com.

destressifying Through Conflict Resolution

Using conscious communication to resolve conflicts should always be our starting point. You are a lot smarter now about the fact that everyone has needs and often they are conflicting. That's why it's critical for us all to be conscious, compassionate, and emotionally aware in all our interactions. In addition, we can resolve most of our conflicts by shifting our mind-set regarding how we approach them.

Use these five guides of behavior as a platform for conflict resolution in your life:

- **Be present.** Use *16seconds* to quickly transport your mind into the present moment. This way you won't bring in any past laden emotional drama. Recognize that this moment is an opportunity for resolving your old feelings about conflicts.

- **Be selective.** You don't have to jump into every conversation, and you don't have to have an opinion about every matter. If you are prone to talking a lot, practice *The Three Gates* and see where that leads you. Choose where you want to place your energy and attention, and let the rest go.

- **Recognize both sides.** We all have differing points of view, and it's not easy for most people to disagree. Acknowledge that in the moment you are both a bit scared, both a bit uncomfortable, and that you both have valid points to discuss. If you can approach every conversation with this as a starting point, you will be amazed by the results.

- **Be compassionate.** Speak to everyone the way you would like to be spoken to. Kindness actually does matter. Start by forgiving all past transgressions and request that you be forgiven also. No need to rub salt in anyone's wounds or to get revenge. Forgive and move forward.

- **Use your energy wisely.** It takes two to solve a conflict. Your attention on a particular issue fuels it with energy. You can always choose not to engage ... not to respond. Remember, you can't control what's in someone else's head. But you can control your words. Choose them wisely and make them valuable.

Listening

Listening is the cornerstone of conscious communication. When we listen, we can hear nuances, detect emotions, and uncover deeper meaning. We also connect on a deeper level with the person speaking. They feel heard. There's a lower likelihood for misunderstanding, and it opens the door to meeting everyone's needs. In the process of listening, you will expand your own perspective—appreciating another's viewpoint as new facts, new emotions, and new needs reveal themselves.

I grew up in a household where whoever spoke the loudest was listened to. Our dinner-table conversation typically had four people yelling at the top of their lungs and no one listening. We all wanted to be heard but didn't have the tools or guidance to allow the free flow of ideas. It wasn't until many years later that I had the opportunity to deconstruct my first ten years of communication "training" and immerse into a more conscious communication protocol.

I had been very well trained in the art of interruption and wisecracking, to meet my Social Needs of attention and appreciation;

and judgment, to validate my Esteem Need of being right. While these may have served me at home—battling every day to be seen and heard—once I stepped out into the real world, none of these skill sets offered any value.

It wasn't until I was in my late 20s that I committed to unconditioning myself and creating a more effective and nourishing communication style. I spent three years reminding myself out loud to listen to every word someone else was speaking in a conversation, to not interrupt when I got bored or impatient, and to play back the other person's words and wait for confirmation. Then I began reinforcing this behavior for the next decade by silently whispering to myself, *Listen,* when I was about to speak while someone else's words were still in the air.

I still slip into my youthful pattern once in a while, but that happens less and less. Learning to listen transformed the nature of my relationships, and it evolved my own sense of what really is going on when people opt to communicate consciously with each other.

So much of the stress we experience is created by our very own words as they ripple into others' ears and lives. When we are able to clearly and consciously articulate our needs to others without emotional charge, and make measurable requests in non-reactive ways, the world opens up to us. Stress—in the form of resistance from others, argumentative conversations, and the ensuing melodrama—becomes a thing of the past. Our personal, home, and working relationships strengthen. And we actually improve the trust, ease, and mutual respect for and from everyone we encounter until, ultimately, flow replaces divisiveness and defensiveness.

• • • • •

CHAPTER 10

destressifying by Mastering Your Purpose in Life

"I think the purpose of life is to be useful, to be responsible, to be honorable, to be compassionate. It is, above all, to matter: to count, to stand for something, to have made some difference that you lived at all."

— LEO ROSTEN

According to the oldest teachings on the planet, each of us is here for some divine purpose. Whether you consider this valid or "out there," the reality is that when we use our unique abilities and our distinctive talents in the service of others, we feel in flow. By *mastering our purpose,* or at least beginning the journey to understand our purpose, a major stressor—struggling over the age-old question *Why am I here?*—is eliminated. In its place appears a deeper fulfillment in each moment as we begin to live a purpose-driven life.

So what is the meaning of life? Why are we here? What is my purpose? These three questions have rippled through the minds of humankind for as long as we have had thought. And the questions don't change regardless of your orientation to God, your belief in a divine creator, or your position in society. Every being has wondered some form of the question at one time or another. According to Maslow, the fifth stage of needs—Self-actualization—is where we truly connect to our purpose.

The need for meaning creeps into every aspect of our being. And if we are not experiencing purpose in our work or home life, then we start a process of detaching from them. We may find ourselves going through the motions, withdrawing from opportunities, becoming mired in malaise, or getting stuck in quicksand. We become directionless and lost from the lack of clarity and passion, and we begin to make non-nourishing choices. So as long as your basic Survival Needs are met, and your safety is ensured, you can begin the exploration of purpose regardless of where you stand with your other needs. Each of us is here to self-actualize, to discover the best version of ourselves, to realize our higher self . . . our spiritual self. Call it source, call it God, call it the universe, or call it the oneness that rests within. But that's what we're all here to do. And we must find out for ourselves that we can awaken the God or Goddess in embryo—the most divine aspect of ourselves that rests deep within—but we can't do it if we are operating from a state of overwhelm or extreme stress.

Whether we are driven by science, religion, or spirituality, the concept of living with purpose has relevance to us. We all want to have a reason for being here—it's our validation on the grandest scale. When we can discover that task, duty, role, cause, or career that fuels the passion in our heart and feeds the fire to do more—that genuinely makes us feel fulfilled—we feel whole . . . actualized. More practically, when we live each moment with purpose, we experience more fulfillment and less stress.

Purpose = Better Health and Longevity

Although the concept of *purpose* has been around for thousands of years, only recently has it been linked to stress. According to a 2013 study whose authors include Stacey M. Schaefer, Ph.D., and pioneering neuroscientist Dr. Richard J. Davidson (possibly the most prolific brain researcher of our time), published in the open-access peer-reviewed scientific journal *PLOS ONE,* "Purpose in life predicts both health and longevity, suggesting that the ability to find meaning from life's experiences, especially when confronting life's challenges, may be a mechanism underlying resilience. Having purpose in life may motivate reframing stressful situations to deal with them more productively, thereby facilitating recovery from stress and trauma."

Those with a higher connection to their purpose in life have lower cardiovascular risk, lower risk of depression, lower weight, and healthier cholesterol levels. In fact, according to Schaefer, "People are more likely to be mobile when they get older, less likely to develop Alzheimer's, and even less likely to die *if they have higher levels of purpose in life.* It appears to be a protective or resilience factor" (emphasis mine). The findings reinforce that if you have a higher level of purpose in life, *what doesn't kill you does indeed make you stronger* by enhancing your emotional regulation, improving your resilience, and increasing your life span.

Purpose Does Not Necessarily Equal Your Job

Now of course, finding purpose and meaning in life does *not* have to come from your job. You can live an amazing destressified life that is richly rewarding and deeply fulfilling where you don't necessarily have the dream job. But I've found that self-realization is a journey to wholeness—where all the pieces of life merge together. So in time, if everything in your life is perfect other than your job, you will most likely take unconscious steps to quit or be fired so that the work component of your life can better fall into alignment with all the other facets of your existence.

I've had amazingly exciting jobs where I was compensated very well, but they fell short in almost every other area. Ultimately, it becomes time to move on. If that's where you are, start saving your money, make your six-month plan, and switch into something you love. I share my own personal story of how I left a longtime unfulfilling career in my first book, *Secrets of Meditation*—but I didn't save and I didn't make a plan. I simply leapt and assumed the net would appear . . . and it did . . . but it took 14 months. That's a lot of unnecessary pain and hardship for everyone else in my life to endure while I searched for my purpose. Take that as a cautionary tale.

You spend at least 2,000 hours a year (1/3 of each day), and more than 220 days out of 365 (2/3 of each year) doing "your job." That's a lot of time, energy, thoughts, and stress for something you aren't passionate about. When you love what you do, it's not work. One of my favorite pieces of poetry regarding purpose is by the Lebanese artist, poet, and author Khalil Gibran, found in his book, *The Prophet*:

> *When you work, you are a flute through whose heart the whispering of the hours turns to music . . . and what is it to work with love? It is to weave the cloth with threads drawn from your heart even as if your beloved were to wear that cloth. It is to build a house with affection, even as if your beloved were to dwell in that house. It is to sow seeds with tenderness and reap the harvest with joy, even as if your beloved were to eat the fruit. It is to charge all things you fashion with a breath of your own spirit.*

Am I Living My Dharma?

In many Eastern philosophies, there is a term for purpose in life: *dharma* (pronounced *"dar*-mah"). It comes from the ancient Indian language of Sanskrit and literally means "pillar"—*that which upholds*. There are hundreds of definitions for this word, which is now part of our general lexicon thanks to a TV show called *Dharma & Greg* that premiered in the late '90s. But going back a few thousand years, dharma referred to the fundamental laws that govern and sustain the universe. So in a sense when we look for purpose and meaning, we are seeking the pillar that will uphold our life—the foundation from which all actions flow. According to these ancient teachings, every being on the planet has a unique gift or a special talent that creates their path of purpose. This talent allows each of us to touch others or heal others or help others or serve others.

Dharma Evolution

Throughout your life, what you think is your purpose or your *dharma* may change, shift, transform, and evolve. Or maybe the vision of what you're trying to accomplish doesn't change, but the methodology does. For example, maybe you were very athletic as a child and that was a way for you to express your unique, God-given talent. But it's a few years later, and you're not so limber anymore. Maybe now you express that by writing about sports, broadcasting, or sharing your insights through coaching or teaching. Maybe you are helping others achieve that same level of fulfillment you once experienced. And so the same vision is there but manifested through a different methodology or channel.

When you're doing that one thing that you love to do, that feels so right that you sense it's what you are here to do, you'll know it. Time stands still. You're joyful and happy and deeply fulfilled. And when you're expressing that talent, the expression takes you into the oneness, the collective.

Take, for example, the famous basketball superstar Earvin "Magic" Johnson, who played for the Los Angeles Lakers for 13 years. After winning championships in high school and college, Magic was selected first overall in the 1979 NBA draft by the Lakers, winning the championship and the most valuable player award in his very first season. We could have said, "Oh, Magic has found his purpose." Over the next decade, he won four more championships with the Lakers—clearly "living his dharma," as the saying goes.

Then in 1991, Magic retired abruptly after announcing that he had contracted HIV. He returned to play in the 1992 Olympics as a member of the "Dream Team," where he won a gold medal, and then in the 1992 NBA All-Star Game he won the All-Star MVP Award for the second time (the first having been in 1990). After protests from his fellow players, he retired again for four years, but returned in 1996, at age 36, to play 32 games for the Lakers before retiring for the third and final time. We could have said, "Oh, Magic—his purpose has come and gone."

Next, though, he became an activist for the issues surrounding HIV and AIDS, and we could have said, "Oh, Magic, now you have truly found your purpose."

Then in the aftermath of the 1992 riots in South Central Los Angeles, where more than 3,700 buildings were destroyed and there was more than $1 billion in property damage, Magic led a redevelopment effort, investing his own money and marshaling the resources of his most influential friends and business partners to help rebuild South Central. We could have said, "Oh, Magic, *now* you've found your dharma."

In 2002, Magic was enshrined in the Basketball Hall of Fame; and in 2007, ESPN rated him the greatest NBA point guard of all time.

And then in 2012, along with the Guggenheim Group, Stan Kasten, and entertainment mogul Peter Guber, Magic led a successful $2-billion bid to buy the Los Angeles Dodgers. For 80 games every season, Dodger Stadium's 56,000 seats are filled with a rapt audience comprising at least 30,000 kids whom Magic gets to sponsor, mentor, teach, and inspire through school programs, team events, and special promotions. We could say, "Oh, Magic, it looks like you have finally found your purpose."

When you look at where you are right now in your life, ask yourself, *What is my purpose?* Look at your unique abilities, your special talents, and see how you can help others using them. Most likely *that's* your purpose for the time being. Remember, your dharma will continue to evolve throughout your life.

Maybe you thought you were living your purpose, but you lost your job, left it for some reason, or got derailed. And now you feel clueless, anxious, or hopeless. That's because . . . most likely . . . you are feeling like a victim, pointing at external forces when the solution rests within. So first you must heal your heart. You must meet those core Social Needs of love, belonging, attention, affection, appreciation, and acceptance, as well as your more internally established Esteem Needs of self-worth. Dharma can wait until you are feeling confident and more connected to your inner voice. Whether or not you are employed, you still have the tools to center yourself and meet your core needs of safety. The answer rarely rests in the outside world. You know the saying "Happiness is an inside job." Once you feel safe emotionally, which destressifying can help with, then your purpose in life will begin to unfold.

Purpose Through Vulnerability

Somewhere along the way, the more macho aspect of our society sent the message that displaying vulnerability is a sign of weakness or cowardice. This couldn't be further from the truth. The most recent research has revealed that vulnerable leaders are:

- Respected more
- Appreciated more for their humanness
- Followed more loyally
- More authentic
- More likely to be self-actualized
- Perceived as being more honest
- Liked more

The true ability they have is courage. The word *vulnerable* comes from the Latin *vulnerare,* which means "to wound." When we can get to that place where we realize we are impervious to the thoughts and words of others, we are beyond being wounded.

Once that fear is gone, we have a window where we can pretty much do anything because our true self is unveiled . . . the part of us that leads from within. We are not guided by what anyone else thinks we should say or do. We are guided by our heart. As the great African spiritual teacher and author Sobonfu Somé said, "If we are going to achieve our purpose in life, we must be willing to fall out of grace and accept its lessons. When we feel righteous about ourselves, or deny our brokenness, we are fighting against the higher states of grace that await us." In this vulnerable state, fear dissipates, anxiety drifts away, and stress is replaced by confidence. In that moment, courage flows (and *courage* comes from the Latin word *cor,* meaning "heart") . . . the courage to risk being wrong, looking like a fool, *be*ing human . . . or as Canadian author Oriah Mountain Dreamer writes in her poem "The Invitation":

> I want to know if you can
> disappoint another
> to be true to yourself;
> if you can bear the accusation of betrayal
> and not betray your own soul . . .

Pretty intense, right? The search for purpose and heart healing requires that you be true to your own self. To get to the place where you can ask the foolish question without fear of reprisal, admit that you don't know the answer rather than making something up, or tell someone how you really feel, you need to find comfort in your vulnerability. This takes courage. It's important to speak your mind, but it's even more important that you speak from your heart. Yet many of us closed that up a long time ago. When you are feeling unworthy, constricted, or less than, remember the words of the ancient Sufi poet Hafiz: "When all your desires are distilled, you will cast just two votes: to love more, and be happy."

Owning Your Impact

As I've mentioned before, a core element of destressifying is owning your impact—essentially, taking responsibility for where you are in your life. Many people point fingers at others or blame circumstances for where they currently are. This is disempowering, because then you have to wait for people or situations to change in order to actualize yourself.

There are some common blockages that afflict all of us as we try to own our impact and move toward self-actualization. If we can acknowledge and own them, then we can take an important first transformational step to mastering our purpose. Recognize any blockages on this list from your own life?

- We don't feel worthy of stepping into our power.

- We are not really present. We feel like we are stuck in the "old life," and that has our undivided attention.

- We haven't given ourselves permission to step into our new destressified life.

- We've grown complacent with our current pain and circumstances. We've convinced ourselves that familiar discomfort is better than potential unfamiliar comfort.

- We aren't taking time for any quietude during our day in the form of stillness and silence. We're not using any destressifying tools like *16seconds* or daily meditation to pattern interrupt us from our nonstop flow of activity.

- We are not aware . . . not paying attention . . . so we are missing the subtle clues, the innocent nuances that are guiding us to meet people, try new things, or discover our divine purpose.

- We blame external forces, usually when we are resisting, and the world around us reflects that resistance back at us. (Surrender rests at the core of dharma.)

- We've bought into the weakest vision we have of ourselves. We see ourselves as unworthy, limited, separate, and fragile. We reinforce this misconception by keeping score of past failures as proof that we aren't deserving.

We can turn it all around in an instant by taking these steps:

- Surrender to the process. Step back and give up control (just for a few moments). Take your hands off the wheel, slide into the passenger seat, and allow the universe to do the driving for a little bit.

- Commit to a daily practice of stillness and silence. In addition to proactively destressifying you, just a few minutes of a daily pattern interrupt will enhance your awareness skills.

- Give yourself permission to step into the unfamiliar . . . the unknown . . . and the undefined aspects of your life that have yet to unfold.

- Listen to your body. Listen to your heart. Listen to your inner guidance, and _trust_ (not second-guess).

- Pay attention and lean in the direction of fulfilling your needs.

- See the world around you as your friend, your partner in the process, something you are deeply connected to and interwoven with—not some harsh environment that doesn't support you.

An Open Heart = An Open Mind

An open heart leads to a greater openness in life. It creates the possibilities of unconditioned responses, leading to a heightened sense of intuition, creativity, and spontaneity. From this more open space, the most profound solutions arise. And this is the birthing spot of purpose. Only when constricted, defensive, desperate walls are removed does dharma effortlessly reveal itself.

Opening our heart is never easy, especially when there's been a heartbreak that has shut us down and we've built walls to protect the tenderness of our heart. But _right now_, you can take some easy nourishing steps to feel again, to love again, and to let love back in. This may sound corny to you, and if it does . . . then that's perfect, because your discomfort with the concept may be the constriction that's preventing you from meeting your needs of the heart as well as your Esteem Needs. And this is standing in the way of finding your purpose. But right here, right now, is the moment of truth.

Heart Breathing to Awaken Your Purpose

Heart breathing begins by following your breath in and out with your eyes closed. There are two techniques for this that will have powerful impact.

The Heart Sutra

The first technique was popularized by Drs. Deepak Chopra and David Simon, who aptly named it the *Heart Sutra*. *Sutra* is an ancient Pali word meaning "thread," and it is used because the exercise holds things together and connects them. Practicing the *Heart Sutra* connects the deepest aspects of our being to the most universal understandings of what the heart truly means. For this first time, keep your eyes open so that you can follow along.

After you've witnessed your breathing for a few moments, place your hand on your heart. Bring your awareness to your heart. Envision a green color in that area. And now, very slowly, silently repeat with your eyes closed: peace, harmony, laughter, love; peace, harmony, laughter, love; peace, harmony, laughter, love; peace, harmony, laughter, love . . . and keep silently repeating it. Then just sit for a few moments and let that settle in. When you notice that you've drifted away to thoughts, sounds, or physical sensations, very gently drift back to peace, harmony, laughter, and love. Let's continue for as long as feels comfortable.

How does that make you feel?

Mindful Flow Meditation

Now let's take it deeper with the second technique, a mindfulness version of heart breathing that I call the *Mindful Flow Meditation.* Let's try it together:

> *As you continue to breathe, now place your hand on the space where you feel the breath entering you. This doesn't have to be your heart; you may feel the breath entering you through the top of your head or your forehead, nose, mouth, throat, solar plexus, or belly . . . even your ears. So place your hand on that space right now and just connect to your breath through this physical location. Take a big, deep breath in through your nostrils to help you find that spot. As you breathe in, feel your breath enter you through your fingers, and then move your attention to the space you've identified. And gently, let the breath leave you through that same space.*

Let's do it for a bit with our eyes closed . . . I'll do it with you. Take your time.

> *As you breathe, feel free to move your hand more closely to the exact space where that wisp of breath is coming into you. And if you suddenly feel that the location has changed, move your hand there. Let's stay in this space and practice this breathing technique for a few minutes. You may even want to lie down for this mini-meditation. Take it slow and easy.*

Okay . . . I'm guessing you're back now.

How does that feel? Do you feel any different? This deeper form of heart breathing is one of the most powerful destressifying techniques that I teach. Even though your hand may not actually be resting on your heart, this technique has powerful heart-opening results. When you're feeling a bit harsh or impatient or judgmental or angry . . . or even if you are struggling to fall asleep, just slip into *Mindful Flow Meditation.* You can do this for a few minutes *anytime* you are feeling stressed, anxious, or overwhelmed. You can practice it as a daily meditation ritual or as an in-the-moment stress buster.

The clarity this practice brings and the sense of calm it evokes will help you make better decisions about life, love, and purpose. Cultivating this ritual as part of your morning meditation will truly transform you. You'll flow throughout the day (or evening) with guaranteed peace of mind. When you open your eyes at the end of the meditation, you will be in a less defensive, less conditioned, less constricted space in terms of unfolding to your purpose. As you proceed, you will notice icebergs of stress melting away.

Awaken Your Courage

In my dharma workshops, I teach many different methods of personal empowerment, emotional release, conscious choice making, and rejuvenation to peel away the layers of constriction and gain clarity. I have found these seven steps to awakening your courage to be an effective starting point.

1. First give yourself **permission** to begin the process. You don't have to give in or forgive someone (or even yourself). Simply granting yourself permission to go to your heart is a *huge step*.

2. **Accept** that you are entitled to receive unconditional love. You are so worthy, so deserving to receive the love of the divine creator . . . the love of the universe . . . the love of others . . . the love of your self. Can you go there and accept that you are worthy? If this feels too mushy for you, feel free to take a baby step.

3. **Acknowledge** that *here you are* in this precious, sacred moment, and whatever broke your heart or continues to make it ache has brought you to this moment where you can love again . . . be loved . . . and feel love again.

4. **Appreciate** your environment. Having gratitude for the world around you allows you to take your attention off your "Oh, poor me" mind-set and inspires you to ask instead, "How can I serve others?"

5. Have **compassion**. This is not just being sympathetic to someone's plight. Compassion is having empathy for another *combined with* rooting for their pain and suffering to end. Having self-compassion (yes, rooting for yourself) and being willing to **forgive** yourself for any big or little sins you've been beating yourself up over will allow you to step through the current pain that may be holding you back.

6. **Share love** with others . . . flow love into the world with your thoughts and words . . . live with a mind-set of knowing that you are neither above nor below anyone else. Leading with love at home and work offers you an opportunity to *be the change* with everyone you know with very little risk to your tenderness.

7. And lastly, **celebrate!** Celebrate your little wins, your small successes. And congratulate yourself for leaning in the direction of *love*.

Once we can be a bit calmer, and a bit more open, an internal dialogue begins deep within. Our rigid limiting beliefs become a little more flexible; we become more accepting and tolerant. Our buttons get pushed a bit less . . . and a powerful destressifying shift occurs as we rewire our DNA and become less reactive. Naturally, we start to feel a greater understanding of our purpose. We see more possibilities simply by getting more connected to our heart.

Find Your Voice

There are many paths to your dharma and certainly many paths to finding your voice in a given moment. So many of us live lives of quiet desperation—deferring our dreams or using the excuses of time, money, or other people for why we aren't expressing our unique abilities and distinctive talents out into the world. If you have been biting your tongue or walking on eggshells in a relationship, then you probably have been self-imposing an unnecessary, masochistic stress burden on yourself. To cut through the swirl, help you awaken your courage, and more effectively find your voice, here are seven powerful steps. Use one, all, or any combination of the seven to spark your voice.

1. **Accept that you have a unique and special voice** that is pregnant with possibilities. As the world lies before you, with each breath give permission to the four unique parts of your being—your mind, body, heart, and spirit—to be their best. By recognizing these magnificent gifts, you will start to feel a glimmer of a shift. Take a look at how they can be applied to your life right now.

2. **Regularly spend time in stillness and silence.** Begin to cultivate a daily practice of stillness and silence. Consider introducing the *16seconds* pattern interrupt right after you wake up; again at 10 A.M., 2 P.M., 4 P.M., and 6 P.M.; and then again right before you go to sleep. These six calming moments that you give yourself each day can have a profound effect, and they build on each other. They will help quiet the fluctuations of your mind and ease some of the emotional turbulence in your life. From that stillness, more answers will come.

An effective way of shifting the energy at work as you move from conversation to conversation, meeting room to meeting room, and office to office is called ***doorknob breathing,*** and it's based on *16seconds.* Every time you enter a room, you can shift your energy, releasing where you were and stepping into a new space. Here's how it works:

As you grip the doorknob—breathe in.
As you turn the handle—hold your breath.
As you open the door—exhale.
As you step in and close the door behind you—hold the breath out.
Your next full breath will bring new energy into the room as

you enter. And more important, you won't be bringing in the thoughts, conversations, or energy that you had only seconds before.

I practice doorknob breathing as I walk out my front door, as I get into my car, and even when I find myself reaching for the refrigerator handle at midnight (it doesn't turn, but you get the point). If there's no doorknob or the door is open, I walk right in; but I've conditioned myself now to practice doorknob breathing as soon as I see a doorknob or door handle, and it has allowed me to always bring fresh energy into a new moment.

3. **Cultivate your ability to listen.** destressifying leads to heightened awareness. What angers you? What makes you cry? What gives you hope? What gets you passionate? What gets your motor running? Listen to your emotions throughout the day and feel what moves you.

4. **Tap into your passion overlap!** Bubbling below your surface are your own personal desires to live a life filled with passion. It can express itself in many ways; but if we take the bold step to *love, live, learn, and contribute* with passion, we will add value to every endeavor we attempt. So where's your voice? Identify the overlap in your life between those desires, and you'll find the seed of your voice!

5. **Get really objective.** We've spent a fair amount of time on the difference between observations and interpretations, and most likely you are already using the tools and feeling the difference. Here's an interesting exercise that is essentially seeing yourself from another perspective:

Take out your journal or a piece of paper and write about yourself in the third person. View yourself as you would a character in a book. Think about who this person is and what *they* are passionate about. Then write about what inspires that person, what their current state of dharma is, and how they will own their impact. Don't hold back—write with passion. When you've been writing for a bit, ask yourself how it feels to express these traits and characteristics (which, of course, are qualities in yourself that you'd like to awaken). See where your heart leads you . . . and go there!

6. **Identify your blockages.** Close your eyes, sit in stillness and silence for a few minutes, place your hand on your heart or your throat, and ask, *Where am I holding back? In what instances am I biting my tongue? Where could I speak up a bit more? Where could I step into the unknown with a little more power? If I knew I could not fail . . . what would be my baby step?* Taking this step and asking these questions from your heart rather than your intellect will drill more deeply into the truth of the matter.

7. **Check your front row.** Identify your biggest cheerleader (a person you know and trust), and practice using your voice with this person, knowing that their response will be compassionate feedback as opposed to ridicule. If someone really believed in you . . . saw your strengths . . . validated your gift . . . and could support your dream . . . then what? Listen to your heart and find a teacher, a coach, a mentor, a confirmer, someone in your front row to help you practice speaking your truth. *Often we believe that time or money are the impediments to fulfilling our dreams or finding our voice,* but in reality we fear that we will not live up to our vision, or even worse—*that we will.* It can scare us into self-sabotage. So take baby steps. Start where you are and give yourself permission to speak from your heart. Remember, all the answers to your life rest within.

Discover Your Dharma

You've probably had a few different jobs in your life, or different roles or incarnations of your current position. Ideally, you love what you do. Maybe you genuinely like the people you work with, or you have a true passion for some aspect of the work. Or maybe you aren't really sure. So how do you figure out what's your dharma? How can you tell if you are in your dharma? How can you find out what your purpose really is?

Start by asking these five simple questions:

1. What are my unique abilities and my distinctive talents?

2. What do I love to do? What am I passionate about?

3. What is it that while I'm doing it, time stands still?

4. The last time I felt joyful, deeply fulfilled, and in the zone . . . what was I doing?

5. How can I help others by using what I'm good at?

The answers that unfold for you are the starting point in discovering your true purpose in life. Ask yourself these questions throughout the course of the day—not to drive yourself crazy, but to invoke the process. Identify your unique abilities. Pinpoint one thing you are passionate about. What do you love to do? What cause are you zealous about? When you realized you were working for three hours and it felt like ten minutes—*and* it was rewarding—what were you doing? What puts you in that zone?

When you break it down into those basic components, it's a lot more digestible and easier to move forward. And your dharma today doesn't have to be your job. The starting point could be a hobby or something you simply love to do. Ask the questions . . . let life unfold the answers for you.

Finding Purpose in Service

As you begin to gain clarity on what it is you love to do, the final question to ask yourself is, *How can I help others using my unique abilities and my distinctive talents?* Then you can truly put your attention on the concept of *How can I serve?* rather than

What's in it for me? The world opens up. When you look specifically for how you can get something out of this, you narrow the possibilities. So often, true self-realization requires a little support from the outside world.

When you are destressified and flowing more easily through life, situations open up for you and opportunities present themselves that were outside your original vision. This expansion occurs naturally through destressifying. This doesn't mean that you can't want something, set your sights on it, and accomplish it. We can all build on our achievements; our success is continually reinforced through the process of understanding needs, meeting them, and moving forward.

But what it truly means is that when we are in pure service, people, situations, and circumstances seem to support us more unconditionally. Our needs and all the needs around us become aligned. The momentum of life allows us to serve, allows us to help, allows us to heal others, and gives us reinforcement and encouragement to keep growing and reach our targets (even if they change as we progress through this evolution).

Dharma does not have to be your job, although there are many people who search for the thing that's going to pay them to use their unique abilities and distinctive talents. Instead, start off by looking at your hobby, something you just love to do, a part-time job, or something you do after hours or on the weekend. And maybe that brings the deeper fulfillment into your life. If you can ultimately merge it with making a living, providing for yourself and your family or for others, then that's beautiful, but that shouldn't be the driving force.

When you have a larger purpose in life—whether it's starting your own business, supporting a cause, raising successful children, or making a difference at work—looking at life through this lens of purpose gives you a filter that helps you decide what's important and what's not. Your true definition of success will become clear.

Your Noble Purpose

A transformational conversation in the banking community was introduced in 2014 when Merrill Lynch CEO John Thiel presented the concept of Noble Purpose to his 13,000-plus financial advisors. It came at an interesting time, considering Merrill's client assets had just reached an industry-leading $2 trillion, profitability was soaring, and this 100-year-old enterprise was contributing more than a third of the net income that its parent company, Bank of America, was reporting. So at the peak of their game, this forward-thinking visionary began a campaign, asking every Merrill Lynch employee, "Why do you do what you do?," encouraging them to explore their noble purpose rather than just focusing on the more traditional goals of other wealth managers in the industry. It was a radical departure from the old line, old school Wall Street mantra of "Show me the money."

In an interview with the *Wall Street Journal*, Thiel said, "I think we overanalyze the process and the techniques and skills, and forget we're all human beings and that 'successful' doesn't necessarily mean money." Several hard-liners within the financial community missed the brilliance of the moment, but the majority of Merrill Lynch financial advisors embraced the new approach, which coincided with an industry-wide shift in focus from a transactional mind-set to a more holistic planning approach based on needs. Instead of simply making purchases and sales for clients while trying to outperform the financial markets, Thiel encouraged his advisors to focus on the bigger picture: helping clients formulate and reach long-term financial goals through a needs-based approach. He must have been channeling Maslow!

Thiel's goal was to tease out the passion of his "thundering herd" in an industry that has become highly transactional and bottom-line focused. He fully comprehends the concept of dharma. I reached out to him and asked him about his vision. He said, "If our advisors are happier and healthier and more aware of their inner motivations, they will perform better in their jobs. If they can find the balance between business and family life, and of defining success to include being a good parent and spouse, they will take better care of their clients." This takes us full circle back to the importance and the reality of living a purpose-driven life. Thiel's visionary message is a game changer in the financial world, where an exclusive focus on quarterly results and monthly commissions has been the standard for a century. Clearly, he is in his dharma.

destressified and Living His Noble Purpose

When the core components of destressifying come together in a lifestyle, the results are magnificent. One of my most engaged destressifying students is Jack Hart, a 16-year veteran of the San Francisco Police Department, an attorney with the department's legal division, and a senior trainer on the Blue Courage team. As a California POST (Peace Officer Standards and Training) certified instructor, he teaches search and seizure in officers' and sergeants' mandated continuing professional training classes, and he has recently completed his 30th SFPD recruit class instruction on search and seizure, laws of arrest, constitutional law, and criminal statutes.

Jack is a brilliant police officer dedicated to service, justice, and fundamental fairness. His record speaks for itself. And most cops are excellently trained on how to use their weapons, drive during a chase, kick in a door, and take down a "perp." As a sergeant, Jack led a street-crimes (gangs and guns) plainclothes enforcement detail in the Bayview SF police district, and as a patrol lieutenant, he was the officer in charge of SFPD's Candlestick Park detail, which included the management of more than 100 officers at all San Francisco 49ers home games. His guiding principle is to keep San Francisco safe for its residents—every moment navigating that fine line of stress, hypervigilance, and guardianship.

Jack meditates every day, practices *16seconds* and *Reaching for SODA*, works on meeting his needs and heightening his emotional intelligence, and lives in service to others. He has learned to fuel himself with nourishing behaviors and let go of the emotional turbulence that does not serve him or others in his life. He not only patrols the streets of San Francisco but is a master facilitator of the *Blue Courage Nobility of Policing* curriculum, through which he teaches trainees and fellow officers at the San Francisco Police Academy how to integrate these destressifying tools into their lives *in addition to* their core policing skills. His life is on the line every day; and yet, because of his commitment to destressifying, he lives a whole, actualized existence while living his purpose.

destressifying at Work

Do you like your job? Are you getting the attention, appreciation, and acceptance you seek? Are your core values aligned with the organization you work for? Do you like working with your fellow employees? Does this work uplift you? Are you serving others?

According to the Energy Project, which analyzed the broad spectrum of personal engagement that workers have, 70 percent of all workers fall into the categories of either disengaged or actively disengaged. Their newest research reveals that workers today are exhausted, emotionally depleted, unfocused, and lacking purpose. It is no surprise they are disengaged considering these numbers:

- 59 percent don't regularly get at least seven to eight hours of sleep and/or often wake up feeling tired.

- 69 percent have difficulty focusing on one thing at a time and are easily distracted during the day, especially by e-mail.

- 58 percent report that there are significant gaps between what they say is important in their life and how they actually live.

Take your job-fulfillment pulse right now: Do you often find yourself watching the clock at work, waiting for the day to end? Do you find yourself feeling anxious on Monday morning, dreading having to show up for another week of work? Do you often wish you were someplace else? Do you feel disconnected from your dharma? Does more than 50 percent of your total stress come from your work? Do you feel you are underpaid? Overworked? Do you have issues with the work, your company, or the values they espouse?

If you answered "yes" once, there's still hope; twice, it's time to find a more rewarding vocation; three times—what are you still doing there? Get out now. If you dread your job, find yourself counting the seconds till you leave, and are totally stressed out, you are damaging yourself unnecessarily.

Spending Time in the destressified Zone

Think about the times in your life when you've experienced being in the zone: You lose track of time, you feel inspired, and life seems to flow easily. Is it when you're doing specific activities such as writing a presentation, motivating people, solving problems, or decorating a space? Or throughout the day, do you find certain behaviors tend to feed you emotionally, such as engaging in conversation, feeling part of something, laughing with friends, or spending time alone? If you can work these nourishing behaviors into your current role, you'll experience deeper fulfillment at work.

"No Problem" vs. "My Pleasure"

Think about ways that your current job helps people or serves others. We have all experienced those in the realm of customer service who clearly hate their jobs and don't want to be there: food servers, flight attendants, front-desk people, cashiers, and sales clerks who act as if we are intrusions in their day. You know the classic line: "If we could just get rid of all these annoying customers, our lives would be so much easier!" Contrast this type of employee with workers who take time to smile, talk to us, go the extra mile to accommodate us, ask about our day, and make the experience special.

We've all had an encounter where upon asking the customer-service person a question, we were met with either, "No problem!" or "My pleasure." They are polar opposites: "No problem" implies that your request will not interfere with their other chores—essentially, "I'll get to it." "My pleasure" means that you—the customer—have become the priority, and the person serving you is going to enjoy their job while they serve your needs.

When you are working, do you find yourself more in a *My pleasure* or a *No problem* mind-set? That should tell you a lot about whether you are in your dharma.

Three Steps to Take at Work

Think of all the needs that might not be met regarding opportunities to use your skills and abilities, and the areas of job security, compensation, communication, and the relationship between you and your boss. That's why fulfilling work that allows you to serve while you use your unique abilities and your distinctive talents has a powerful destressifying impact. How does your job allow you to touch people's lives? Jobs that help others, heal others, serve others, or make the world a better place create a sense of deeper satisfaction by their very nature, and therefore have the potential to be destressified jobs.

Here are three powerful steps you can take every day to keep you destressified at work:

1. **Gain clarity on expectations.** Stress is easily dissipated through clarity. And if you can have clarity around what all your co-workers expect from you, you will have less stress. Using conscious

communication, ask them. This doesn't mean you have to fulfill everyone's needs regarding your behavior, but at least you will know what the expectations are so that you can either meet or exceed them. This also opens up the dialogue for you to express your needs and expectations to everyone else.

2. **Look at your job through the lens of dharma.** Seek meaning and purpose in every thought, word, and action. Think big picture and look at every task with the thought, *How can I use my unique abilities to help, heal, and serve others?*

3. **Make sure you meet your need of appreciation.** Being recognized for your contribution and what you bring to the table is core to destressifying at work. You don't want to become addicted to constant feedback, but a little recognition goes a long way. Start by recognizing the contributions of everyone around you. The ripple effect will flow back to you.

Burnout

Are you heading for burnout? Starting to feel crispy? In the 1970s, psychologist Herbert Freudenberger coined the term *burnout* as it applies to work, and wrote the book *Burnout: The High Cost of High Achievement.* Very quickly, this term, which he defined as "the extinction of motivation or incentive, especially where one's devotion to a cause or relationship fails to produce the desired results," became part of the language of stress and wove itself into our social lexicon.

Even though it's not a disease or an acknowledged clinical disorder, burnout is distinctly real. It's more pervasive than chronic stress, depression, and diagnosed mood disorders, and it shares many of their symptoms. The good news is that it's quickly identifiable and easily solvable through destressifying! Take your burnout pulse now.

The Burnout Quiz

- Do you feel like you want to give up? Is the glass half empty? Not seeing any silver linings?

- Are you feeling run-down? Is it a chore to get out of bed in the morning and face the day?

- Are you feeling overwhelmed? Is your emotional intelligence at a low? Are you oversensitive, not listening to others, or unaware of nuances in others' emotions and your own?

- Are you experiencing health symptoms of chronic stress, such as more frequent colds, aches, pains, or flu-like symptoms? Are you sensing that your immunity is down? Suffering from back issues? Feeling unsupported?

- Are you struggling with your core relationships at work and home?

- Are you phoning it in at work? Just showing up and going through the motions of whatever you are attending?

- When you think about the future, do you imagine a life in a different place, with a different job, surrounded by different people?

There are 16 possible yes-or-no answers. If you have more than ten yeses, most likely you are burned out. But *do not despair*— destressifying will cure you!

Stress at Work: Heading to Burnout

More than 40 years after the word *burnout* became part of our vocabulary, we still use it to describe any kind of *long-term exhaustion leading to diminished interest* in a relationship, a physical location, or—most commonly—our work. Many factors contribute to burnout. And not meeting our needs, expectations, desires, and dreams on a daily and consistent basis will burn anybody out. Now that you understand the concept of destressifying, burnout is obviously a form of chronic stress.

No matter where you find yourself in any company or organization and regardless of what your job is—from CEO to assistant, from entrepreneur to right-hand man or woman behind the scenes—there are certain distinct job-related features (which also apply to your life at home) that are stress inducing and will ultimately lead you to burn out.

Beyond your answers to the Burnout Quiz, the following symptoms are signs that you are heading to burnout or at least a job change:

- **Never-ending work:** One day rolls into the next with no break in the action.

- **Random surges in the intensity:** It doesn't feel like you are building toward something.

- **No vacation time:** Everyone needs to take a week or a few days off every few months.

- **Lack of alignment:** Your core values aren't the same as your organization.

- **No group, departmental, or team support:** You're all alone—it's all on you.

- **Feeling micromanaged:** You aren't told the big picture, just the task at hand.

- **Feeling underpaid and undervalued:** You're not receiving the attention, appreciation, or acceptance you need.

- **Flailing around looking for leadership:** There's a lack of clarity in the vision.

- **Pulling in a different direction from your co-workers:** You feel at cross-purposes.

- **Porous rules of engagement:** No one is really sure how to interact.

- **Fearful of making a mistake:** You're working under the threat of spank rather than the spark of inspiration.

If you are living or working under these circumstances, you need to make a shift *now!* So right now, let's take a powerful step to slow you down, destressify, and gain some clarity. I refer to this practice as the *destressifying Body Scan.* Get comfortable . . . and let's do it together.

destressifying Body Scan

As you read these words, feel the air flow in and out of you. Feel your lungs stretch and relax. Feel your chest rise and fall. Now close your mouth, and gently breathe in and out solely through your nose. Feel your belly fill as you inhale. Feel it release as you exhale. Again, don't consciously do anything to alter your breath other than closing your mouth and breathing both in and out through your nose. Just observe your breath for about a minute . . . simply be aware that you breathe in, hold it in for a moment or two, exhale for a moment or two, and hold that out for a moment or two before you inhale again.

As you breathe, silently notice: I'm breathing in, I'm holding the breath, I'm breathing out, I'm holding the breath. Maintain this awareness for the next few minutes. I'll wait right here . . .

Now become aware of your physical body . . . how does it feel? Are you hot or cold? Relaxed or tense? Do parts of your body hurt, and are there other parts you don't even feel right now? Notice that as your awareness drifts over different parts of your body, you become more aware of your physiology. Let's make our calves tingle right now. Feel the tips of your nostrils without touching them. Become aware of your lips. Isn't it funny how our awareness truly does dictate our experiences?

Keep breathing . . .

Look at your hands right now. Look at your palms. Rest them on your thighs, and feel the sensation in your thighs suddenly come to life. Out of sight, out of mind . . . but within sight, within mind. Now bring your attention to the blood flowing into your hands. Keep your focus on your palms. Feel the blood move into your palms. Feel them begin to get warm in the center. Keep focusing. Keep breathing.

Where attention flows, energy goes. Do you see how as soon as you become aware of something, your mind starts to interpret your experience? Do you notice how your mind instantly wants to define it, label it, categorize it, or assign it meaning? Do you see how your awareness is connected to your body as well?

Now move your awareness beyond your hands and down to your feet. Start on your right side. Flex your right foot. Wiggle it a bit. Roll your ankle around for a few moments. Now relax your foot. Feel each toe as you move your attention from one toe to the next, and then from one side of your foot to the other.

Feel that flow of attention move from your toes down the sole of your foot into your heel. Then move your attention slowly up the back of your calf until you arrive in your mind's eye at your knee. Now, gently breathing in and out and using only your mind, massage your kneecap in a circular motion and move around to the back of your knee. Next, move up your right hamstring and then energetically feel the front of your thigh without touching it. Let a relaxing sensation radiate from the top of your thigh. Slowly breathe in as you keep the attention on your thigh. Feel it.

Close your eyes for a few moments and gently breathe.

Open them and just feel. Feel all the sensations and interpretations you are experiencing in your right leg.

Now bring your awareness to your left foot. Flex it. Wiggle it a bit. Roll your ankle around for a few moments. Relax your left foot, and feel each toe as you move your attention from one toe to the next, and then from one side of your foot to the other. Feel that flow of attention move from your toes down the sole of your left foot into your heel. Then feel it slowly move up the back of your calf until you arrive in your mind's eye at your knee.

Gently breathing in and out and using only your mind, massage your kneecap in a circular motion and move around to the back of your knee. Next, move your awareness up your left hamstring, and then energetically feel the front of your thigh without touching it. Let a relaxing sensation radiate from the top of your thigh. Slowly breathe in as you keep the attention on your left thigh. Feel it. Close your eyes for a few moments and gently breathe.

Open your eyes and feel all the sensations and interpretations you are experiencing in your left leg.

Now let's bring our awareness to both feet. Wiggle them. Roll both ankles around a bit. Relax your feet and let them melt into the floor. Feel each toe on both feet as you move your attention from one toe to the next, and then from one side of your foot to the other. Feel that flow of attention move down the soles of your feet into your heels. Remember to keep breathing as you drift to each part of your body. Then feel your attention slowly move up the back of your calves until you arrive in your mind's eye at your knees. Now, gently breathing in and out and using only your mind's eye, massage your kneecaps in a circular motion and move around to the back of your knees. Next, slowly move your awareness up your hamstrings, and then energetically feel the front of your thighs without touching them. Let a relaxing sensation radiate from the tops of your thighs. Slowly breathe in as you keep the attention on your thighs. Feel the energy in your thighs. Sit there for a few moments and gently breathe. Feel it.

Now move your attention to your pelvis. Sit with that feeling for a moment or two; simply observe it as you consciously move all your awareness to your pelvis. Feel the blood flow in and out of your pelvic region. Feel any discomfort you have get lighter as you witness the area from the tops of your thighs to your belly button becoming more vital and warmer from the attention you place on your pelvis. Sit with this sensation for a few moments with your eyes closed.

And then drift your awareness up into your belly. Feel the blood flow into your belly. Do you see how subtly shifting your awareness has actually brought blood flow and other physiological changes to these areas? Feel the blood flow against gravity from your pelvis up into your belly.

Simply awakening the lower half of your body with your mind has brought all these body parts into your awareness. Moments ago your attention was on reading. Where attention flows, energy goes. Pretty interesting, isn't it?

Now with your breath, see if you can gently breathe and move your awareness from your belly up your torso to your heart. Feel the power center of your physical body—your heart—become more open and more full. Notice how right now you are able to take a deeper breath than you could before. Your rib cage can expand more with every inhale. Once you truly feel full in this region of your body, breathe in again; and as you exhale, move your attention even higher up your chest. Breathe in and pull your energy from below your heart to the area around your heart; feel the sensation in your chest. Sit with that for a few moments. Feel your heart fill with love. With gratitude. With compassion. With forgiveness. With joy. Notice as you do this . . . a smile unfolds on your face.

Now push it up even farther as you inhale. At this moment, you are experiencing present-moment awareness. As your attention goes, there you are in that moment. Not thinking about the past . . . not thinking about the future. Totally present. Totally here. Right now.

Lift your eyes from the page after you've read these directions. Look around, and take in all your eyes observe. Don't judge; just witness . . . like a video camera simply absorbing all it sees in total witness mode. Take in the colors; see the depth and shade of everything around you. The shapes . . . the distances between objects, their shadows, how the light is falling, their denseness. Just stay with this for a minute or two as you receive all these waves and particles of light that you are turning into meaning.

What do you hear in this moment? Are there noises around you? Music? Sounds of nature? Sounds of a busy world? Any internal noises, like your stomach rumbling? Or the sound of your breathing?

Remember to keep breathing through your nose as your awareness heightens. Are you aware of any aromas? What is the smell of your surroundings? Keep breathing and bring your awareness to some part of your body that feels tight or heavy or constricted. It might be your heart, belly, temples, back, legs, arms, throat, or any other area. Don't do anything other than drift your awareness to that place and ask yourself how it feels. Now, with your awareness on that place, breathe in deeply to the count of three. And slowly exhale, bringing even more attention to this area.

Now slowly breathe in and out three times with your eyes closed. I'll wait.

How did the experience change with your eyes closed? Did you feel a difference? Did you become aware of your thoughts? Were you thinking *more* or *less*? Did you visualize your surroundings on the backs of your eyelids? Did your other senses become more aware? Did you hear better? Relax more? Did it seem comfortable or unfamiliar in any way?

And what does the area of your body you focused on feel like now? Is it a bit lighter, looser, more open? As you begin to answer this question, your mind is drifting into the past. But the present-moment awareness you experienced only moments ago is now part of you here . . . now . . . in *this* present moment. You can use this powerful tool at home, at work, and in any kind of situation, whether you are sitting, standing, or lying down. The *destressifying Body Scan* actually slows your body and entrains your mind to follow it into a place of calm, relaxation, and peace.

This whole exercise took less than five minutes. Imagine if you took just five minutes each day *right in the middle of your work process* to nourish yourself, heighten your awareness, and release any tension you've stored up while talking on the phone, sitting at your keyboard, crafting a strategy, or immersing in a project.

• • •

Discovering your purpose is an ongoing journey. When you live your life using your unique abilities and your distinctive talents in the service of others, you feel in flow. Through this process of *mastering your purpose,* or at least beginning to own your impact, you will struggle less when you ask the question, "Why am I here?"

Mark Twain is quoted as saying, "The two most important days in your life are the day you are born and the day you find out why." We can destressify through discovering our purpose, and we can experience powerful gratification simply by exploring meaning in our life and awakening our dharma. Once we have gotten comfortable with pursuing our divine purpose, many other stressors simply drift away. And if stress is not in our awareness, then neither our body nor our mind is interpreting it—in a good or bad way. When we are immersed in purposeful activity, stress is invisible.

And that is the height of destressifying.

• • • • •

PART III

Living a destressifying Life and Keeping It Real

Welcome to Part III. If you've made it this far, you definitely get it. As you read these words, every cell in your body is destressifying. Bravo! You've absorbed and integrated the core teachings; you've practiced more than 15 different techniques to bring you into the present moment; and you've made a few quantum leaps into the best version of yourself. You've immersed into the five principles of mastery: mastering your awareness, needs, emotions, communication, and purpose. And beyond that cellular immersion comes a real-life journey like no other, filled with clarity, growth, connection, success, contentment, joy, deep satisfaction, and self-actualization. The key is to simply keep moving forward *as you journey*—the results take care of themselves.

You recognize that the starting point for greater happiness and the platform for self-actualization is mastering your awareness. Through daily use of the destressifying tools and locking in a daily meditation practice, you will continue to feel calmer throughout your routine activities, experience more restful sleep, temper your conditioned emotional responses, make better choices, and truly experience peace of mind—that feeling you experience as you rest your head on the pillow right before you go to sleep *where you know inside* that all is well.

You realize that to truly experience satisfaction and fulfillment in life, we all have to meet our needs. You understand all the categories of needs, and you now have an important tool to help you look at your entire life: the lens of the Five Realms. Using this tool on a regular basis can help you meet your core needs and determine what you can let go of and what you can invite into your life to assist and accelerate your journey to destressifying.

You also have a deeper understanding of your emotions, your emotional intelligence, and the value of emotional awareness. You have learned specific techniques to heighten your understanding of your own and others' emotions and to shift from your conditioned reactions to more purposeful, unconditioned responses.

By mastering conscious communication, you can support getting your needs met on a more consistent basis with the help of others. You will also live a life of deeper fulfillment and less emotional charge as you create less turbulence and disappointment with your words, hold fewer grievances, and ask for what you truly need rather than demand it or keep your needs bottled up.

Living a purpose-driven life allows you to accurately see the big picture, to realize what is truly important, to find meaning in all the little moments, to cultivate gratitude, to appreciate and celebrate your unique abilities, and to experience the deep fulfillment that comes with helping, healing, and serving others using your special talents.

Staying Connected

I really don't want our connection to end here, so I've created a dedicated destressifying section on davidji.com where we can keep the practice alive in real time. If we stay connected, your destressifying will accelerate. This dedicated treasure trove of exclusive destressifying online resources includes how-to videos for each of the Five Masteries, all the destressifying meditations we've practiced in a guided audio form for you to stream for free or download to your device, the most recent research on stress, and additional bonus chapters for all those who have journeyed this far!

We've gotten to know each other pretty well over these pages. Let's keep our connection alive, and let's keep destressifying together. Feel free to visit davidji.com/destressifying whenever the moment moves you. But before you go there, let's dive into some core real-world practices to keep the teachings flowing.

destressifying Day-to-Day

Living the Five Masteries alone will deliver you to a new place in your life. Yet sometimes on our journey to destressifying, we all benefit from ongoing support—a few quick steps, a meaningful sound bite or directive, a new research study, a tip on how to deal with a specific situation, or a nourishing behavior to help keep us on track. You already have a strong footing and you know all the techniques; but because stress is so personal, we can often benefit from daily, consistent, customized guidance to help us destressify when the moment strikes. I've crafted Part III to help you navigate life more effectively and bring you back to clarity when you see the first signs of the tsunami of stress coming over the horizon.

• • • • •

destressifying Through Lifestyle Choices

*"I do not weep at the world—I am
too busy sharpening my oyster knife."*

— ZORA NEALE HURSTON

As we work longer hours, become more engaged in social events, take care of all the members of our family, meet all our obligations, get busier and busier, and try to become self-actualized, the stress of life can be overwhelming. One of the core aspects of destressifying is simplifying. Just as we de-clutter our closets, de-cluttering our life brings a sense of order or structure, which is very relaxing for a lot of people. If you have a room in your house that's out of control, if your car has cereal embedded in the backseat, or if your garage is filled with boxes from your last move, these can be tip-offs that you are at risk for massive chronic stress. Paring down, cleaning house, and living a "less is more" lifestyle is massively destressifying. In an innocent way, it fulfills unmet

Safety Needs by inserting order and structure into the chaos to which you've grown accustomed.

We've learned that there are so many triggers in our life that exacerbate the challenge of nonstop stress. Here are 18 daily lifestyle choices you can make to shift quickly back onto the path of destressifying. Experience teaches that if you try too many new techniques at once, you're likely to fail, stop trying, and slip back into the clutches of stress. So be smart: Select one—only one!—and own it until it flows effortlessly through you. Then move on to the next technique that resonates with you.

1. **Simplify:** Look at all the moving parts in your life. Find items, behaviors, and relationships that distract you more than nourish you and prune your life down. Don't do it all at once—that will create more stress. Take five minutes every morning or evening, identify something that's taking up space in your life, and release it. Six years ago, after I realized that I was holding on to many material things that added little or no value to my life—old birthday cards, trinkets that no longer had meaning, printed-out e-mails, clothes that no longer fit—I committed to a program of releasing one thing every day and cleaning my closet as the seasons changed. These rituals have become liberating as I feel lighter; comforting as order returns; and even rewarding as my unworn older clothes get gifted to Goodwill. In the process, I have become less attached to many of my material possessions, and that has freed up some space in my mind.

2. **Get comfortable with *no*:** Saying yes to life opens you up to more opportunities, expanded horizons, and more abundance in every area of your life. But if you live every moment with an open-door policy, you'll quickly feel the stress of this abundance. Don't shift your abundance consciousness—instead pick one day a week where you say no to everything. Create more definite boundaries and un-commit yourself from overreaching obligations where your needs probably won't be met and most likely you will not meet someone else's needs either.

3. **Evolve a relationship:** Every month, using the Five Realms of My Life Personal Worksheet and your deep knowledge of your needs and the Five Realms, commit to shift, repair, or end a relationship that doesn't serve you in its current state. The process may take you a few weeks, but once the relationship is actually meeting your needs, the benefits will be exponential as someone who once absorbed much of your thoughts no longer takes center stage in your mind or pushes your buttons.

4. **Start saving and lessen your debt:** Make the commitment to get out of debt. Owing money, especially to a credit-card company, can be one of the most stressful aspects of your life. If you have a constricted relationship with money, reach out to master of abundance T. Harv Eker, author of *Secrets of the Millionaire Mind*, who has inspired hundreds of thousands around the world to be their best versions of themselves financially. You can also find very helpful debt-management guidance from any of Suze Orman's or Dave Ramsey's numerous books. And if you are looking to manage your wealth at a higher level, don't try to do it yourself. Focus on your skills that made the money to begin with, and reach out to a wealth-management firm with integrity, a long-term goals-based orientation, and solid core values that align with yours. This is not meant as investment advice—this is pure destressifying. Make the commitment today to shift into abundance consciousness.

5. **Meditate:** Start slowly and build your daily meditation practice into the foundation of your day. It will quickly evolve into a cornerstone of your life. Once you start to feel the positive ripples from this painless destressifying practice, your life will blossom and bloom. This is a core mastery of destressifying, so as I strongly encouraged in Chapter 5, aim to meditate for at least a few minutes every day upon waking and before bed; and practice *16seconds* at 10 A.M., noon, 2 P.M., and 4 P.M.

6. **Celebrate:** Take the time at the end of each month to celebrate another successful 30 days of destressifying, meeting your needs, heightening your emotional awareness, communicating consciously, and moving closer to self-actualization. Oftentimes

when the month ends, you may roll right into the next month without skipping a beat. This feeds the nonstop swirl and the relentless intensity of daily living. If instead, you break your year into 12 celebrations where you reward yourself with an experience, a trip, or a treat you've been desiring, prepare a special dinner, pay off some debt, or put some money into savings, then you will fulfill many of your unmet needs as you close the loop and move closer to self-actualization. In addition, take some gratitude time each day—even if it's only a minute—to celebrate your small wins and your blessings. (See technique #13.)

7. **Get perspective:** Don't dwell on solving situations you can't control, such as weather, traffic, flight delays, what someone else might be thinking about you, and the like. Solve one small problem every day that is within your control—something easy, like taking a walk, putting some attention on a neglected relationship, reading a few pages of a book, going to an exercise or yoga class, putting the cap back on the toothpaste, taking out the trash, cleaning a room or your car, washing the dishes, paying bills, watching a training video, doing the laundry, or bettering yourself in some way—to remind you what is within your ability to influence. This "win" will reinforce your moving forward and will actually fuel the meeting of your Esteem Needs with greater consistency.

8. **Go to bed:** Lack of sleep is a huge stressor. There are a few hundred reasons we don't go to bed early and sleep restfully through the night, but the most common are the food we ate for dinner (usually too much caffeine or alcohol), the evening urge to stay online or watch TV (catching up on e-mail or mind-numbing social media), and the fact that we resist slowing down after 7 P.M. (often just beginning our evening dining and socializing). Set a target to be in bed by 10:30, and start by going to bed 15 minutes earlier every week until you get there.

9. **Exercise regularly:** We know the value of getting our blood flowing and the nourishing chemical and hormonal response we experience from a good workout. In order to thrive physically and emotionally, the bodymind needs to cultivate strength, flexibility, and balance. Daily exercise of at least 22 minutes (the minimum

threshold for capillary development) makes that possible by building our resilience, and it releases physical tension. Exercise also allows the mind to release anxiety—and you don't even need to leave the house to do it. Every TV content provider offers free programming for physical workouts, Pilates, yoga, and dancing. Find an expert in an exercise category that interests you. Visit davidji.com/destressifying to read a life-changing bonus article from fitness guru and certified *Masters of Wisdom & Meditation* teacher Laura Bender on the practical and transformational fusion of meditation and exercise, where she explains the powerful benefits of a bodymind workout.

10. **Create a nourishing environment:** Ideally, one of the steps you are taking toward destressifying your life is decluttering. Clutter in the home can create stress for everyone who lives there. A messy home equals a stressy home! If you can make the commitment to create all your physical spaces with balance and nourishment, your outer world will begin to mirror your inner destressified self. Being in any space that you consider calm, orderly, and reflective of your values will support you in your projects, relationships, and choices. You don't need to jet off to Tahiti right now; even making regular trips to tranquil places in nature where the sounds, sights, aromas, and "vibe" continue to nourish and relax you can have a powerfully destressifying long-term impact.

11. **Prepare:** Living in the moment is very relaxing—until you have to show up and be your best! Taking the time to plan and prepare are two present-moment activities that ensure the future will arrive as close to your expectations as possible. If you have a big presentation next week, take the time to look at all the possibilities, and practice—even if you just read it over a few times. This applies to any big moment, whether it's preparing for an interview or planning to quit a job, training for a race or a competition, or rehearsing a difficult conversation. Being your best means practicing so that your muscles and your mind have a familiar groove to flow into at the critical moment. Attention invested in advance will help the moment unfold with greater ease and with a higher likelihood that your needs will be met.

12. **Cultivate self-referral:** If you think life is rushing at you too quickly, remind yourself that the world comes at you at the speed and frequency you choose. It's easy to fall into the trap of believing outside circumstances and obligations control your inner dialogue and that you're at their mercy. Develop clarity regarding what is within your control and what is not. The outside world will only bring us temporary happiness—true, long-lasting happiness rests within. As the famous 12-step prayer reminds us: "Grant me the serenity to accept the things I cannot change, the courage to change the things I can, and the wisdom to know the difference." By developing your understanding of these teachings, you cultivate your own innate empowerment and stress less about things beyond your control.

13. **Practice gratitude:** Having a daily gratitude practice allows you to see the magnificence in each moment and can shift your sense of internal optimism or pessimism to a more life-affirming place. Seeing the silver linings in each moment allows you to be more creative with your problem solving and shift from a "poor me" mind-set to a "lucky me" perspective. Throughout your day, ask yourself, "What am I grateful for?" and "Who am I grateful for?" In the realization of your good fortune and blessings, you'll feel the positive effects of your actions and connect to greater joy in your life.

Why Do I Get Angry?

We all get angry sometimes. It's a human emotion that leads to a biochemical reaction, which then feeds on itself in a circular pattern. Earlier, I mentioned the very real benefits of anger as a motivating force to help us get and stay motivated. It has a profound ability to inspire us to leap out of self-pity and take action.

Anger is one of the oldest, most primitive emotions in the animal kingdom. It's a primal reaction to feeling that something is unfair. This all made sense way back in the jungle when not getting our fair share of food, shelter, or sex meant possible extinction. But in the 21st century, in those moments where our sole emotional response is anger, how can we keep it from getting the best of us? How can we transform our personal fire into a process that radiates more light and less heat?

Anger is a comparison emotion, and it's all based on expectation. Brain science has discovered that when we get less than what we thought we were entitled to . . . when we look at our reward compared to somebody else's . . . when we see or experience a moment that we don't think is "fair" . . . our response is frustration, which morphs into anger as we identify the "one" responsible for the unfairness. Our brain can't stand being treated unfairly. Its primitive self-preservation coding is always looking out for us and feels we deserve a better chance at any rewards being offered. When we feel like we're being cheated or when outside forces stand between us and the reward we think we're entitled to, our brain sends out an alarm that things aren't right.

When anger gets personal, we need to ask, *What am I really mad about?* We'll find that 99 percent of the time, it isn't about what's really going on in that moment; rather, it's more often about something else that we didn't think was fair. But in the moment, the lines get blurred, we scramble to make ourselves whole, and usually everyone suffers. We are never our best when we're angry, unless we are fighting a threat to our safety—then it makes sense. But think about how many times you've gotten angry when your life, home, career, or significant other *was not* being threatened.

When you feel challenged regarding your food, shelter, mate, or turf, your emotional control center sends out testosterone and adrenaline; and as you know, these two key hormones prime the body for physical aggression. Your heart

> starts to race; your palms sweat; it becomes difficult to think as blood flow decreases to the reasonable, thinking part of your brain; and *blammo!* The battle to "make things right" begins, physically and emotionally.
>
> *Reaching for SODA* in the moment will save you from doing or saying something you'll regret. And your emotional awareness of the *true* threat will allow you to simmer down. Each time you catch yourself, you build your resilience; and each time you take a step to meet your unmet need in a calm, conscious way, you evolve as a person. Anger can teach you about your inner demons; destressifying can help you finally put them to rest.

14. Get in tune with the rhythm of life: There's no such thing as a daytime raccoon, and there's no such thing as a nocturnal human. Just like plants, most birds and mammals, and the majority of *diurnal* creatures on the planet, our bodies are wired to rise with the sun, be productive during the 12-plus hours of sunlight everyday, and wind down when it sets. People who say, "I'm a night owl" are confused or conditioned with a non-nourishing behavioral pattern. When we can align ourselves with the rhythms of nature—the daily, lunar, tidal, and seasonal—we are not struggling against universal forces of nature. We are flowing with them.

The occasional late night won't hurt you, but believing you will thrive by consistently resisting circadian rhythms and the laws of nature is madness. All the hormones and chemicals in your body are specifically designed to support you during sunlight and nourish you in sleep during darkness. Those who work while the sun is "sleeping"—train conductors, ER nurses, pilots, swing-shift and night-shift workers—all experience the negative impacts of poor sleep and confused biorhythms, such as apnea and reduced performance. They are continually stressed and struggling against the damaging schedule that is hindering their path to self-actualization. If your job "forces" you to buck the natural rhythms on a daily basis, consider introducing a more healthy pattern interrupt into your weekly schedule to get you more closely aligned with the universe's flow. If it's not your job that's driving this schedule, then revisit number 8 on this list, and start going to bed 15 minutes earlier each week to normalize your sleep patterns.

15. **Keep breathing:** If you find yourself in the throes of chronic stress, where you are living in a state of emotional fight-or-flight, then most likely your breathing is probably pretty shallow or erratic and your sympathetic nervous system is calling the shots. Making a conscious decision every hour throughout the day to take a few deep, relaxing breaths in through your nose—and long, sighing exhales out through your mouth—to activate your parasympathetic nervous system will offset the initial surge of the sympathetic nervous system and the subsequent constricting physical effects. Additionally, just *16seconds* of deep breathing fills your body with nourishing, calming oxygen and activates your relaxation response by quickly introducing a pattern interrupt into the first few conditioned waves of emotion or tension. Proactively practice *16seconds* throughout the day at 10 A.M., 2 P.M., 4 P.M., 6 P.M., and whenever you find yourself in an idle moment—in your car, waiting in a line, while you're on hold, and so on.

16. **When you're going through hell, keep going!** These words attributed to Winston Churchill during World War II can be a subtle reminder to keep leaning, keep moving in the direction of your dreams. destressifying works, and it works in a relatively quick period of time if you trust the process. We know that the most successful people get clear on their plan and give it 40 days to unfold. It's been said that Thomas Edison failed more than 15,000 times in his attempts to create the incandescent light bulb and that Michael Jordan—the greatest basketball player to ever live—missed 50 percent of all his shots. But small irritations and blockages never stood in their way for long. They understood the "forge ahead" mind-set. And if you choose to keep going, even when it looks pretty dark out there, you will rally those around

you to support your efforts. So keep destressifying, keep practicing, and as Churchill also is reported to have said, "Never, never, never give up."

17. **Go back and change things:** Oftentimes, once the regrettable comment leaves your lips or the unfortunate decision begins to take hold, you may shut down and ruminate on it for hours, days, months, and even years. But you are never really stuck. Even though your actions are carved in stone, you can always revisit the scenario and apologize, request another chance, and recast the trajectory of your words and actions. Chapter 2, verse 47, of the ancient Indian text the Bhagavad Gita says, "We have total control over our actions, but no control over the fruit of our actions."

And yet we spend so much time in the fruit—the part we can't control. Instead, let's go back in and perform new actions, make new decisions to shift our lives from where they are to where we'd like to be.

18. **Remember the power of your ripple:** Every word you say and every action you take has a powerful impact and huge consequences. When you smile at someone, authentically thank them, pay them a compliment, apologize with remorse, ask for forgiveness, forgive them, offer a hug or a kind word, congratulate them on a job well done, or recognize their accomplishments, you start a ripple of energy that takes on a life of its own. They in turn flow their energy out into the world, and so on . . . and on. Every time you express yourself in a word or deed, a new ripple begins. You are a magnificently powerful being. Remember the power of your ripple.

• • • • •

CHAPTER 12

In-the-Moment destressifying

"Here we are in this sacred, precious present moment.
What are you going to do with it?"

— DAVIDJI

You have all the tools you could ever need to live a self-actualized, stress-free life. No equipment is necessary. Continue to develop your mastery of all you've learned in this book:

- Increasing your awareness
- Identifying and meeting your needs
- Heightening your emotional intelligence
- Communicating more consciously
- Discovering your noble purpose

As long as you do so, you will experience a profound inner shift as you interpret most of your stressors in a more positive light and quickly move through the stress that you once perceived as threatening.

Back to the Breath

It seems so obvious, and I know we've spent a lot of time on it, but we don't breathe enough. Let's review several breathing techniques that will quickly ground you, center you, relax you, and help you destressify.

Releasing Tension from the Body

Following your breath and relaxing your muscles gives you a dual benefit: mind *and* body destressifying. You can use this in addition to the *destressifying Body Scan* in Chapter 10, or in place of that meditation when you want a faster, in-the-moment technique.

As you follow your breath in and out, start with one muscle—pick the one that you are aware of right now. Hold it tight for a few seconds, and then relax it. Just as in the destressifying Body Scan, continue this process with all your muscles. After the first muscle, move down to your toes and feet. Then work your way up through the rest of your body, one muscle group at a time. As you reach your shoulders, roll them, since they hold on to a lot of subconscious tension. When you get to your neck, roll your head in a gentle circle and feel the tension release. Finally, reach toward the sky, and then practice the eight destressifications of the spine.

Present-Moment Breathing Techniques

You know the destressifying power that simply taking a deep breath can bring to you. We've meditated together using our breath many times throughout these pages, and by now you are pretty comfortable with the *16seconds* process, the *Heart Sutra,* and the *Mindful Flow Meditation*—which is my number one recommendation as a tool to use if you're having trouble sleeping. Building on this new skill set is a key to your destressifying when the stressful moment arises. Throughout your day, when you find yourself constricted, anxious, or panicky, feel free to use one of the additional destressifying techniques that you learned in Part II:

- Doorknob breathing
- Quiet continuous breathing
- Sipping breath
- Gargling breath
- Ocean breath
- Alternate-nostril breathing
- Metta meditation

While you are cultivating your new destressifying mind-set, there may be moments in between when you will want to deploy some of the many in-the-moment destressifying techniques to move you from conditioned responses to your best version. Select the one that resonates right now.

Which Meditation Is Right for My Personality?

There are many different types of meditation that can shift your state of mind; and depending on your personality and your emotional need in the moment, you can easily summon the perfect destressifying tool to balance yourself and bring you back to center:

I. **You're holding a grudge, comparing yourself to others, or feeling less-than:** metta meditation

This is a nourishing and healing meditation, and an example of putting the oxygen mask on yourself first before you rush to put it on someone else. But don't worry—after you're filled with loving oxygen, you get to flow it out to every corner of the galaxy! Use this technique when you've been sulking, blaming others for your circumstances, or when you're about to connect with a larger group of people. You may even want to start your holiday dinners with everyone holding hands, saying grace, and doing a two-minute group metta meditation. Everyone will feel the shift. Remember, we transform the world by transforming ourselves . . . it happens one heart at a time.

2. **You're filled with anxiety and you need to get calm** *right now*: mindfulness meditation *or* alternate-nostril breathing, if you have more time

You know that feeling you get when doing something you love? You're totally absorbed, yet your mind is super clear? A simple mindfulness meditation can help invoke that feeling. Stop yourself for two minutes a day and bring your attention to your breath. Just follow your breath in your mind's eye, going in and out through your nose. The idea is that by staying with your breath, you're not going to the past or future in your thoughts. If you're extremely busy or a beginning meditator, this method works really well because it's quick and you can do it anywhere. It's also beneficial for combating stress and anxiety in the moment. If you are willing to take a full five minutes, you can take it even deeper and practice alternate-nostril breathing.

3. **You're an emotional eater, reaching for food when you need some love:** sensory meditation

Mindful eating is a form of sensory meditation. Choose a meal—or even just a piece of chocolate—and focus on the flavors and experience of eating it, savoring every bite and connecting to the moment without any other distractions like television, work, or other people. If you struggle with emotional eating or weight concerns, or if you just haven't been taking the time to notice what you're putting in your body, this is a great tool for gaining more awareness of the process of eating and bringing more joy to the experience.

As you take your first bite, connect to the flavor, and then become aware of the nuances—the subtle changes in texture, taste, aroma, and how it makes you feel.

4. You're a perfectionist and you're focusing on the one percent that isn't right or the thing that's not working instead of the 99 percent that you've done well: the Heart Sutra

Instead of searching for the things that didn't work out that you need to fix, celebrate your humanity and place your hand on your heart, while you silently repeat *peace, harmony, laughter, love* to yourself, as you learned in Chapter 10. Do this for five minutes, repeating the words slowly. They'll become positive affirmations and will help you experience self-compassion, remind you not to take everything so seriously, and perhaps even move you to celebrate your accomplishments.

5. You need to let go, shake it off, and have fun more: eight destressifications of the spine

Do this physical meditation as you blast your favorite song and sing along. This doesn't have to be a serious practice. You can hum under your breath for the first few destressifications, and then bust it out when your arms are raised at the end. Make it fun!

Daily Opportunities

Take a look at all the various opportunities you have through-out the day to move beyond stress. Once you are living a destressifying life, these in-the-moment tools will matter less; but as you journey to full-on self-actualization, your interpretations of stress can take their toll.

1. **Destressify while traveling:** If you have any anxiety or discomfort about flying or being on a plane, use the following methods to help you destressify while traveling.

- **Heading to the airport:** Play calming music and destressify through your senses, or dive in and sing along with a flying theme. Some possibilities include "The Letter," by Joe Cocker; "Back in the U.S.S.R.," by the Beatles; "Coming into Los Angeles," by Arlo Guthrie; "Aeroplane," by the Red Hot Chili Peppers; my personal favorite, "Learn to Fly," by the Foo Fighters; or pick one of your favorites.

- **Once you're inside the airport:** Take it slow and breathe as you allow all the activity around you to drift right past. Stay centered in your heart. Practice mindfulness meditation, drinking it all in and coming back to your breath. Keep coming back to your breath.

- **Checking in:** Get focused on the flight details, your desired seat, checking your baggage, and sending kindness to the ticket agent if there's a snag in your seat assignment or a flight delay (do a mini metta meditation). Put your phone in your pocket. Don't multitask. Do one thing at a time and stay present.

- **Standing in the TSA line:** Use *16seconds* as you drift your attention to the soles of your feet and feel your unshod feet connecting with the floor. Slowly and methodically put your watch, phone, belt, shoes, and so on into the bin. Take your time. Go through the scanner. Keep going through several rounds of *16seconds* until you have collected all your belongings . . . breathe and smile.

- **Waiting at the gate:** As soon as you sit down, do a few rounds of *eight destressifications of the spine.* Reach out to someone you love and text them to let them know you are thinking about them, and then practice a relaxed *destressifying Body Scan* as you wait for your seating zone to be called.

- **Walking onto the plane:** Start with *16seconds;* then practice *Reaching for SODA* as you stow your carry-on. Silently repeat to yourself, *Stop, Observe, Detach, Awaken.* As soon as you sit down, close your eyes and breathe deeply for a few minutes as the boarding process continues. Feather your nest; practice *eight destressifications of the spine.*

- **Taking off:** Settle into a *Mindful Flow Meditation* or try *alternate-nostril breathing.* This is also the perfect time to practice a *destressifying Body Scan.* Remember: If there are any areas of your body that feel tight, constricted, or painful, breathe deeply into them until they release. Since there's very little you can do for the first ten minutes of the flight, drifting back to Mindful Flow during that time can ease you into the trip.

- **While flying:** Meditate during the flight for a few minutes here and there—use any technique you've gotten comfortable with. Drink lots of water, and set your watch to the current time as you cross time zones—this will keep you present. Do a few rounds of *squeeze&release,* and every 30 minutes practice the *eight destressifications of the spine.* If you commit to this regimen, you will feel refreshed and limber when you get off the plane. When you see someone rubbing their sore back or looking haggard, remember that could have been you in your pre-destressifying years!

- **Getting ready for landing:** Focus on the seat back
  directly in front of your eyes, and lock into a trance
  of *quiet continuous breathing*. Then close your eyes as
  you continue the practice until you feel the wheels
  hit the runway.

2. **Destressify on the phone:** Throughout the day, there will be moments where you feel on call to the universe or tethered to uncomfortable or difficult phone conversations. Use the phone as an extension of your mind, keeping your phone on silent for stretches of time where you are dedicating your time and attention to *your* needs. This will help keep your internal ringer on silent as well. When you are ready to commit your time and attention to incoming calls, take a deep breath in as you put the ringer back on low, and . . .

- **As the phone rings:** Upon seeing an anxiety-
  producing number or name appear on your phone,
  begin *Reaching for SODA*. Just as you get to *Awaken*
  (the best version of yourself), answer the call.

- **Starting the conversation:** Practice *16seconds*. Let
  the other person reach out and speak first as you
  breathe. As the conversation winds down, do a mini
  metta meditation and send the person you're talking
  to unconditional loving-kindness.

- **As you hang up:** Smile and congratulate yourself on
  a job well done.

3. **Destressify at your computer:** Introduce a pattern interrupt by looking away from your screen to a pleasant image and stretching every 15 to 30 minutes; play the sound of trickling water, or listen to a guided meditation from davidji.com. Take a break every two hours—get up and take a lap around the office or your house; practice a few rounds of *alternate-nostril breathing*; and next do *eight destressifications of the spine*. Then dive back in with renewed vigor!

4. **Destressify after hearing bad news:** Immediately practice *16seconds*. Then take a few deep breaths, and sigh as you exhale. In this moment—as the first wave of stress hits you—you are in a state of confusion and overwhelm. Slow yourself down with long, slow deep breaths in and out. If you need to be levelheaded to help others, breathe in and notice that space between your breaths—your still-point—and remember that you are the calm amidst the chaos. See yourself as the solid, strong pillar upholding the space all others are in. When you have your chance to be alone, allow your emotions to flow. Practice emotional awareness and surrender to a 20-minute practice of *Mindful Flow Meditation*. Then practice a metta meditation or the *Heart Sutra*, and begin to reach out to—and connect with—those closest to you for support.

Five Realms Transformation Exercise

I've shared with you the most cutting-edge research and some of the most profound guidance on destressifying. We've begun the journey together; now the following steps can help you further activate your transformation process.

During times when it seems as if you can barely catch your breath, if you can look at your life through the lens of the Five Realms, you will continue moving forward while keeping everything in perspective and bringing greater clarity to the moment.

Maybe your to-do list is bursting at the seams. You've got expectations about what needs to get accomplished, several obligations you've committed yourself to, and then a brand-new set of circumstances arises . . . and the basic day-to-day tasks and chores still need to get done. So let's slow it all down. Simply walk yourself through the Five Realms and spend just a few minutes on each one. You'll want to take a moment at the start of your day: perhaps after you've meditated, or maybe during your morning commute, or right after you've checked your messages. Just take some quiet time, close your eyes, and settle in for a few minutes.

*Start with your **physical realm**: your body. Take a long look at what comes in and what goes out, what strengthens it and what weakens it. Pick one action to definitely do, and one behavior to let go of just for today . . . don't torture yourself. As you breathe in, in your mind's eye imagine bringing in one physical behavior to your life that will nourish you, and as you exhale, release one that's not nourishing.*

*Then drift your attention to your **emotional realm**, and walk yourself through your ability to monitor your own and other people's emotions, to discriminate between different emotions and label them appropriately, and to use emotional information to guide your thinking and behavior. Place your attention on your levels of empathy and compassion, hot buttons, trigger points, assumptions, and conditioned responses. Recommit to one emotional behavior that is serving you, get clear and breathe it in, and keep it in your awareness as you go about your routines and tasks. Create a mantra that you can keep flowing throughout the day, such as "patience . . . patience . . . patience." And every time you feel that you're about to respond in a way that might not serve you, take a deep breath in and . . . as you exhale . . . silently repeat the mantra.*

*Then drift your attention to your **material realm** for a few minutes. Make one decision today regarding how you will view the material abundance in the world. Seeing yourself as a never-ending conduit will flow through how you treat your money, finances, debt, status, position, possessions, dharma, saving, hoarding, or giving. Allow abundance consciousness and wealth circulation to transform any feelings of poverty consciousness or less-than thinking. And throughout the day, remind yourself of that shift. Reinforce it by keeping the subtle intention "I Am" running in the background of all your thought processes.*

*Next, spend a few minutes on the **relationship realm**, and reflect on one relationship you have—with yourself, a core family member, a friend, an extended relationship, or someone with whom you have a grievance. Leading with love, take a step to birth, repair, shift, or end it. Throughout the process, breathe* *in deeply as you allow the virtues of acceptance; forgiveness; compassion; honesty; and impeccability of your word, your thoughts, and your actions to be cultivated within you.*

*Then spend a few minutes on the **spiritual realm**: your connection to your soul and to divine spirit, and your daily practice of prayer, meditation, and devotion to the divine. Contemplate your dharma or noble purpose in this life. Breathe in, plant a seed of oneness in your heart, and let the universe kiss your soul.*

Last, briefly reflect on each realm and the intentions or commitments you made to yourself. If you really want to ground them in the tangible world, write them down and place them somewhere you will regularly see the document. But the key is to live them—live your intentions, lean into them. As Krishna says to the warrior Arjuna in the Bhagavad Gita, "Yogastha kuru karmani"—essentially, "Establish yourself in the present moment, and then perform action."

The swirl will slow. Clarity will unfold. Your choices will become more evident. Your decisions will start to truly nourish you and those in your world. With gentle repetition, this can become a daily practice. And it takes only a few minutes of attention on each realm.

Integrating destressifying Techniques into Your Day

The goal is not simply to live your life in bliss (although that would be nice), but to cultivate your ability to connect to present-moment awareness and then come into the next moment with greater calm, clarity, creativity, intuition, and fulfillment. Intellectually, it's easy to understand the scientific benefits of introducing a pattern interrupt into your nonstop flow of thoughts, words, and actions. And once you lock in a daily practice, the results will effortlessly circulate through your life.

Ten In-the-Moment destressifiers

In the morning at home: Ideally you've already completed your first meditation of the day using RPM. Creating stillness as the starting point for your next 24 hours sets a powerful trajectory. But unknown stress can lurk right around the corner. As soon as you feel stressed, implement any of these steps to bring you back into the moment:

1. Spend five minutes holding your child, your lover, your pet, or yourself. This will instantly ease your blood pressure. Bask in the glow.

2. Take a ten-minute walk, connecting to nature to ease anxiety and replace it with calm. Leave your phone at home and don't plug in any music. Just drink in everything you see, hear, touch, and smell as you walk at a leisurely pace.

3. Start with five minutes of deep *alternate-nostril breathing*. Then practice 15 minutes of yoga or gentle stretching to awaken your energy, release tension, and rejuvenate your body. Even taking a long, slow walk will suffice. Then finish by lying on your back with your eyes closed, and practice the *Mindful Flow Meditation* for five minutes. Just let all the physical and emotional sensations settle in.

At work: Ideally you are walking into the workplace with stillness and silence already flowing through you. But as soon as you notice frustration, irritation, or intensity starting to build, take these steps:

1. Upon feeling the spark of your emotional tell, *Reach for SODA*. Stop, Observe, Detach, and Awaken to the best version of yourself.

2. Pour some lavender- or sandalwood-based oil or lotion gently into your open hand. Massage your

palm with your thumb; then massage each finger from the base to the tip, and then the webbed area between your thumb and index finger. Close your eyes and breathe in the vapors of destressifying.

3. Step away from your desk and go outside or to an unoccupied place where you can sit for a few moments. Close your eyes and breathe in and out deeply through your nostrils ten times to lower your heart rate and reduce your blood pressure.

4. Take three minutes and chew a piece of gum to loosen the stress in your jaw. While you chew, roll your neck around to ease any tightness.

After work: You're carrying the past 12 hours of the day inside every cell in your body. So either as the very last thing you do before you head home or the very first thing you do when you get home, take time to release the day:

1. Shake the tension right out of your body. Roll your shoulders backward and forward. Reach your arms to the sky and stretch and elongate your whole body from your toes to the tips of your fingers, and then do a few arm circles. If you're feeling sprightly, finish off with ten jumping jacks or the *eight destressifications of the spine.*

2. Shake the tension out of your mind with recapitulation. Spend five minutes playing your day in fast-forward from the moment you woke up. Don't linger for more than one second on each activity or event that unfolded throughout the day—don't harp on the drama or the words. Just keep playing your day at high speed as if you were holding down the fast-forward button on your remote.

3. After dinner, *slow* down. Light a candle, brew some tea, take a bath, or nibble on some chocolate.

These ten steps can keep your body and your mind on a steady destressifying regimen; and if you can commit to them, fewer crises will arise in your day-to-day activities. Of course, if you use the Five Realms worksheet on a regular basis, practice the Five Masteries, and use any of the myriad destressifying techniques with any level of consistency, you will very quickly feel the benefits of a life that transcends stress.

• • •

If you're reading this, you've come light-years from where we started more than 200 pages ago . . . so stay the course. Clarity will crystallize, stress and anxiety will become experiences of the past, solutions will start to unfold, your relationships will begin to thrive, and waves of fulfillment will ripple through every fiber of your being. destressifying will percolate through every cell of your body, and the grace and ease you feel in those present moments will become *you.*

Know that you are always stronger in your vulnerability,
you are always more courageous in your trust,
you are always more abundant in your acceptance,
and you are always more empowered in your surrender.
You ARE the calm amidst the chaos.

And throughout each day, when you realize that chemicals, hormones, and conditioned behaviors are starting to dictate your thoughts, words, and actions . . . when fear of the future or anxiety of the past starts to grip you . . . remember that you have all the tools you could ever need to live a brilliant, destressifying existence. Then close your eyes, practice *16seconds,* and remind yourself,

When I let go of who I am, I become who I might be.

When you open your eyes, acknowledge,

Here I am in this sacred, precious moment.
What am I going to do with it?

Fully destressified, you can now take your next step into magnificence . . . into the best version of yourself.

• • • • •

Afterword

Over these pages, we've journeyed through life a bit together. We've gazed into each other's eyes, watched each other breathe, shed tears, laughed, held each other close, listened to each other's hearts, learned a lot more about what rests inside, awakened our dreams, supported each other, connected our souls, raised ourselves up, and made transformational breakthroughs. And now we must separate as we integrate what we have experienced and forge our own paths, hoping to meet again at some special celebration in some distant place—maybe in another incarnation. Life is a constant intertwining of the energies we absorb and the wisdom we inherit. I am grateful to you for connecting with me, immersing in this powerful body of knowledge, and choosing to take your life to the next level.

As you continue to meet your needs, heighten your emotional intelligence, enhance your conscious communication, lean into your dharma, and practice daily meditation, your life will shift, your relationships will flourish, and you will start to approach each day with a sense of wonderment and awe. You truly will experience deeper fulfillment as you live a destressifying life. When we meet again, we may not recognize each other—but know that we are connected forever, in this life and the next. Let's keep it going. The best is yet to come!

It is my intention that destressifying has and will continue to help you fulfill your needs on a daily basis, raise your emotional awareness and emotional intelligence, allow you to lean more deeply in the direction of your dharma, guide you on how to communicate with greater consciousness, and lead you to live each moment with greater awareness and presence. This will allow you to truly self-actualize and to serve others at a higher level.

You are not alone on this journey. We are all together, stumbling through each day to put some food in our bellies and receive

273

a little bit more love. In the process, we can share patience, friendship, acceptance, forgiveness, encouragement, and peace with everyone we touch. If we can do this—even just a bit more than we did yesterday—then this life of ours, as transient and uncertain as it is, will be the most amazing journey we could ever fathom.

Remember that we have an obligation to nurture and protect all the sentient beings on the planet, starting with ourselves and those closest to us. This also includes animals in shelters, zoos, and on factory farms; the billions of birds that swirl through the skies; the animals in forests and jungles . . . the elephants, rhinos, hippos, bears, gorillas, and great cats nearing extinction; and our beautiful oceans home to highly evolved mammals, whales, and dolphins, as well as the other vast varieties of marine life that teem within. Remember the power of your ripple, remember to love thy neighbor, and remember to adopt your next pet. We transform the world by transforming ourselves.

Visit www.davidji.com to connect with me and more of these timeless teachings.

• • • • •

Index of Meditations
and Exercises

• • • • •

Acknowledgments

None of us do anything alone. I am humbled by the support, friendship, and devotion of those in my front row. Deep gratitude to the following people for making this journey of destressifying possible:

My sweet mothers Mae Harrison and Olga Lenore Cohen

My unconditional parents, Stanley and Naomi Drucker

My amazing dad JayJi, and Charna Glasser

My sister, Susan Gilbert, for always being there for me

Rosanne Drucker for your relentless wisdom, life-affirming courage, undying love, and unwavering trust

Somyr Perry for your daily brilliance, selfless support, openhearted guidance, and ability to see the big picture, as well as the granular, in every moment. You are Ganesha!

Nancy MacLeod—the bravest person I know—for being my steady rock, never flinching at the challenge, and always making it look easy

Helena Maniti for your enthusiasm, professionalism, and dedication

Dianne Star for your creativity, flexibility, and lightning-fast execution

Tiffany Murray for your loyalty, friendship, style, and grace

The amazing team at davidji SweetSpot productions

Louise Hay and Reid Tracy—thank you for unconditionally nurturing me, encouraging me to soar, and inviting me into your magical sandbox to share, love, and play with the magnificent Hay House community

Karla Refoxo and TulkuJewels.com for the love you tenderly flow into the world and into my life. I am grateful for your infinite heart!

Diane Ray and the magnificent Hay House Radio team who help me be my best every week—Steve, Rocky, Mitch, Joe, and Mike

The amazing Donna Abate, Stacey Smith, Bryn Starr Best, Christy Salinas, and Diane Ray—the original members of the Hay House Meditation Club

Lupe Barajas, Shay Lawry, Mollie Langer, Jodie Shull, Jessica Polson, Maryann Riccardi, Jennifer Simmons, Teri Vodden, Dani Riehl, Wioleta

Gramek, Michelle Ocampo, Melissa Brinkerhoff, Kate Riley, Heather Tate, and Margarete Nielsen

Eternal gratitude to my beloved friend and mentor Dr. David Simon; and to my most powerful archetype, Dr. Deepak Chopra, the greatest translator of timeless wisdom

John Thiel, Caroline Brown, and Laurent Potdevin for lighting the way with your vision and courage

My spiritual brother Lubosh Cech, the Fearless Terri Cole, the transformational Dr. Barbara DeAngelis, the Boston Buddha Andy Kelley, game-changer Shawn Achor, generous heart T. Harv Eker, Gabrielle Bernstein, Nirmala Raniga, the "Father of Motivation and Inspiration" Dr. Wayne Dyer, Lindsay O'Brien, Alisha Olivier Park and Tranquility, Benji Mosiman, the visionary and divinely creative J. Ivy, pure and authentic Shauna Piscitelli, the voice of an angel Ariana Grande, Damien Rose, crazy sexy Kris Carr, Carolyn Rangel, Megan Monahan, Amanda Ringnalda, Danielle Mika Nagel, Gordon MacGregor, Mike Garro, Steve Samuels, Janet Ashley, Anna Callori, rock-star yogi Gabrielle Forleo, Frank Elaridi, Trista Thorp, my heart partners Peter Platel and Luc Acke, the "eye of God" Gordon Wong, Krystal Wilson, Jeffrey Gilbert, Marsha Seahorse Perry, Jennifer Johnson, Wendi Cohen, Tracy Persson and Soul Remedies, Veronica Piñerua, Monica Campos, Jenna Guarneri, Joann Gwynn, and Suze Yalof Schwartz of Unplug Meditation

Tracy Hutton for living your dharma, leading with love, and shining your light

Those who've trusted their inner guidance to journey with me, meditate with me, study with me, and manifest with me at my davidji workshops, immersions, and retreats

The ever-expanding hearts, minds, and souls of the 100+ *Masters of Wisdom & Meditation* teachers whom I have had the honor of certifying in sharing this timeless body of knowledge throughout the world. I am so grateful for your passion and brilliance. You inspire me each day to raise my vibration, die to the past, and lean into the future with greater grace and ease.

The members of the davidji SweetSpot Community—100,000 spiritual warriors and growing strong—you have helped me to keep it real, study more deeply, and be my best version

The bold, creative, and beautiful Beings of lululemon athletica for your authenticity, support, and evolutionary values

Hay House U.K. for helping me share my writings in Spanish, Dutch, Russian, Arabic, French, German, Swedish, Danish, Norwegian, and Bulgarian

My magnificent reindeer-sister Marianne Pagmar, my dream-sister Rosalinda Weil, and my Kundalini-sister Julia Anastasiou

Pam Cammarata for the bravery and brilliance you flow to the millions you touch with your ceaseless energy

Dean Richards and MJ Vermette of SacredFire

My dear friend and guardianwarrior Michael Nila for your vision, velocity, and the transformational work of the Blue Courage Team

Next Generation Yoga and my undying bestie Jodi Komitor—the most prolific kids' awareness teacher of our time

My dear friend, yogi, and forward-thinking publisher Sonnia Valverde and Espacio Cosmico

The divine destressifiers Alicia Florrick, Carrie Matheson, Jack Bauer, Annie Walker, "Red" Reddington, Tyrion Lannister, Jax Teller, and Harvey Specter for offering me nourishing stress throughout the years

The magnificent soul seekers in Amsterdam, Centrum de Roos, Suzanne Henning, Anaïsa Bruchner, Marita Dibrani, Marije de Jong, Richard Kwakernaak, Rene Brandjes, Suzanne Fink, *Code* magazine, my Dutch publisher Altamira, and the *Happinez* magazine team

Patty Gift for her enthusiasm, boddhicitta, guidance, and encouragement to write "a special book"

My brilliant Hay House editorial team of Lindsay DiGianvittorio, Jessica Kelley, Lisa Bernier, and Alex Freemon, and the Hay House design team that has graced me with your creativity and genuine appreciation of my work

My dear companion Peaches, the Buddha Princess, the Mindful Morkie L.A. rescue who teaches me every day: resist nothing and you will receive unconditional love

And you, the reader, who has taken the time, effort, and commitment to journey with me and embraced destressifying to manifest our collective dream

• • • • •

About the Author

davidji is an internationally recognized stress-management expert, meditation master, corporate-wellness trainer, public speaker, and author of the award-winning *Secrets of Meditation: A Practical Guide to Inner Peace and Personal Transformation,* now translated in 11 languages. He is credited with launching the 21-day global guided-meditation movement for personal transformation, and his voice can be heard on more than 500 guided meditations, including his best-selling meditation CD *Fill What Is Empty; Empty What Is Full* and his critically acclaimed Ayurvedic opera *Journey to Infinity* with SacredFire, which have been streamed and downloaded more than a million times. Each Thursday, he hosts *LIVE from the SweetSpot,* now in its fifth year on Hay House Radio.

After a 20-year career in finance, business, and mergers and acquisitions, davidji began a new journey to wholeness by apprenticing under Deepak Chopra for ten years as the Chopra Center COO and lead educator, and as the first dean of Chopra Center University. He now travels the world teaching business executives, corporate groups, and work teams the practical integration of business and wellness, stress mastery, wealth consciousness, meditation, mindfulness, and conscious communication into our real-world, modern-day experiences. For more than a decade, davidji has trained hundreds of thousands of people around the world to be more reflective and less reflexive, make better decisions, sleep better, find more happiness, enhance their relationships, experience abundance, and live a purpose-driven life.

davidji is a certified Vedic Master and has a passion for working with those in high-stress, high-pressure situations, including business leaders, world-class athletes, entertainers, members of the military, Special Forces, law enforcement, the medical community, and those in crisis. He is the co-developer of the Blue Courage Awareness Training curriculum, a revolutionary approach to policing using present-moment life tools for conflict resolution, stress management, resilience, and mindfulness, which is now practiced in some of the largest precincts and police academies in the country.

To learn more and join the davidji SweetSpot meditation community, visit davidji.com.

• • • • •

davidji

Transform the world by transforming yourself.

Visit **davidji.com** for information on meditation, conscious choice-making, stress management, heart healing and integrating timeless wisdom into your daily life.

Sign up for the davidji SweetSpot Meditation Community and get access to tools, tips and techniques to lessen your stress and anxiety and bring greater balance into your life. You'll be able to sample exclusive guided meditations, stress busters and ways to connect with meditators around the world.

Connect with davidji

- facebook.com/flowoflove
- twitter.com/davidji_com
- google.com/+davidjimeditation
- pinterest.com/davidjidavidji/
- davidjimeditation.tumblr.com
- davidjimeditation

Hay House Titles of Related Interest

YOU CAN HEAL YOUR LIFE, the movie,
starring Louise Hay & Friends
(available as a 1-DVD program and an expanded 2-DVD set)
Watch the trailer at: www.LouiseHayMovie.com

THE SHIFT, the movie,
starring Dr. Wayne W. Dyer
(available as a 1-DVD program and an expanded 2-DVD set)
Watch the trailer at: www.DyerMovie.com

• • •

*BECOMING AWARE: How to Repattern Your
Brain and Revitalize Your Life*, by Lisa Garr

*DE-STRESS EFFECT: Rebalance Your Body's Systems for
Vibrant Health and Happiness*, by Charlotte Watts

FRIED: Why You Burn Out and How to Revive,
by Joan Borysenko, Ph.D.

LIFE LOVES YOU: 7 Spiritual Practices to Heal Your Life,
by Louise Hay and Robert Holden

*MIRACLES NOW: Inspirational Affirmations and
Life-Changing Tools*, by Gabrielle Bernstein

*THE WAY OF THE HAMMOCK: Designing
Calm for a Busy Life*, by Marga Odahowski

All of the above are available at your local bookstore,
or may be ordered by contacting Hay House (see next page).

• • •

We hope you enjoyed this Hay House book. If you'd like to receive our online catalog featuring additional information on Hay House books and products, or if you'd like to find out more about the Hay Foundation, please contact:

Hay House, Inc., P.O. Box 5100, Carlsbad, CA 92018-5100
(760) 431-7695 or (800) 654-5126
(760) 431-6948 (fax) or (800) 650-5115 (fax)
www.hayhouse.com® • www.hayfoundation.org

• • •

Published and distributed in Australia by: Hay House Australia Pty. Ltd.,
18/36 Ralph St., Alexandria NSW 2015
Phone: 612-9669-4299 • *Fax:* 612-9669-4144 • www.hayhouse.com.au

Published and distributed in the United Kingdom by: Hay House UK, Ltd.,
Astley House, 33 Notting Hill Gate, London W11 3JQ
Phone: 44-20-3675-2450 • *Fax:* 44-20-3675-2451 • www.hayhouse.co.uk

Published and distributed in the Republic of South Africa by: Hay House SA
(Pty), Ltd., P.O. Box 990, Witkoppen 2068 • info@hayhouse.co.za

Published in India by: Hay House Publishers India,
Muskaan Complex, Plot No. 3, B-2, Vasant Kunj, New Delhi 110 070
Phone: 91-11-4176-1620 • *Fax:* 91-11-4176-1630 • www.hayhouse.co.in

Distributed in Canada by: Raincoast Books,
2440 Viking Way, Richmond, B.C. V6V 1N2
Phone: 1-800-663-5714 • *Fax:* 1-800-565-3770 • www.raincoast.com

• • •

Take Your Soul on a Vacation

Visit www.HealYourLife.com® to regroup,
recharge, and reconnect with your own magnificence.
Featuring blogs, mind-body-spirit news, and
life-changing wisdom from Louise Hay and friends.

Visit www.HealYourLife.com today!